A Fighter Pilot's Call to Arms

This book is dedicated to all the Czech airmen who fought and died with the RAF during WWII.

A FIGHTER PILOT'S CALL TO ARMS

DEFENDING BRITAIN AND FRANCE AGAINST THE LUFTWAFFE, 1940-1942

Stanislav Fejfar

Edited by Norman Franks with Simon Muggleton

GRUB STREET · LONDON

Published by
Grub Street
4 Rainham Close
London
SW11 6SS

British Library Cataloguing in Publication Data
Fejfar, Stanislav
   A fighter pilot's call to arms: defending Britain and
   France against the Luftwaffe, 1940-1942.
   1. Fejfar, Stanislav. 2. World War, 1939-1945 – Personal
   narratives, Czech. 3. World War, 1939-1945 – Aerial
   operations, British. 4. Great Britain. Royal Air Force.
   Squadron, No. 310 – Biography.
   I. Title. II. Franks, Norman L R III. Muggleton, Simon.
   940.5'44'941'092-dc22

ISBN-13: 9781906502768

Cover design by Sarah Driver

Typeset by Pearl Graphics, Hemel Hempstead

Printed and bound by MPG Ltd, Bodmin, Cornwall

Grub Street Publishing only uses
FSC (Forest Stewardship Council) paper for its books.

Contents

Introduction

Squadron Leader Henry Prokop at the end of the war.

In November 1994 I was contacted by a fellow medal collector and good friend, the late Chris John who was aware that I had an interest in the Battle of France and Battle of Britain periods. Indeed, I had obtained several medal groups in my collection from Chris over the years, and he knew I was particularly interested in the part played in both air battles by the Czechs and Poles. Chris informed me that he had just returned from the Czech Republic searching for interesting medal groups and associated militaria, and had found something which may be of interest to me. He had located a copy of the personal diary of Flight Lieutenant Stanislav Fejfar along with his medals, photograph album, some official papers, and his pre-war leather flying coat, gloves and helmet.

This was an opportunity not to be missed as a quick search in my reference books showed Fejfar to be a famous Czech flying ace, who had been killed in action in 1942 flying over the Channel, shot down by the well known German fighter pilot, Oberst Josef 'Pips' Priller. Although the diary was obviously written in Czechoslovakian, as were most of the official papers, I knew when I saw them I had somehow to get these published in English and tell this heroic pilot's story.

So I started my quest for further information on Fejfar, beginning with contacting Wing Commander Gordon Sinclair OBE DFC, the senior flight commander in 310 Squadron during the Battle of Britain. He in turn suggested that I make contact with Henry Prokop, a retired Czechoslovakian squadron leader who had served as a flight engineer with 310 Squadron during the war.

As soon as Henry Prokop saw the papers and photograph album he was enthused to start translating the documents straight away. Henry had escaped from Czechoslovakia at the same time as Fejfar taking virtually the same route through Poland and serving in the French Foreign Legion before travelling to England in order to join the RAF.

On occasions Henry had actually worked on Fejfar's aircraft in both 310 and 313 Squadrons, and had spoken to him many times whilst doing so. It is due to his magnificent effort and love of the old Czechoslovakia that this book began to be written in its present form.

Since acquiring Fejfar's effects in 1994, enquiries revealed that the hand-written copy of the diary was given to an English girl-friend called Yvonne after his death in 1942. He had met her whilst recuperating in hospital at Torquay and she is mentioned in the diary. She retained it for many years after the war but eventually decided that it should be returned to Stanislav's native land. Its current whereabouts, however, are unknown.

The diary was published in 1970 in verbatim form and Norman Franks and I decided that Henry Prokop's translation should be annotated with information pertaining to his early life, the operations in which Fejfar was involved, as well as presenting a useful background to the war and battles in which he and his Czech comrades were engaged. This brings the whole story alive and gives it a more rounded presentation.

In 2007, Ladislav Kudrna had his book *Na Zemi A Oblose Západní Evropy* published, again in the Czech language (see Bibliography). The book is written around the story of Fejfar and his diary, and is quite comprehensive, but again not in English, and is different in format to this present offering.

Simon Muggleton

Foreword

On finishing reading this magnificent translation of Stanislav Fejfar's diaries my first thought is to congratulate the translator in producing such a vivid and readable English version. He has made Fejfar's thoughts come to life in a way which prompts many nostalgic memories of those far-off days.

Stanislav Fejfar was one of a group of Czechoslovakian pilots, who formed the nucleus of 310 (Czech squadron) of which I had the honour of helping to form and build up immediately before the Battle of Britain in June-July 1940.

Like the other pilots and the ground crew, Fejfar spoke no English when he arrived at Duxford, but his intentions were clear from the outset, to get at the Germans.

That he and his fellow pilots fulfilled their intentions became abundantly clear from the moment that 310 Squadron was declared operationally fit to join the Battle.

I flew with Fejfar on many sorties, over the Thames estuary in particular, meeting up with Luftwaffe bombers and their escorting fighters. I can only say that it was a wonderful comfort to me knowing that I was fighting with such gallant and determined men as Fejfar and his fellow Czechs.

His diaries are a vivid reminder of what he represented in gallantry and courage.

Wing Commander G L Sinclair OBE DFC

Acknowledgements

Over the years the authors have received very welcome encouragement, assistance and correspondence from a number of veterans, some of whom they have had the pleasure of meeting. Simon in particular has contacted a number of people from the Czech Republic. In particular, he wishes to record the tremendous help from the late Henry Prokop, not only in translating the diary into English but also in providing anecdotes. This book could not have been written without him.

Pavel Vancata in Prague is thanked for his help in identifying photographs, documents, and his tremendous knowledge regarding the Czechs and their involvement with the RAF in WW2. Others who have freely given their help and support are: Andy Saunders, for his unending knowledge of the Battle of Britain. Gordon Leith of the RAF Museum. Christopher F Shores. The Free Czech Air Force Association. Lucie Harmer (née Cernamska) for additional translating. Tania Spottiswoode for typing up the original translation. The Keeper and staff of the National Archives at Kew.

Finally, our wives Heather and Jill, who put up with our hobby, which is a pretty solitary occupation, but is helped with their unswerving love and support.

Preface

I am sweating a bit and immediately order the 'Tally Ho!' At this altitude this fight is for life and quite possibly, death. I attack the nearest 190 in that micro-second and after pressing the firing button I see the enemy pilot climbing out of his cockpit, but I do not see the subsequent parachute canopy. I cannot and must not muddle my thoughts because I now notice white tracers approaching my Spitfire. I flick my machine into a spin at once – what else can I do? – to avoid two FW190s that suddenly appear. However, they pass me and head towards some Spitfires below.

Whatever happens and whether the Spitfires are flown by Polish, Czech or English pilots, I have to dive at once to help, lining up one in my gun-sight. I fire without hesitation but in my mirror I spot another Fritz, this time the horrible yellow propeller hub of a FW190. My knees tremble. My usual trick is to close the throttle, but I almost black out from the g-force effect, and I go into another flat spin. When I recover and start to climb, a 190 without one wing, just passes me by.

The battle is far from over and I see another three FW190s are after me. I am alone and can only do one thing – full throttle, engage emergency boost for more power – and I aim for England. The German pilots do not like the Channel much and this has saved my bacon I believe! Yet the danger is still present because I estimate my remaining fuel is no more than ten gallons; Merlin engines consume 40 gallons an hour, and I am now over the sea with nothing below but a milky fog.

Prologue

The Story Begins

This is the tale of a fighter pilot, Stanislav Fejfar, trying to help his Czechoslovakian fatherland to survive and regain its freedom from oppression and domination, and fighting in the skies of two other countries, France and Britain, during the Second World War.

His is not a unique story, for like many of his contemporaries, it was for him necessary to leave the homeland to prepare for and then take part in the struggle for freedom. What is different in this case is that he kept a diary of his travels, adventures and finally his time as a fighter pilot with the French Armée de l'Air, and the British Royal Air Force.

The force and reasons behind his and his companions' motives started before the Second World War began in September 1939. It goes back to the previous year. On Friday 30 September 1938, the British prime minister, Neville Chamberlain, returned triumphantly from the Bavarian town of Munich to Heston Airport, just to the east of London. He had been part of a momentous meeting with the German chancellor, Adolf Hitler, the Italian dictator, Benito Mussolini and the French prime minister, Edouard Daladier, called to discuss ways of preventing a second disastrous war in the 20th century. The somewhat frail Chamberlain, holding aloft a famous piece of fluttering paper on a damp and windy airfield, declared with a somewhat pathetic smile, that they had achieved 'peace in our time'. The piece of paper was in fact the Anglo-German declaration that the two countries would never engage in war against each other and had been signed by Chamberlain and Hitler, independently of the other leaders.

However, this scrap of paper held dire consequences for the people of Czechoslovakia and as it turned out, the whole world. It had been agreed by the four leaders that the improperly named Sudetenland should be annexed to Germany, which was an area of Czechoslovakia where most of that country's border defences were located, and therefore of great strategic importance. The four powerful nations of Britain, Germany, France and Italy, had decided between themselves on

11

the new borders. There were no official representatives of Czechoslovakia invited to the meeting. The Czech ambassador to Berlin and a Czech foreign office official were seated in an adjoining room and not asked to contribute.

Under pressure, the Czech government had been informed that the German-speaking residents of the Sudetenland would be part of Germany by 10 October that year, with Poland and Hungary also staking land claims. The territory in the north of Moravia (Tesinsko) would go to Poland while the southern borders of Slovakia, with Carpathian Ruthenia, would be Hungarian. The document was actually signed at 0130 hours on 30 September, although dated the 29th, and became known as The Munich Agreement. There was little to be joyful over and the best the British, and Chamberlain, might claim is that it delayed any immediate conflict with Germany for a year. It was a year that helped Britain prepare for the unwanted second great war in twenty years.

*　*　*

The area of Europe under the Munich spotlight had a colourful and intriguing history and it is worth recording how Fejfar's life had been shaped by the history of this emerging country.

Before the Czechoslovak Republic was founded in October 1918, the Czechs and Slovaks, although sharing a very similar language, had experienced a very different history, both economically and culturally. Originally part of the Old Hapsburg Empire they were separate nations, with the Czechs occupying the Austrian part and the Slovaks the Hungarian. The Slovaks were very conservative and under the heavy rule of Hungary with a strong catholic following, whilst the Czechs forged their own liberal-minded kingdom.

After 1918 Czechoslovakia was made up of Bohemia, Moravia Silesia, Slovakia and Ruthenia, and all were aligned with France, which gave them its guarantee of independence. In 1921 there were 13.6 million people living in the country, made up of 6.8 million Czechs (51%), and 1.9 million Slovaks (14.5%) forming two thirds of the country's population. The remainder consisted of 3.1 million Germans (23.4%), 750,000 Hungarians (5.4%) 460,000 Ruthenians (3.3%), and 75,000 Poles (0.5%).

At Heston Airport, Neville Chamberlain declared to the cheering crowd:

> 'This morning I had a meeting with the German chancellor, Herr Hitler, and here is the paper which bears his name upon it as well as mine. My good friends, for the second time in our

history a British prime minister has returned from Germany bringing peace with honour. I believe it is peace for our time.'

(Chamberlain was making reference to Lord Beaconsfield's speech following the Congress in Berlin in 1878.)

Chamberlain made his way to 10 Downing Street and was greeted by a further crowd, singing: 'For he's a jolly good fellow...', and where he repeated the speech he made at the airport.

The Czechs were naturally devastated by the Munich agreement. Not only had it been decreed that the Sudetenland should be part of Germany, and heavily fortified, but southern Slovakia would then be occupied by Hungary with Poland taking some land as well, making Czechoslovakia's borders indefensible. The country would lose approximately 70% of its steel and iron resources, 70% of its electrical power, 66% of its coal, 86% of its chemical industry, 40% of its timber, and worst of all, most of its world-famous Skoda works, not to mention 3.6 million citizens who had now became part of the Third Reich.

Winston Churchill, who a year afterwards would succeed Chamberlain as prime minister of Great Britain, would later denounce the agreement in the House of Commons in October 1938:

> 'We have suffered a total and unmitigated defeat; you will find that in a period of time which may be measured in years, but may be measured in months, Czechoslovakia will be engulfed in the Nazi regime. We are in the presence of a disaster of the first magnitude, we have sustained a defeat without a war, the consequences of which will travel far with us along our road, we have passed an awful milestone in our history when the whole equilibrium of Europe has been deranged.'

On 15 March 1939, the German Wehrmacht [armed forces] invaded Czechoslovakia (under codename Operation Southeast), with Germany declaring it needed to protect its own borders, and Hitler ranting that Germany was being encircled by other western powers.

With Slovakia seceding from Czechoslovakia a day before, and Carpathian Ruthenia declaring its independence, the Czech president, Dr Emil Hacha (who had replaced Dr Eduard Beneš after his resignation on 5 October 1938) was forced to accept the occupation of the rest of both Bohemia and Moravia, with the Germans making it a protectorate.

Six months later, Adolf Hitler derided the Munich Agreement as just 'a scrap of paper', and regarded Prime Minister Chamberlain with utter contempt. Making a speech to his generals on 22 August 1939, the Führer declared: 'The enemy did not expect my great determination. Our enemies are little worms; I saw them at Munich.'

Sir Ivan Kirkpatrick in his book *The Inner Circle*, quotes Hitler talking about Chamberlain after the Munich Agreement, and being overheard to say: 'If ever that silly old man comes interfering here again with his umbrella, I'll kick him downstairs and jump on his stomach in front of the photographers.'

A week later, on 1 September 1939, Germany invaded Poland, an act that would envelop the whole world in conflict for the following six years. Chamberlain's 'peace in our time' had lasted just twelve months.

* * *

Just how aware Stanislav Fejfar was of Chamberlain's famous speech, will never be known. What is obvious though is that he, along with many others, was determined to kick against the oppression and humiliation Germany had brought them. No sooner had he planned and then executed his escape from the country of his birth, than he began keeping a diary of his new life. The actual reason why he began writing it is unclear. Perhaps just a desire to record his adventures so that one day, when he was finally able to return home, he could remind himself of all that had happened, and especially to tell his story to his mother in a factual and accurate way.

As it turned out, the diary, written in old exercise books, did eventually reach his homeland, but sadly not before his mother had passed away. That it survived is in itself a miracle and the life of this young, patriotic and brave airman has not been lost to the world.

* * *

EARLY DAYS AND MILITARY LIFE
Stanislav Fejfar was born on 25 November 1912, the only child of Marie Kuhnova and Josef Fejfar. The family home was located in Stikov, a small village within the district of Nova Paka, part of the region of Hradec Kralove.

Stanislav was devoted to his mother and makes many references to her in his diary. She died in hospital in Nova Paka in May 1960 never believing that her son had been killed and confident that one day he would return home. Apparently her last words were: 'Please do not close the doors of our house, Stanislav did not take a key.'

His father had died fighting on the Italian Front in 1918, whilst

Stanislav Fejfar with his mother in the late 1930s.

Fejfar's father, who died in WW1. This picture was in a tiny metal-framed brooch that Fejfar carried with him during WW2.

Fejfar's grandfather, Jan.

serving with the Austro-Hungarian army, and this affected Stanislav greatly, leaving him only with his grandfather Jan Fejfar for male company and influence while growing up. Stanislav kept a small round photo of his father within a small frame along with a charm of an aircraft attached to it, with the number 1,000 on the wings. This was returned to his family along with other effects, after the war.

By 1932, his mother had re-married another Czech, Alois Junek, who later fathered a step-sister Helena, whom Stanislav was never to see. The family home was now at No.11, Zizkova, Nova Paka, which was a public house run by his step-father.

Stikov was a very small village in the 1920s, and even today its population only stands at around 3,000. It is now part of Nova Paka, and nestles in the wooded northern part of the Czech Republic, some 120 kilometres north-east of Prague, and not too distant from the border with Poland. From here Stanislav would travel to the next town, along the upper reaches of the Elbe river, to Smirice, famous for its baroque church. Here he attended five general classes in the local grammar school, and then four classes in the town school of Nova Paka.

Having shown a leaning towards science and mechanics, Stanislav enrolled into the higher technical school in Pardubice, completing four further classes, and graduating finally on 20 June 1932.

It seems Fejfar was something of an introvert at school, becoming very intent on his studies, and fully determined to gain top honours. Thus he did not make friends easily and was a bit of a loner. However, he had set his heart on a course that drove him to study intensively. From his very early days his dream was to become a pilot and to fly aeroplanes. His other main interest was photography, and he was given a camera on one of his birthdays. From then on he would record the events and people in his life. This would later prove to be invaluable in illustrating the training he received, and the fellow comrades he met at the military academy, as well as his service in North Africa, France and then England.

One person he did make friends with in those early years at the academy, was František Fajtl, who went on to become a famous Czech general and a modestly successful fighter pilot with the Royal Air Force, and also be awarded many decorations. Recalling Fejfar in 2004 as a very dear friend, he said that he once told Stanislav that: 'If you don't appreciate happiness for your friends being happy, then you don't understand what friendship and life are all about.' Fajtl was only a few weeks older than Fejfar, and came from Donín, in the Louny district. He would see service with his friend in both France and England.

Fajtl also confirmed that Stanislav was, in his view, an excellent fighter pilot and flight commander, who changed his attitude to others once he became a pilot and took on the responsibilities of being the leader of a flight. 'Stanislav was always ready to help others, and impart his knowledge.'

Another good friend was Karel Mrázek, whom Fejfar first met in 1933 at the military academy. He would later become the second man to lead the Czech Fighter Wing in the RAF. The trio of Fejfar, Fajtl and Mrázek would become known by their colleagues as 'The Three Musketeers'.

On 20 April 1932, at the age of 19½, Stanislav Fejfar was called up for national service. Still determined to become a pilot he enrolled into the Czech air force at Prostejov on 29 September. Two days later he was sent to the technical flight of No.1 Air Regiment *T G Masaryka*, which was situated in Prague. Eight days after that he went to the training school for reserve air force officers back at Prostejov.

He graduated from here on 15 June 1933, being placed 21st out of a class of 34 pupils. Although he was classified as being 'a good student', Fejfar wrote home to his mother saying that he was far from satisfied with this result. He was then attached for a short period to No.15 Flight of No.4 Air Regiment, located at Hradac Kralove. On the first day of September Fejfar entered the military academy based at Hranice, and at Prostejov, both situated in Moravia. With this came the rank of sergeant – *Četař, Aspirant.*

At the academy he undertook training alongside the army officers, where they were assessed daily by the teaching staff who would eventually confirm or deny the pupil a place. The regime was much the same as RAF Cranwell in England, or the army at Sandhurst, but much more harsh and basic. The military codes in the Czech army and air force were also completely different to those of the equivalent forces of the United Kingdom. A loose minute found in the files of the post-war Allied Administration Committee, referring to the Czechs, shows the penalty of death could be applied to cases of mutiny, desertion to enemy forces, cowardice in the face of the enemy, or the surrender of a fortified position.

The pupils at the military academy would not only have to study intensely in their chosen subject but were encouraged to take an active part in all sports and in field events. For his part, Fejfar became a very proficient swordsman with the epee and a good shot with both the rifle and the shotgun, all designed to enhance the fighting spirit. He also undertook gymnastics and cycling, both part of the curriculum. In Fejfar's photo album there are pictures of men fencing, and uniformed troops out on bicycles and undertaking physical exercises. In these photos he is always smiling, so he obviously enjoyed himself within this regime.

His report at the academy for 1933/34, however, is not a particularly good one overall. Fejfar's certificate for this period shows him attached to Sandhurst Troop 1, with the following results:

Military Training	3
Service Rules	3
Radio Communication/Theory	4
Physical Training	3
Organisation	5
History of War	5

Daily exercise by bicycle at the academy.

Field Engineering	4
Weapon Theory	3
Landscape Theory	4
Military Admin/Correspondence	3
Physics	5
Chemical Technology/Hygiene/ and First Aid	3

The highest mark a student could obtain being a 1, while the lowest was a 5. Not a 2 in sight, let alone a 1, in any subject.

A good insight into the life at the academy was recently provided in the autobiography of General František Fajtl (1912-2006), entitled *Z Donina do Oblak* (From Donina to the Clouds), which was published in the Czech Republic in 2008. (Ostrov Publishing, George Stegbrauer).

'Our life was a daily routine of the alarm going off at 6 am, and onto the parade ground for a half hour of exercise in all weathers. We would return to the barracks in order to wash and shave, after which we made up our beds and cleaned the dormitory. Breakfast was served in the large communal hall after which we split into different groups to continue with further exercise, or onto the parade ground for drill, or back to the classroom. Around noon we returned to our barracks, where we again washed and prepared ourselves for communal lunch, during which our daily orders would be read by the duty officer. After this short break we then had to prepare our uniforms and clean our kit, including our rifles and small arms, before further work in the classroom. At 5 pm the whole platoon attended the reading of further daily orders by the duty officer, and then it was supper time. We then returned to the classrooms for private study, after which it was time for bed, changing into long night shirts that reached down to our heels. We tried to remain calm and drift into sleep knowing that the alarm would be going off in a few hours time, looking forward to the weekends when we were allowed some time off.'

Along with Mrázak, his other contemporaries in the same year's intake were Josef Hanuš, Tomáš Vybíral, Josef Keprt and Josef Hýbler. All were destined to become fighter pilots and take part in the Battle of Britain with the RAF in 1940. All would survive the war, except Fejfar.

Fejfar graduated from the academy on 1 July 1935, gaining a commission as a *Poručík* (air force lieutenant). This time he was assessed as 'very good', and was placed ninth out of the 27 graduates. A military parade for all the graduates was held in the town square at Prostejov on 22 September 1935, attended by all the instructors and high ranking Czech air force officers. Fejfar's personal photograph album contains many images of this parade along with a picture taken later at a grand ball held at the academy. This shows the graduates lined up in their dress uniforms along with girlfriends in their ball gowns.

His first posting after graduation was to No.6 Reconnaissance Flight, and then to No.61 Scout Flight of No.1 Air Regiment, *T G Masaryka*, in Prague, from where, on 2 September he was sent on an Administration Course of Air War at Prostejov. He finished this course on 21 December, again being assessed as 'very good', finishing fifth out of 12. On 15 June 1936, Fejfar was transferred to No.38 Flight, during which time his commanding officer wrote of him:

'A well disciplined officer who is loyal and subordinate on duty, and of very good behaviour when off duty. He is mentally flexible, with rapid perception, and logical thinking. He is a good and capable section leader. He has proved his interest as a fighter pilot, and is a good disciplined pilot. He is recommended for the post as a section leader which includes administration duties.'

Passing-out ball, 1935. Fejfar is 4th from the right with his assigned lady.

Zdena Hylmorová, Fejfar's girl-friend in the early 1930s.

Following this he was appointed as a field pilot (*Polni Pilot Letec*) on the first day of January 1937. At the conclusion of his fighter pilot training he was sent on a night-fighter course at Piestany, in Slovakia, which he attended between 1 July and 14 November, finishing 5th out of 18. His assessment at the end of the year by his CO had now greatly improved:

'His capability as a section (schwarm) leader is good, and he is very capable as an instructor. He is very good as a fighter pilot, well disciplined and courageous, and a good marksman, being skilful in his clerical duties. I recommend him for duty as a flight commander.'

Fejfar was then attached in turn to three fighter flights of No.3 Air Regiment (*General a Letce M R Stefanika*), Nos. 38, 45 and 59. These flights were located at Vajnory and Soisska in Nova Ves, and Piestany airfields in

Slovakia. The Czech air force (CzAF) at this period had six air regiments, one fighter (the 4th), with three mixed fighter/reconnaissance (1st, 2nd and 3rd), along with two bomber regiments (5th and 6th). The force had more than 1,500 aircraft, of which 320 were fighters.

The standard fighter aircraft at this time was the Avia B-534 biplane, which was armed with four machine guns. Some reports at the time heralded it as the best fighter in Europe during the early 1930s.

Although it had a biplane wing assembly of fabric and steel, plus a static undercarriage, it also had an enclosed cockpit which allowed a ceiling of up to 30,000 feet. With its 850 hp Hispano-Suiza engine, providing a speed of around 245 mph, it was highly manoeuvrable and deadly in combat using its four 7.7 mm synchronised machine guns. Although only approximately 300 came off the assembly line, the German Luftwaffe held the Avia B-534 in such high regard that they later briefly employed it to form a squadron of captured aircraft.

On 1 May 1938 he was given the post of temporary flight commander of No.45 Fighter Flight. During the Munich crisis, this unit was the first squadron assigned to the 4th Army Group in Southern Moravia, and later as part of the 3rd Army sent to Slovakia, between 24 September and 21 November. Here he became a flight commander and then promoted to the first officer of the flight. Fejfar excelled in this post and was given an outstanding final assessment in December 1938.

'Although he is a young officer, he has proved an extraordinary capability in the post of flight commander. He is conscientious, energetic, reliable, and always shows initiative. He is an excellent pilot who enjoys flying.

His cheerful nature is without any bad tendencies. He has good theoretical knowledge and is mentally flexible and logical with a good education. He is a member of the literary circle and tries to increase his general and military knowledge by studying professional journals. He is an active participant in winter sports, especially skiing and skating, and is very capable as a motor-cyclist, and an excellent marksman.

He is more than capable for the position of flight commander.'

* * *

In the meantime, Czech intelligence officials who were in the field, reported on 11 March that they had discovered plans for the occupation of Bohemia and Moravia, but the Czech government failed to act as they didn't want to 'upset' the Germans, and the events in Slovakia regarding the separation. On 13 March 1939 the heads of the army of both the Czechs and Slovaks had a meeting with the head of intelligence to discuss the situation and decided against destroying weapons/transport, etc., and to wait for events to unfold!

Also on 13 March, the day before Slovakia became independent, Fejfar was forced to return to his homeland. Hitler had given his support to the Slovak separatists, willing them to break away from Czechoslovakia.

Like other Czechs, Fejfar felt this division of the country was a hard pill to swallow, and by then he must have had serious thoughts, as others were having, that leaving his homeland, perhaps forever, was his only real course of action. His mind was quickly made up for him as German troops began marching into Czechoslovakia two days later, on the snowy morning of the 15th, then raising the hated swastika over the historic city of Prague. Czech radio announced that: 'Today at six o'clock this morning German troops crossed our borders and proceeded to Prague by all routes. Stay calm and go to work as usual.'

Suddenly his country had ceased to exist. The next day the 'Protectorate of Bohemia and Moravia' was proclaimed to be now under the protection of Hitler's Third Reich.

The German Luftwaffe quickly took control of the Czech air force, consisting of 1,625 military aircraft of all types plus civilian aeroplanes, along with its airfields and aeroplanes, leaving Stanislav Fejfar and his fellow officers with no aircraft to fly, and seemingly, no future. In the Czech aircraft factories five new prototypes were captured, including the Avia B35.

On the ground, the superior air officers stood around in groups, not knowing quite what to do, just discussing the situation. One member of the air staff was quoted as saying, 'It was though we were in a bad dream'. From this day on Fejfar planned for his escape.

*   *   *

Fejfar was on the move. He and others like him with strong feelings for liberty and freedom, knew the only way to help regain their country's independence was to fight for it, even if this meant fighting from another country. Between June and August 1940 more than 900 Czech airmen eventually found their way to the UK, and 88 of the most experienced of these took part in the Battle of Britain. Knowing too that this was the start of a whole new life and adventure, Fejfar decided to keep a record of his future life, so as the month of June 1939 arrived he began to jot down his thoughts in diary form.

Like most diaries it consisted of personal reflections and recordings of events as they involved him and his comrades. The entries of course were in his native Czech language and Jindřich (Henry) Prokop's generous translation is recorded here. There has been no major editing from the translation, only the occasional correction of spelling, or using a better word or improved grammar. However, it is plain that Henry Prokop did edit his translation, no doubt keeping the story simple and perhaps more straightforward. The authors of this book have added more flesh to the story from a historical perspective as well as giving the reader a better understanding of the background to Fejfar's life and involvement in the events that were about to envelop him.

We will start with Prokop's own words about the translation, which he carried out between 1996-7, and how he came to know him from mid-1939:

'I knew Stanislav Fejfar first in Poland, in June 1939, on our journey from our beloved homeland to Western Europe, so as to be free to fight the Nazi criminals. We served in the French Foreign Legion in North Africa, where we transferred to the French air force, then through France during the invasion of 1940 and finally to England where we joined the Royal Air Force. Fejfar was a fighter pilot through and through; I was technical ground crew and later an engineering officer. He showed a determination to get at the Germans from the moment he decided to leave his homeland in 1939.

'The discovery, by Simon Muggleton, of Fejfar's diary, published in Czech by the communist regime, amongst other memorabilia of Fejfar, in Prague, was a touching revelation of the wartime thoughts of an indomitable spirit.

'It was this that made me determined to translate the diary into English, in the hope that others might share the thoughts of a gallant man, who was so representative of his many compatriots flying alongside him in the Royal Air Force.'

Prokop was two years younger than Fejfar and came from Olomouc. After the war he remained in England and was living in Worthing when originally contacted by Simon Muggleton. He died in October 1998, and this translation is a testament to him and shows his love for Czechoslovakia.

The Diary

Stanislav Fejfar as a trainee pilot, 1933.

Chapter One

The Escape

1st June 1939

At twelve o'clock I leave home. I cannot describe my feelings as I contemplate life in exile. At the railway station I meet Otto. A meeting has been arranged and organised in Prague by the underground organisation, where we can also have a last dance, together with our friends. At 11 pm we sit on the express train which will take us to the Polish/Czech frontier town of Moravská Ostrava. Otto and I are now joined by Hudeček, our Czech comrade pilot officer from Pardubice town.

5th June 1939

At 5 am we arrive in the town and real life begins, because we are now in the hands of the local escape committee and have to await further instructions. We stay in the Hotel Blanik where we meet another pilot officer, Stránský.[1]

6th June 1939

Everything is too quiet (apart from us who are feeling nervous). Waiting to kill time, we play cards. If we stay here much longer we shall become experts in the Czech card game called *Marias*.

7th June 1939

We are not happy waiting for something to happen. The local underground organisation has gone off somewhere until its organiser suddenly appears at 5 pm and announces: 'We are going tomorrow!' We are told to go out and purchase rucksacks because we shall have to become tourists. We change our suits and abandon our luggage deliberately in the hotel just to foil any Gestapo informer,

---

[1] Josef Stránský was 24, from Borová. He would eventually be a Mosquito pilot with 21 Squadron RAF, win the DFC, but was killed in action two weeks after D-Day, 21 June 1944 as a squadron leader.

should there be any, who may report about our group. We now move to the Hotel Atlantic and are painfully aware of the fact that we are living in Nazi-occupied Czechoslovakia.

8th June 1939

Reveille at 4 am and after breakfast we walk to the railway station at Vítkovice and board the train for Frýdek. We have another breakfast in the waiting room restaurant and await the arrival of our contact man, Mr H, who can only be identified by him waving a blue handkerchief. We wait for this man when along comes his wife accompanied by Captain Pavlíček, who takes charge, and we begin to march. In the lead is our contact man followed by his wife, while we three follow this group from about 300 metres behind. Later, we pass through the village of Dobra, where we know the Gestapo has a representative. We proceed to the tourist office of Pazderna and begin to feel we are nearing the Polish frontier. We walk past a Czech public house where at least four German customs men are drinking beer. Now we approach a little brook, where the lady and husband vanish. We have no idea yet that we are now just ten steps from a Polish border post.

We jump across the brook and suddenly we are in Poland. It is now 09.55 am and we walk to the Polish side of the Pazderna tourist office. Our courageous lady re-appears and we are now, seemingly, a German group of tourists. At 10.20 her husband joins us and we then say goodbye to this brave couple. We now continue our trek through the wooded countryside until we reach a bus station.

By now it is 11.30 am and we board a bus that takes us to Czech Tczesin, named by the Poles, and we have lunch whilst waiting for the train to the town of Cracow. In charge of our group now is First Lieutenant Kral, who is also a pilot, and we follow him through the streets of the town to another tourist office.

The general consul from the consulate is now in charge and he informs us (we hope jokingly) that we may be transferred to the [French] Foreign Legion. Until now we have had no idea what we shall do, but obviously everything is proceeding smoothly under the supervision of a man named Znojemský, who is a doctor of international law.

9th June 1939

In the morning we fill in our identity forms under the personal supervision of Vice Consul Henzl, another doctor of law. At 3 pm General Prchala of the Czech army and all of us 29 officers, and 80 other ranks who have gathered here, have to swear allegiance to fight for the future liberation of our country.

Our group also contains some Slovaks, whose country was deliberately not occupied, thus spoiling all this fight against him [Hitler] in future, but Slovaks do not think much of this and they are now joining us.

The lists of all are checked and re-checked and we are now duly registered as military exiles with permission of the Polish military attaché and obviously agreed by the Polish government. Food is a problem because the Poles do not feed us, [and] in the infancy of this anti-Hitler planning and grouping [things have not been organised]. Czech organisations in various cities are being asked to assist us but the response is not speedy enough. We share amongst us some Polish zloty currency, especially from those officers who do not smoke. As officers we are offered officer's flats nearby [to stay in] but they are filthy and even then two people have to share. This is Poland and not our country.

12th June 1939

Our military resistance group is increasing every hour. Rumours about joining the French Foreign Legion abound but our consul from the Czech embassy persists that whatever happens we shall definitely be flying. We are delighted when he is so emphatic because that is why we left our dearest ones behind in order to fly and pay back the Nazi swine for the humiliation of being occupied. The next morning we find that one officer and four other ranks were discharged from our military unit because they were communist party members and that is against our Czech pre-war regulations for armed forces. They are asked to leave at once.

13th June 1939

During the morning we walk around Cracow town and in the afternoon we are asked to sign a contract with the French Foreign Legion. Those who will not sign will be returned to the Nazi occupied homeland.[2]

15/16th June 1939

We are getting ready for our journey to France and at 07.20 on the 15th there is a religious service for our first group who are soon to sail. At the end of the Mass we sing our national anthem. Further groups of escapees arrived today.

---

[2] Henry Prokop was with the group of other ranks and NCO men and he remarked that this statement was not true. Apparently the Polish military authorities would have been delighted to accept any Czech air force regulars with open arms. However, it must just be that as far as the Czech officers were concerned, Fejfar's comment was an 'official' line at that moment.

Our first selected group is nervous, this being the last day in Cracow (16th), and we begin by furious showering and are ready to 'fall in' by 6 am. Our commanding officer, Staff Captain Duda,[3] presents himself to the other 106 ranks and 36 pilot officers. After this Lieutenant-Colonel Svoboda of the Czech army, who is staying behind, asks us to promise him that whatever happens we shall faithfully serve our fatherland without dishonour. Again we sing our national anthem. Our departure precipitates our fears that not all will be well with our Polish Slavonic nation. Finally the train leaves at 7.35 am and at the last moment the brother of President Beneš arrives, describing how he escaped in an empty coal train heading for Poland.

17th June 1939

We arrive at the port of Gdynia at 9.15 am following a tiring journey via Warsaw. This is the first time I have seen the sea and could observe little white sails of yachts and watch the seagulls. What awaits us beyond these waters? At 2.30, Polish customs officers insist upon an inspection but all I have in my possession is a comb, a handkerchief and what I stand in – one pair of trousers, a shirt and tie.

At 3 pm we are finally allowed to board the ship, a huge liner named SS *Sobieski*, which is sailing to South America via England. Once on board we have no idea how to behave or what to do! At long last the ship's sirens blow and we begin leaving poor Poland at 5.15 pm. Somebody arranged for a Polish military band to play on the quay, although we doubt it is for our benefit, since the Polish military authorities never visited us. We were told later, though, that the Poles were far too slow to appreciate how many trained Czech air force men passed through their country.

Soon we sail into the Baltic sea and we still walk around the ship on this (for many of us) the first sea crossing of our lives. The first-class cabins are allocated to officers, but since our fares are the cheapest, two officers must share a cabin, but [in the event] this only happens for Staff Captain Duda. We lieutenants are to have four men to a cabin. Fifteen other officers sleep somewhere else in the second-class area. The dinner gong sounds and this is the first time we see food served properly and in sufficient quantity. Not only good food but for us officers we have access to the first-class smoking rooms and the [promenade] deck.

Darkness comes soon and it begins to rain. Having had my trench-coat stolen in Cracow (no doubt to exchange for food) I have to retire

---

[3] Josef Duda, from Prague, was a pilot and later, with the RAF, became a group captain. Served with 312 Squadron and then Czech HQ in London. Was made a CBE. Died in 1977, aged 72.

early to my cabin, where, at 10 pm I write these notes. I end by adding remarks, wondering about how we will achieve the defeat of our German enemy, who are such formidable opponents!

18/19th June 1939

We have left Danish waters and are now sailing parallel to the German coast. The skies are blue but the sea is rough and all the Czech air force heroes are lying in their cabins cursing the seasickness. My stomach is also affected and I have no intention of having a meal however tempting the menu might be.

We hear and then see two bombers flying very high above us but have no idea as to what nationality they are, but it indicates to us that we shall land in France tomorrow.

20th June 1939

This morning I am still sea-sick and can only observe the sea through the port-hole of my cabin. By 10 am we are approaching the English port of Dover and can see the [famous] White Cliffs above the harbour. As soon as we dock we hear that some more Czech airmen are joining us. We leave to cross the Channel and finally arrive at Boulogne at 2.15 pm. Our ship is so large that we have to wait for high-tide before we can enter the harbour. However, seeing the French coast makes us happy and we disembark at 7.30 pm.

We are welcomed by our military and air attaché from Paris, Captain [Jan] Pernikář.[4] As the last train has already left for Paris, our destination, we must find somewhere to sleep here. The only building available is one formerly occupied by Spanish soldiers and it is so filthy that we refuse to use it. Some of us search and find some fourth-rate Bistro restaurant and with some Polish zloty and in exchange of a few wrist-watches we manage to eat and sleep here. Although we do not speak the language, the atmosphere is very friendly. Some Czech army passengers will proceed tomorrow to Agde, which is on the south coast of France somewhere.

21st June 1939

Reveille is at 5 am, as if anybody slept anyway. Taking the 7 o'clock train we arrive at the Gare du Nord in Paris at 10.45 where we are welcomed by a very popular Slovak ambassador by the name of Osusky. We board French air force lorries with bench seats and the petrol fumes seem unusual to us. We end up in the air ministry staff dining rooms at 11.30. The building is situated by the River Seine and is very spacious.

[4] Later squadron leader with Czech HQ in London. A pilot aged 36 at this time.

We all eat together disregarding our ranks, and the food is out of this world, including bananas in abundance, that hardly any of us could ever afford back home. Quite frankly we have never seen such quantities of everything as this on our first day in France. Most of us snooze by the Seine, and after supper we stroll through Paris. Once more everything is overpowering and these impressions of Paris will last me through this life and the next one. I return from this walk at 11.30 pm.

22nd June 1939

This morning is taken up by studying the French language and at 2 pm we have our photos taken – guess what for? – our documents for the French Foreign Legion. So far this is only done for us officers. Other ranks will be forced to be inducted via street recruitment offices. I note that the five-year contract is sub-titled: *For service in the French air force*, and the French officers with us could not believe this. This clever, typically French diplomatic gesture is only for those serving in peacetime and this contract will be void, once a war is declared. Other ranks called up by a staff captain every morning had to go to the recruitment office. The first party was of about 50 men, but everything moved so slowly I do not think many others will be forced to receive a Sidi-bel-Abbes [type] training for weeks to come.

Perhaps I should record in my diary the daily menu of the ordinary French airman. Breakfast consists of black coffee, bread, cheese and a bar of chocolate, which one eats with dry bread. Try it! Or a huge solitary sardine. Lunch begins with sardines, mostly in jellied form, or a liver pâté, followed by a pork cutlet or a rump steak called a *biftec*, served with fresh vegetables. Dessert is mostly fresh fruit such as bananas, all washed down with red wine. Supper starts with soup and a meat dish with potatoes, followed by a camembert cheese and wine. One does not queue since one airman carries a large tray for six from the serving hatch. I cannot imagine any other nation providing such food for their servicemen but this is, of course, a country of food [lovers] and according to French people, the hub of the universe.

We officers form an excursion party of walkers and proceed to inspect and admire the French capital. The genius of French engineering is, of course, the Eiffel Tower.

23rd June 1939

This morning we had a medical examination and during the afternoon Captain Perníkář asks us to write down details of our Czechoslovak air force career, such as pilot, observers, etc. These details are needed by the French air ministry. Nobody hurries and after this is all taken down we take a leisurely walk back to the Eiffel Tower because it is the 50th anniversary of it being built. But tragically, one of the Czech embassy officials informs us that one of his staff has committed suicide by jumping from the top. None of us can understand why anyone should do this in such a free and wonderful city.

24th June 1939

A week has gone by and there is no news for any of us, and being Czechs we are the only ones enquiring about the possibility of flying. However, French bureaucracy does not permit haste. Yet we are, seemingly, not forgotten by the colonel commanding the nearest French air force base. The news is that we officers are to be moved from the airmen's billets to the sergeant's mess. All very clean, modern and spacious. Also a pool table is provided.

We study intensively the French language every morning and the afternoons are spent at the pool table. We also consume champagne like water. If we are not soon transferred we shall become masters of this pool game.

We also observe the departure of 28 poor devils of NCO rank being taken to a Paris recruiting office. Most of the NCO group are the pilots I served with on Czech airfields and we are sorry that they will be marching as infantry soldiers, but what can we do? Military orders must be obeyed. God only knows when we shall see them again in the blue uniforms of the French air force. We are all patriots, which is proved by our being here, instead of remaining in our homeland, but this foreign legion idea seems quite preposterous and quite unacceptable.

Henry Prokop noted that he was among this group of 28 NCOs, but being an officer, he and the other officers would not be inducted this way, while those who went would serve as sergeants. Some of those that went are named by Fejfar in his diary, and later served with the Royal Air Force. Vladimír Kyselo, who would later fly with 32 Squadron RAF and be killed in March 1941. Karel Lang, would die with 311 Squadron RAF in October 1940, his Wellington bomber (L7786) hitting some HT cables by Needham Market, Norfolk. Otokar Hrubý would later serve with 111 Squadron late in the Battle of Britain, and afterwards flew with 313 and 310 Squadrons, RAF, and be awarded the DFC. He died in his homeland in 1993. Jaroslav Novák flew with 311 Squadron as a navigator and survived the war as a flying officer. František Buliš became a pilot with 311 Squadron RAF and lost his life on 18 October 1942 as a pilot officer. His Wellington (T2564) suddenly spun into the ground near Uxbridge. Oskar Valošek was another NCO pilot to fly with 311 Squadron and he too lost his life, in October 1940. Somehow a Very pistol was discharged inside his Anson and the aircraft crashed near Peterborough. Adolf Musálek became a flying officer pilot with 311 Squadron, and also died with this unit, on 29 August 1943, in an accident 30-seconds after take-off in Hampshire, in Liberator BZ775.

Perhaps the most well known was František Doležal. He flew in France with the French and escaping to England saw action during the Battle of Britain with 19 Squadron. Commissioned in August 1940 he went to 310 Squadron but quickly returned to 19. Back with 310 in early 1941 he would later command this squadron and in 1942 won the DFC. The following year he commanded the Czech fighter wing, ending the war as a wing commander with the DSO. Sadly he was killed in a flying accident in October 1945, flying as a passenger in Czechoslovakia.

30th June 1939

Today is an unhappy one because we are to be moved from the sergeant's mess to a former Zig-Zag cigarette paper factory which is empty and will be refurbished as our Czech air force centre. However, the advantage is soon obvious, for we love to be all together. The bedding with white sheets is impeccable and although we officers keep together in our groups, we are perfectly happy with this arrangement. I was told that refugees of any description are allowed by the International Red Cross to write home on a special form but using only some 25 words. Perhaps our families will receive them so I fill in my card to my mother at once. This leads us to discuss what the Gestapo swine may have done with our parents and wives. Obviously I cannot write to my mother about the repulsive feeling we have that we shall soon be departing for the French Foreign Legion, for it is such a waste being a fully trained officer pilot, but as always I am a serviceman and orders must be obeyed.[5]

1st July 1939

We went to Versailles today, marching all the way, since the 10 francs given to us by the Czech embassy is insufficient, even for cigarettes. I have never seen anything like this [palace], especially the gardens and bush arrangements. It was staggeringly beautiful and during the afternoon there were some fireworks. This was a typical French gesture and idea, to set off fireworks in daylight.

9th July 1939

I have not written anything lately because there is nothing much to comment upon. If somebody would send us to Indo-China we would go at once. This period of inactivity leads to quite a few quarrels amongst ourselves. Today we visit – that is we are invited by the Czechoslovak army – to see how they live in a tented camp by the River Marne. Our

---

[5] Again Prokop added a comment here, that many families of these escapees were interned in labour camps for the full five years of the war until the collapse of Germany.

French language teacher, hearing about this, provided us for this outing a free lorry and driver.

The camp is situated next to a gymnastic stadium which is rather nice for any PT minded Czech citizens. Some, we are told, like the summer camping but we are all agreed that it will not be much fun during the autumn and winter. Some local French people do not understand why all these foreigners are brought here, although the local council agrees that the camp is spotless. We later celebrate a day of the Bohemian countryman of ours, Jan Hus, who centuries ago was burnt at the stake for being against the opulence of the RC church. Hus was the follower of the English John Wycliffe. In our homeland today it will be a state holiday.

14th July 1939, Bastille Day

The biggest fête in France and empire is soon pretty obvious by the special preparations in every village and town. We awake at 4 am in order to secure the best places on the Champs Elysées route which we reach on foot by 10 am. The celebrations are begun by two British squadrons followed by two French escadrilles. It makes me sad that a year ago we held a similar fête in our homeland. The marching begins to the sound of a Scottish regiment pipe band with their curious bag-pipes. Then a group of British guards, followed by French regiments and the French navy, with their typical red pom-poms on their hats. These are followed by the *Légion Étranger*. The enthusiasm of the French civilian bystanders was unbelievable. Not surprisingly since they were all six-footers, and their marching was absolutely 100 percent. These 'cut-throats' whom we are soon to join, simply out-marched everybody. They were followed by the regiments of mostly coloured soldiers, such as Spahis, in their blue ballooned trousers of the French empire, with others from Africa, Morocco, Tunisia, Syria, Levant, Indo-China and Madagascar.

I am moved by this parade because as a military person I am also a judge of such assemblies and I do not think that what I saw today can be matched by any other nation on earth now in 1939. I try to visualise the parade when all this [conflict] is over and we march across Prague's Wenceslas Square!

The programme ended at one pm and we marched quickly back to our air ministry dining room because the French government especially favours servicemen today with a special meal. What a beautiful meal it was too, with tender beef rump steaks and more expensive château wines in abundance. Naturally after such a feast we do not intend to return to our Zig-Zag billets, but begin singing, as usual, with our Czech marching songs – marching or sentimental – and soon the French groups begin with their own. As we get progressively more intoxicated we sing more loudly and the French 'Copains' naturally follow. Gradually we begin, whilst singing a mixture of French/Czech songs, to embrace our French air force comrades in bear-like fashion. We have thus ended this Gaullist evening which I will remember forever.

How I got to my lodgings and bed situated two miles away I do not know but I awoke the next morning lying on the floor beside my bed with everyone around me still snoring vigorously.

15th July 1939

France is celebrating the 150th anniversary of the Republic. Even we continental-born citizens are amazed to observe how strangers in the streets embrace each other. Some of the streets are completely closed to traffic and everybody is dancing and singing. We went to the Trocadero to listen to the best military bands with Standa Zimprich and Venca Šikl.[6] Our French teacher, Sergeant Jean Breton, was responsible for this enterprise and we returned to our Zig-Zag billets at 8 am the next morning. I was told that I was seen swimming in the [fountain] in the *Place de la Concorde*. The French police never interfere with citizens behaving absurdly on these occasions, and only do so when somebody intends to jump into the Seine while intoxicated. The river here is quite fast running. Also they close the Eiffel Tower. I suppose it reduces the Parisian population quite a bit by people jumping from it.

18th July 1939

Unbelievable! Through the Red Cross I received a 25-word letter from my mother. I was crying when I read it for I knew she was crying too when she wrote it. So the paper I kissed to taste her tears of happiness, knowing that I was still alive and well. I was never, of course, allowed after the decision to escape, to contact her, and what hope have I to return to her in one piece?[7]

And now back to further waiting. The French air ministry have decided that we Czech aviators will be serving in the French imperial air force bases overseas. Therefore I fill in a questionnaire that I would like to serve in Madagascar or Indo-China, which was entirely French, or alternatively in North Africa, or Syria. Nobody was going to fly in France during peacetime.

---

[6] Both Stanislav Zimprich and Václav Šikl later flew with 310 Squadron in England. Zimprich was killed in April 1942, but Šikl survived the war.

[7] Henry Prokop noted here that the next letter she received about her son was in 1945, telling her of his death in a Spitfire three years earlier, which of course she did not believe or accept.

The questionnaire, once sent off, proves only that the French air ministry at least have a list of all Czech air force personnel at their disposal.

I write now about how many officer pilots are here with me in our billets. They are Staff Captain Duda, our CO at present. Pilots, Hudec, Šnajdr, Mrázek, Janouch, Zbořil, Zimprich, Nezbeda, Hájek, Šikl, Vancl, Hochmál, Čermák, and myself, Fejfar.[8]

26th July 1939

Twenty-five years ago saw the beginning, and end, of the Austro-Hungarian Empire since they declared mobilization [in 1914]. We Czechs originally belonged to it and it seems to me that this mobilization was only the beginning of the end. I wonder what will happen in the next 25 years?

Today our military attaché told us the happy news that a ship leaving Gdynia in Poland contains 180 NCOs and 92 officers, all being the cream of the pre-war Czechoslovak air force. More will arrive later. However, we also receive the alarming news that the German ambassador has discovered that hundreds of Czech airmen are in Paris and is demanding our return to the Third Reich as their citizens. The French, as we know by their foreign legion, would never ever allow us to be sent to certain death without moving us to some of their far distant colonies.

2nd August 1939

I receive a letter from a former NCO pilot in my regiment, complaining about the behaviour of the legion staff. I will not reply and I would expect this mummy's boy to act as a grown man for a change. After all, we officers, who have gone through the high academy of the Czechoslovak forces, are compelled by circumstances to be inducted into the French Foreign Legion as a special favour by the French bureaucracy, to serve as 'sergeants'. I personally think that apart from we Czechs, no other nation would ever consider it, never mind accept it as a *fait accompli*!

5th August 1939

Saturday and Sunday proves a quiet weekend, but unknown to us, our departure is to be Monday the 7th. Although this is a bombshell, never-the-less *something* is to happen in our deadly silent, uneventful existence. So during Sunday we all walk the Paris boulevards and taste

[8] From this list, the following became operational during the Battle of Britain: Josef Duda (312 Sqn), Karel Mrázek (43 and 46), Svatopluk Janouch (310), and Fejfar.

French civilization, before we shall undoubtedly begin to march in the legion-issue infantry boots.

7th August 1939

Our favourite French teacher, Jan Breton, took us by his transport to sign the 'Act of Engagement' as the French call it. We sign this contract for five years with the subtitle of the 'French air force service' underneath. The recruiting officer was amazed to see the *Légion Étranger* will have its own pilots. Some of my colleagues were in fact jokingly going to sign and present the contract with the name of the puppet president of former Czechoslovakia – Hacha – but quickly realised that if anybody calls out for Hacha, they would not know which of them it was.

Sergeant Breton took us to the Gare de Lyon rail station and off we went, reaching Marseilles, and the Fort St Jean headquarters of the foreign legion's European base the next day at 9.40 am.

The train carriage was also full of other legion recruits with the guards having fixed bayonets in case somebody suddenly changes his mind and wants to go home. It can happen when you have quarrelled with a loved one or mother-in-law, and now that you are the property of the legion, going home is not allowed.

The next morning we begin to queue for our first uniform which will be used only for here and in transit before we reach North Africa. We notice that a sergeant in charge of stores is a 'god' here. We have to give up our civilian clothing which is not so bad as we have sometimes slept in them and never changed even a single shirt.

8/10th August 1939

We are allowed to go out and walk to the nearby beach. Mostly we stand and watch the huge trans-ocean ships leaving Europe's biggest port. Our departure is to be at 2 pm on the 9th from the fortress and as sergeants we are given a squad of 30 recruits to march to the quay where our ship, the SS *Sidi-bel-Abbes* awaits us. As sergeants we are allocated a cabin with four of us sharing. Our sailing time will be at 5 pm.

The food is reasonable, with wine – government issue – that tastes like water which probably it mostly is. The weather is absolutely beautiful and when night falls we are sitting in the restaurant where everybody is dancing. This ship, normally employed by the legion on a 24-hour basis, is transporting officers, NCOs and some business people to the port of Oran. As we have almost no money and with only a few unattached ladies available, we are just watching, and only drink the cheapest red wine [from the bar].

11th August 1939

We are still asleep when we hear commands to wake up. We dock and march off the ship at 6.30 am, and are obliged to march under a fierce sun, to the French Foreign Legion fortress, Durier. A car comes for us four and takes us to the Oran hospital for a medical examination, although we already had one in Paris. A sergeant at Sidi-bel-Abbes, who happens to be of Czech birth, takes us to the railway station and directly onto the platform. It is unbearably hot and our new uniforms are not tropical issue. A sergeant in Marseilles told us that whatever unit we serve in on French soil we should always have the top button belonging to the foreign legion. It causes a lot of envy because the ordinary Frenchman respects this button as a symbol of tough, virile men.

Arrived at Sidi at 9.25 pm and in proper formation my squad of 30 reached their destination. In the case of the recruits, they go into CP3 huts, where the poor devils disappear, whereas we are proceeding to the sergeant's mess. My friend Šikl was told that he overheard someone say that drinking 12 to 15 beers the first night at Sidi is the norm, and indeed, he drank 15 beers. Thus ended our first night in North Africa (Algeria).

12th August 1939

First thing in the morning we are issued with two uniforms. One is for work, the other for going out. The thin denim one is for work. We all admire the huge headquarters compound housing various regiments, mostly here before they sail for Indo-China. The yard is full of flowers and small palm trees. It is not surprising that with so much cheap labour available the place is picturesque and orderly. Part of the base is a gymnasium and a volley ball court, along with a swimming pool and also a library. We are officially welcomed by a long-serving officer, Major Hájek, who is of Czech nationality.

We are told that we shall be paid a daily sum of 1.80 francs and we shall have to submit to preliminary training of four to six weeks. We are not satisfied and tell him that Paris never told us about any 'square bashing' at all. As grown up men and regular officers we should have been told. But here we are supposed to set an example as officers to all those who arrive after us.

19th August 1939

After yet another medical examination we are finally admitted to the legion and are informed that we are one of the 52 nationalities here. Looking around in the dining room I can see an Englishman, a Swede, a Dutchman and two Germans. Another one I could not even guess at. We are told that regulations do not allow offensive nationalistic

Czech airmen in the French Foreign Legion uniforms and top-coats.

remarks. Anyone found stealing is punished with a one year sentence in a prison block.

We soon become accustomed to a 4.30 am reveille, in order to fall in at 5. At 5.30 we begin our infantry training, including rifle drill. Every second day we march out of the gate and trek a distance of about 30 miles. We are also taught theoretical military assaults by soldiers but our knowledge of French is insufficient to comprehend anything and frankly it is a waste of time. At 11 am we have lunch in the sergeant's mess which lasts for 45 minutes, after which comes an enforced siesta for two hours, and everybody must stay in bed for that time. At 3 pm we work for another two hours and then change from our working uniforms for supper at 6.30. We hear nothing about Europe but continually talk about it. We do not see any newspapers either.

26th August 1939

Today we hear that France and England are mobilising and that Stalin and the Germans have concluded a non-aggression pact. Poland is now in the same situation that we found ourselves in March and the German Wehrmacht is on the march again. We are told that some Czech infantry regiments are coming here but later the order was rescinded and they sailed from Oran back to Europe.

For us at present, it is 'Legion Patria Nostra', which means that the legion is our fatherland. We find it difficult to adjust to the North

African heat and according to the legion regulations, everyone at night must lie under a sheet, so you sweat continuously. The regulations do not allow us to open windows because of the mosquitoes. We think about our homeland and our loved ones and gaze at the ceiling where you can read the painted slogan: 'Legionaires, you are soldiers of death and I am sending you where death is waiting for you.' In the French language it sounds very romantic!

27th August 1939

We return from our march very early, at about 8 am, because the Sahara Sirocco wind has reached Sidi-bel-Abbes and the heat, along with the strong sandy wind, produces a temperature of 45 degrees (112°F). One must remain in the shower for a ridiculous time because with the Sahara wind the mosquitoes become embedded in your skin.

28th August 1939

Unbelievable day. The last one as far as we are concerned in this confounded place. It is a bombshell when the legion ceases to give any more orders. Captain Adam, a pilot and former military attaché, arrives at 2 pm with Major Hájek of the legion, and announces immediate postings to various North African air bases. One by one we enter an office to avoid misunderstanding. I am to be sent to Oran with Rudolf Holečka. Others are posted to Tunis, including Mrázek, Šikl, Zimprich, Janouch, Hájek. We are excited by the news of the mobilization of France, and can almost smell the exhaust fumes of our future aircraft.

We fervently hope that the Führer is not going to ask for negotiations because we are more than keen to acquaint ourselves with his Luftwaffe miracles in the air. The general excitement is observed by us in the dining room because some regiments are to sail for Europe at once.

This is the news for which we have been waiting since our escape from our homeland, and although this will result in many pilot sacrifices, this is what we have been training for in our peacetime forces. The only disappointment is that I am to go to a bomber squadron with others, except for the three lucky devils, Šikl, Zimprich and Sýkora, who are posted to a fighter base. We are also furious that we as the elite of the fighter school are to fly in those horribly slow French bombers.

Chapter Two

War

31st August 1939

Today we are told that on 3 September we shall be officially transferred to our French air force bases as discussed with Captain Adam. We are all very pleased that the three days of waiting will be the last ones in this hole.

1st September 1939

At 9 am we are told by someone who had been listening to the wireless that some Polish towns have been bombed by the Luftwaffe. Although we are sorry for the Polish population, it means something more to us at long last. The war with the Luftwaffe! A special order delivered after our day's work, arrives with a duty sergeant that we must all depart tomorrow.

2nd September 1939

By 8.45 am we are assembled at the Sidi-bel-Abbes train station, but discover that the train is not due to depart till the evening, so back we go to headquarters. However, the delay is a godsend, because the legion treasurer discovers that we can be paid with a 'primo', that is, we have come to the end of our training and are therefore fully eligible for back pay. This amounts to 350 francs, and having up till now only been receiving 1.80 francs a day, I consider myself rich.

By 8.30 pm we leave Sidi for the journey to Oran. The Tunis pilots will change at Oran. During our journey we naturally sing happy marching and sentimental songs. We still belong to the legion during this transit though, and regrettably, in Oran, we still sleep in fortress Durier with the bed bugs. We are joined here by other Czech pilots and a ground staff specialist – Pátaček – who served in the legion with us as an ordinary soldier.

3rd September 1939

At 8 am a vehicle takes us to a base in Oran called 'De la Senia'. We report to the commanding officer: Captain K, J Štefan, Holeček, Zimprich, Janouch, Hájek, Zadrobílek[1], Přihoda and myself. Also Warrant Officer Pátaček joins us as a group staff specialist. We are now informed that our escadrille is Number 10 and it is in the process of being established on a war footing but in the meantime we are transferred to No.572 Escadrille. During the morning we are equipped with flying suits and helmets, and we are welcomed in the officer's mess, and a lot of champagne flows once more. As we are still in NCO uniforms we will have to stay in the sergeant's mess. What a pleasant crowd, with their charming wives, but our language still mainly consists of five fingers. How annoying when you want to speak to a charming French woman.

4th September 1939

Today we shall remember forever because news came through that war had been declared by France and England yesterday. The news of war is always depressing in normal circumstances but not for us Czechs, who have been waiting for our chance to get our homeland back from the master race. We are also aware that the situation will perhaps change in our homeland. We are just trembling with excitement. Who will shoot down the first Luftwaffe pilot?

We are told that [men in] Oran and other bases will remain here because of the threat from the Italian air force. This depresses us because we want to be in Europe and not fight 'Macaronis'. The first flight began today in a two-seater and I feel very happy. No.572 Escadrille is commanded by Capitaine Tricaud and we do not think much of their ancient aeroplanes. The Nieuport has only 230 kilometres an hour speed and the Spad only slightly more. The flight instruments are also ancient but every French pilot talks about the new French fighter planes but where are they?

A further problem for us now, is that we are considered as reserve pilots and therefore have less priority in the flying programme. The escadrille consists of 20 French pilots and they are good comrades with plenty of jokes, if only we could understand them.

9th September 1939

Today Escadrille 572 celebrates its founding which gives us an opportunity for both pilots and ground staff to get together and, as usual, the champagne is flowing in buckets.

---

[1] Ladislav Zadrobílek was another pilot who later flew with 310 Squadron in England and survived the war as a flight lieutenant.

Ground staff have manufactured in metal, a Pegasus figure which is 572's emblem and this was displayed under a plush cover until the commanding officer arrived. He thanked everyone who not only conceived the symbol but also made it. He was very touched I must say.

Obviously the latin French race differ from us who are more pensive and sad, and as the celebrations continue we Czechs would have complained about the lack of activity in the air, while they [commiserated] with us by bringing on more champagne. Typically, Zimprich declared that whilst we are gradually getting intoxicated, people in our occupied homeland may be wondering where their next meal will come from.

11th September 1939

The whole French air force celebrates the 22nd anniversary of the death of their famous ace of the First World War, fighter pilot Georges Guynemer.[2] His life history, and his dog-fights with the Germans are well known to every recruit in the French air force, together with his 53 victories in air combat.

Our commanding officer ended his speech with: 'I know that you will all fulfil the tasks set by your commanding officers for the glory of your fatherland.' I was thinking whilst he was speaking that we Czechs having just emerged from the Austro-Hungarian Empire, have not hundreds of years of military conquests, or a Napoleon, but we already feel quite adequate to avenge ourselves when the opportunities arise!

21st September 1939

And so life goes on.... The normal routine of this escadrille is full and idyllic for us with some flying. For me as a Czech it is impossible to take the situation so calmly because I remember how at this moment Poles are suffering and I would not have thought that their turn would come so quickly. After the painful lesson of the Munich betrayal ending the existence of our independent nation, I feel truly sad....

Now a change of routine. We are told during a lecture on the use of the machine gun that we are being sent to a night [flying] school in Blida (an aerodrome near Algiers) and so there is another celebration by our French comrades, all of whom wish us – *Bonne Chance*. We leave Oran rail station at 8.15 pm and are all quite merry on the train having spent the whole day drinking. I began this diary entry on the 21st, and must go back to state that we arrived during the evening of the 19th. The

---

[2] Guynemer disappeared over Poelcapelle on the morning of 11 September 1917. He fell in the German front line and although buried by his enemies, his grave was lost in the subsequent fighting over the area. There is a memorial to him at the cross-roads in the town of Poelcapelle, Belgium, and his life is celebrated there every year.

aerodrome is new and the buildings and technical equipment are perfect, but the billets are still full of bed bugs. We meet Czech comrades already residing here and they are talking about flying continuously. On the night of our arrival we sleep in the other ranks' billets but the next day demand a sergeant's mess accommodation.

Two Czech pilots arrive from a mine-laying operation and we are also informed that more Czech pilots are arriving here tomorrow. We report happily to the commanding officer of the base, but he regretfully informs us that there are no planes to fly. The relationship between us and the French pilots is strained because they resent the influx of foreign pilots seeking their jobs. They have no idea where we come from and the word Bohemia or Czechoslovakia appears meaningless. They ask imbecilic questions such as whether we have a dancing orchestra, whether we eat meat, and if not what else. In addition they are bewildered as to why we are not black! Other questions are even more bizarre, such as do we eat potatoes and if not, what *do* we eat?

The flying instructor is pathetic, reminding us that the earth is not flat. This sort of thing must be due to the fact that we were, as a kingdom of Bohemia, incorporated in the Austro-Hungarian Empire, and only since 1918 became Czechoslovakia. The French airmen are always well dressed and their peak caps in Africa are covered with a white cloth. There are no aeroplanes available and for everybody to be fully occupied presents a big problem.

Yet more Czech airmen are coming here from other parts of North Africa since this is to be the last staging post before returning to Europe. I walk into the town of Blida, often on my own, and disappear into a cinema, in order to see some Pathé newsreels [so as to discover what is happening with the war].

1st October 1939

I have to report to the commanding officer of the escadrille and with the limited number of aircraft available our flying is to be evaluated one by one. My first aircraft type is a Potez 25, which should be in a museum. The second is a Nieuport, and then a Morane 211, both of which I flew in Oran, so altogether I have had four hours of flying since arriving in this country. Unfortunately dog-fighting simulation flights are out of the question. So we have ended the evaluation trials and have now an embarrassing amount of time on our hands. We attend lectures, but merely sitting and perusing some maps, and after lunch we march into the countryside to see all those orange groves, which is always pleasant for central Europeans. We also visit the Barbary Coast and laugh at the monkeys. The mountain range is absolutely bare, peaks are very sharp and being situated so close to the aerodrome, an engine failure must end in a funeral for the pilot.

It is not surprising that Fejfar thought the machines they had to fly should have been in a museum. The Potez 25 was quite a large aeroplane and had been produced in some number since 1919. The French air force took them on strength in 1926. A two-seat biplane with fixed undercarriage it went through several engine types and had a large radiator in front. The Nieuport he talks of was probably something like a Nieuport-Delage 29, 42 or 62, again vintage biplane types with fixed undercarriages. The Moranes were no real improvement.

8th October 1939

The sun is blazing in Africa, even in October and we have to take cover after lunch. The compulsory siesta of the legion, with closed doors and windows is now a distant memory although we know there is another group still marching around Algerian Sahara, whilst we at least are living among Europeans and will not be knifed in the back while walking along in the streets of Sidi-bel-Abbes. I begin to think of my native town of Mala Paka where I was born and the top of Atlanka mountain where I often pondered about my future after leaving high school. I am very sad. My soul is deep in thought and I have no friend close enough in relationship, or of similar background, who will partake in this experience. The nights are warm with starry skies every night. You fall asleep until the bed bugs awaken you. Only then do you realise that nothing has changed since yesterday and another day has arrived.

18th October 1939

We are at long last ending our time at Blida aerodrome and are being posted to No.10 Escadrille at Oran. Our group consists of: Mrázek, Krajina, Bieberle, Vrecl, Novák, Jicha, Kučera, Popelka, and myself. We say goodbye to a lot of our friends and drink more champagne. It costs so little here and is suitable for any occasion. We all board the night express train and like other trains in France, it is fast and never late!

19th October 1939

We end our journey at La Senia base, near Oran, where the weather is much cooler. While we are searching for our billets, a couple of Morane 406 fighters fly over. They carry out simulated dog-fights and we think that this is the best welcome anyone from 10 Escadrille could arrange for us.

There can be no doubt that Fejfar and his comrades felt happier seeing this more modern fighter aircraft after their period on ancient biplanes. The Morane

406 was a single-seat monoplane fighter with an enclosed cockpit and retracting undercarriage. It was a vast improvement on the old biplane fighters and had started to re-equip a number of front-line escadrilles. None-the-less, it would have its work cut out when pitted against German fighters.

20th October 1939

Today I visited my former 572 Escadrille and they were pleased to see me, the old Czech *aviateur*. Behind the hangar I saw for the first time the most advanced fighter aeroplane in the French air force, equalling anything the Luftwaffe has to offer, but what are they?[3]

The commander of Escadrille 10 has now divided us into sections which they call groups. Number one consists of myself and Popelka, Number two: Bieberle, Jicha and Kučera, Number three: Mrázek and Janouch, Number four: Krajina and Novak. These are the sections we shall be flying in from now on.

28th October 1939

Today is like any other day in North Africa and it does not seem like anything special, but for us Czechs this date celebrates the re-birth of our new nation from the old Austro-Hungarian Empire in 1918. I dress very carefully today; my white shirt is especially white and the trousers I have had under my mattress all night and they look perfect. We are all dressed but inside our soul, it is a black day in reality, because our homeland has been taken over by the Third Reich. It does not feel right somehow.

Then a surprise! Our commanding officer orders the whole escadrille to assemble and had probably been told of our feelings. In a speech encouraging our future while not forgetting our past, he tells us that France's desire is to fight and finish the Nazi master race so that we may all return to our beloved country. After this remarkable speech for a French military person, he gives each of us an envelope in which we find 100 francs. We go to town immediately after lunch but we do not drink too much, for we are all thinking of our loved ones at home.

19th November 1939

Life goes on. We prepare for target shooting and other military pastimes. Our commanding officer, Captain Mauvier, is in charge of four officer pilots, 11 sergeant-pilots, and 18 mechanics, but we only have nine aircraft between us. Our Morane 406 has not enough horse-

---

[3] What fighter indeed? Fejfar does not enlighten us but one might assume it to be one of the new Dewoitine 520s, the newest French fighter and far better than the Morane 406. Looking at both aircraft, one can be forgiven for likening the Dewoitine and Morane to the RAF's Spitfire and Hurricane.

power for climbing to any German fighter. The sand-saturated atmosphere here may lead to a sudden seizure of the 850 hp engine and the temperature outside is mostly 100 degrees Fahrenheit or more, which makes the engines very hot indeed. Quite a sobering thought. The sooner we get out of Africa the better.

25th November 1939

It is Saturday and our day off. It is my birthday and I have bought myself a pair of new white gloves. Frank [František] Bieberle, my best friend, runs with me to the bus stop because if we miss it the next one is not for two hours. I do not feel 27 years old at all, but much older in fact. Although, just as any other Czech, I go to the cinema, I do not take anything in as I am thinking of my mother and how she might be coping. I also see the face of my girlfriend and wonder if she will ever wait for my return.[4]

I wake from my day-dreaming suddenly because a newsreel brings me back to reality. It is full of shooting somewhere near the French Maginot Line. Upon our return a pleasant surprise awaits me. I have been chosen to join our fighter pilots in France. There are, altogether, six of us going, but in fact this is only an advanced notice that we shall be going. Like everything else about France, it will always be later.

Further flights are allowed and I am beginning to get used to the Morane 406 quite a bit. I roam the African skies and the sun is strong, even so late in the year. As I fly I think of my homeland. Adam, the pilot from Paris, has brought us the news that some students in Prague were shot and many are interned in Ruzyne prison. I am therefore more than prepared spiritually to avenge all those countrymen of mine, given the chance.

On an internet site there is a quote, which if correct, must have come from the original diary entry and deleted from the first printed version due to its content. It is noted to be on this same 25 November, it must have been in response to the shocking news from home. If it was so written, we show it here: 'Mother, forgive me that I want to be cruel to my enemies. You have raised me in the love for my country, therefore I must take an eye for an eye and a tooth for a tooth.'

11th December 1939

A definite order arrives, telling us we are to leave in two days time, but I now, paradoxically, feel less inclined to leave this Africa of the legion and all the flying in this glorious sunshine today, and every day. Even the miserable pay of 1.80 francs a day no longer matters.

---

[4] In the early 1930s Fejfar was seeing Zdena Hylmarová, but having to choose between her and flying, flying came first.

Czech airmen wait to board a ship from North Africa to France.

13th December 1939

They say that number 13 is an unlucky number but on this day we sail from North Africa. We shake hands with all our French friends, pilots and ground staff, including our Czech comrades who are awaiting their own turn to sail. We six pilots are now finally on board the SS *Sidi-Barahim*, which makes its way across the Mediterranean to Europe.

15th December 1939

A very foggy day welcomes us in Marseilles. Our unit is the 6th Escadrille, which consists of 22 pilots, including the officers. We disembark and wait for further orders, when a lorry arrives at 11 am and we are taken to the newly-built aerodrome of Marignane. Although everything is new, French disorder prevails and French officers disappear into Marseilles which means we Czechs will have to sleep somewhere on the base. There are two escadrilles assembled here, ready to go to northern France. We are, at any rate, prepared for anything so long as we are flying against the Boche.

26th December 1939

We celebrated Christmas Eve two days ago on the outskirts of Marignane aerodrome, where in a small restaurant, a table was set for seven of us. We wonder why since we are only six, but Janouch brings his girlfriend Suzanne along.[5] On the table is a small Christmas tree and underneath it are a lot of presents. We have a good meal but I cannot help thinking of my homeland. We open our presents and however modest [they are], everybody is very pleased with the simple offerings. My friend Bieberle[6] knows that I am always complaining about my cold feet so I receive a pair of warm slippers. We end as usual by singing the Czech songs of our youth. Suzanne was quite drunk but managed a French song for our benefit. We reach our billet well after one o'clock.

30th December 1939

Work begins today and the escadrille is now equipped with new machines, but while we are supposed to have nine aircraft, only six have arrived so far that are fully serviceable, so we cannot yet be classed as fully operational. The first few days of flying these new machines are difficult because the cloud base is dangerously low and if we get above it into the blue sky there is the danger of trying to get back below the clouds and finding our airfield.

---

[5] Svatopluk Janouch came from Holín, and was 26. He would later fly with Fejfar in 310 Squadron in the Battle of Britain, and survived the war as a squadron leader.
[6] František Bieberle was 27 but did not survive the French campaign.

par le milieu, de façon à ce que l'inscription soit à l'intérieur. FORMAT : 11,5 × 16,5. Article 24 du Règlement.

EXTRAIT DU LIVRET INDIVIDUEL

Nom *Fejfar* Classe : *1.929*

Prénoms : *Stanislav* Grades *Sergent*

N° d'incorporation : *3210* successifs

Corps ou service *2ème Escadre aérienne*

SIGNALEMENT DU TITULAIRE

Unités successives *Unité Administrative Polée 1/9*

Signature du Commandant d'unité et cachet du Chef de corps,

CHANGEMENTS DE CORPS	Signature des commandants d'unités
Passé le au comme nouveau n° d'incorporation :	
Passé le *au 1940* au *G.C. 1/6* comme *Lieutenant* nouveau n° d'incorporation :	
Passé le au comme nouveau n° d'incorporation :	

Le Capitaine *[illegible]* Commandant *[illegible]* G.C. 1/

Observations au sujet de l'établissement de l'extrait du livret individuel. — Le corps (ou service) dans lequel l'homme est incorporé établit l'extrait du livret individuel ; celui-ci est signé par le commandant de l'unité. Les changements d'unité, ainsi que les grades successifs, dans ce corps, sont portés à la partie supérieure de l'extrait, par les soins du nouveau commandant d'unité.

Lorsque l'homme change de corps (ou de service), il conserve son extrait du livret individuel. Mention est faite du changement de corps, à la partie inférieure de l'extrait, par les soins du nouveau commandant d'unité. A chaque changement de corps, sur la ligne commençant par « au », indiquer le corps et l'unité ; sur la ligne commençant par « comme » indiquer le grade.

(1) Cette case est réservée au signalement du militaire.

NOTA IMPORTANT. — Le présent extrait ne donne droit au tarif militaire sur les chemins de fer que s'il est présenté conjointement avec une feuille de route ou un des titres qui suppléent cette pièce (ordre de route, sauf-conduit, congé, permission ou ordre de service).

Fejfar's French I/D document as a sergeant in GC1/6.

31st December 1939

We all receive a gift today from our Czech embassy, which is a substantial sum of money, despatched to hundreds of Czechs in France and her colonies. This very welcome gesture enables us to celebrate the end of the year that saw our successful escape from the Nazis and also the end of our French Foreign Legion engagement. At midnight I drink with my friends and we are promised by our commanding officer that a Czech fighter pilot trio will show the French fighter brethren a simulated dog-fight over the aerodrome tomorrow. Exciting news and we are thus ending with every breath and drink, to a year of disastrous occupation of our homeland and at the same time a hope that the new year with be the time for *revenge.*

10th January 1940

I prefaced my diary today by copying a poem from the Czech poet, George Wolker, when he was dying from tuberculosis at the age of 24. It goes thus: *I am not afraid of death, death is not bad, death is only a piece of hard life. What is terrible, what is bad, is the actual act of dying.'*

20th January 1940

The military attaché sends us a questionnaire along with which I have to sign a form to be discharged from the foreign legion. I write on the attached paper, that I demand my return to my previous rank of lieutenant pilot in the Czech air force. But after my experience of ponderous bureaucracy in this country I am convinced it will take weeks before I become the equivalent of a French lieutenant. The commanding officer, after our mock dog-fight show on the 1st, is so impressed that he has decided to make one section of myself, Jicha and Popelka, while the second section will consist of Janouch, Bieberle and Kučera.[7] This delights us since three of us are officers and three sergeants. We are, therefore, flying like comrades and not by rank.

27th January 1940

Perhaps a few but excited words in my diary because somebody managed to obtain for us a strong wireless receiver so that we are able to listen to Prague radio. Wonderful music after hearing nothing but French music and songs here. We receive the news that some Czech

---

[7] It is unfortunate that Fejfar did not record anything about the mock dog-fight between the French and Czech pilots, but obviously they acquitted themselves well. One imagines that the Czechs were just that bit older and therefore a shade more experienced than their French counterparts.

pilots are to be posted to Syria because of some political situation and this departure from Europe is not welcomed by any of us.

5th February 1940
We gradually receive some more news from the Czech military attaché in Paris. It is very bewildering how many aircrew officers were transferred and posted to the air force training schools, etc. And today we are absolutely disgusted because owing to some mishap in French bureaucracy we are not paid the fortnightly money due to us. When you smoke it is a disaster, and bearing in mind that we are officer pilots still being paid at the legion rate of 1.80 francs a day. Also, because of the thinness of our mattresses, our backs are [becoming] painful. We ask for more straw filling but to no avail.

I spend the whole day with my machine and the mechanic. I want it to be in perfect working order and I also learn the layout of the cockpit. I paint my personal slogan on the side of the fuselage, which is permitted, and name it 'Resultant'. We finish the day by going to a cinema which is not a happy suggestion since the tickets have been increased to nine francs, when we previously paid five. We find that ordinary soldiers only have to pay five francs, so we go out and tear the sergeant stripes off our uniforms, then go back in again.

23rd February 1940
Another circular arrived today from the Czech embassy in Paris. It is bulky and contains the documents promoting me to the equivalent rank of a French pilot officer. This long awaited agreement between the governments of France and Czechoslovakia guarantees our pre-war rank and pay. For NCOs, they are promoted one rank higher. Czech insignia will be worn on all tunics and the French air ministry is also hoping that we shall learn their language faster.

A wonderful surprise this afternoon because three Curtiss aircraft flown by Czech pilots arrived here for a rest. They are tired after destroying, along with their group, 21 German planes. Our morale with the money guarantee increases and also hope that we shall soon encounter 'Le Boche' – as the French call the German bastards. We talk to our comrades but notice they are quickly asleep in their armchairs.

The Curtiss fighters referred to here by Fejfar were Curtiss H-75 Hawks. The Curtiss Hawk was an American single-engine monoplane fighter, known in the USA as the P36. With the urgent need for more modern fighters, France had placed an order for 100 of these machines back in May 1938. The early type carried just two machine guns located behind the engine and firing through the propeller, while later two additional guns were fitted one in each wing. The 1940 version carried two more wing guns, making six in total. By the time the war got underway the French had four fighter groups equipped with them.

The first combat involving Hawks was on 8th September 1939, an action which resulted in GCII/4 aircraft claiming two German Me109s shot down. By the end of that month a total of 27 enemy aircraft had been claimed, most of them by Hawk pilots. These early fights continued and on 6 November GCII/5's Hawks claimed eight for the loss of one Hawk, and even this was repaired after a crash-landing.

Unfortunately Fejfar does not mention the French unit, but one wonders if it was GCI/5, for amongst its pilots was Sergeant František Peřina, who would end the French campaign with 11 victories and two probables. The 29-year-old Peřina had joined the Czech air force in 1929 and after the fall of France eventually found his way to England and the RAF. With 312 Squadron in 1942 he gained one kill and one damaged to add to his total. Whilst with the French he had received the Légion d'Honneur and the Croix de Guerre with at least six palmes and four stars.

In Peřina's escadrille were a number of top French aces, amongst them being Edmond Marin La Meslée (16 victories), Jean Accart (12), Léon Vuillemain (11), Marcel Rouquette (10), and François Warnier (8).

On 2 January 1940, Corporal Vladimír Vašek had been the first Czech pilot flying with the French to lose his life on active service. He suffered oxygen failure during a high-level patrol in a Hawk and crashed to his death.

26th February 1940

Today our Czech commander-in-chief of the Czechoslovakian air force arrived for an inspection. He visits one base every day or so. With him is the military attaché, Captain Pernikar.

The newly awarded increase in officer's salaries will take effect in due course, we are told, because the treaty has not been officially signed yet, so our pay remains at 1.95 francs per day and is still paid by the legion. This is bureaucracy and imbecility of the worse kind.

1-7th March 1940

Some gift parcels arrived from the USA on the 1st, all donated by the Czech citizens [over there] now that they have organised themselves to help their poorer brethren during this period. I received a scarf, two handkerchiefs, a sewing kit, a razor, socks, 200 Camel cigarettes and chocolate. We are pleased that they are acting on behalf of our families, so to speak....

Received orders on the 4th that we are to be ready to fly within five minutes, but nothing came of it. We are still dissatisfied that this rich country cannot pay their fighter pilots their due. If this was in Germany or our country they would specify the necessity for saving, but here in this rich land it cannot be justified....

The 7th is the birthday of our beloved first president, T H Masařyk, who made Czechoslovakia possible along with the president of the

United States, Woodrow Wilson, in 1918.

8th March 1940
We are told that we shall be leaving here today. My cockpit is full of my personal belongings and we are also issued with emergency rations. In France when you are posted you must carry food with you. We take off and at 12.02 are heading towards Chissey, via Marignane and Lyon, a journey of 640 kilometres. Our destination is a grass landing field which is only 300 metres long. Once down, we are not allowed to leave the base until all our aircraft have been refuelled. We have been booked into a nearby hotel, one man to a room, and I have never slept in such a wonderful luxurious feather bed since leaving home.

9th March 1940
Our commanding officer tells us that we are to defend this area right up to the Swiss frontier. We are also ordered to shoot down any German aircraft approaching our zone. The next day we are sent off and German fighters fly overhead but our machines are so slow in climbing that we lose them over Dijon. We are unhappy about this because the sky is clear and we could have shot down quite a few of them. Alas, the Morane 406 does not climb very fast, and certainly not as fast as German aircraft. We return to the aerodrome and go to our hotel dining room for a meal. Suddenly there is a sound of anti-aircraft fire and it finally dawns on us that we are now in the middle of the war in Europe.

11th March 1940
Still the sky is clear and although the Germans are ever present over France they never seem to veer towards this corner of the country. Suddenly, at 12.30, the alarm sounds and I take off with Jícha. We are ordered up to 30,000 feet from where we can see the Alps clearly and close by. We remain circling here as instructed but find no enemy aircraft so eventually – at 14.05 – we are ordered to land. Jícha was so frozen inside his cockpit that his mechanics had, with some difficulty, to help him out. We are told later that one German aircraft was seen flying close to the Swiss frontier, but on no account are we allowed to cross this border.[8]

---

[8] Fejfar does not mention that on this day Svatopluk Janouch had a lucky escape when his Morane 406 suffered an engine fire during a patrol. He attempted to get his machine down but was finally forced to bale out despite only being at 200 feet. He survived without injury as his fighter crashed at Chissey.

Fejfar writing up his diary in front of a Morane of GCI/6.

20th March 1940

I am still asleep in my comfortable bed when at 5 am I am rudely woken by a strong knocking on my door. Then the alarm sounds and within a quarter of an hour we are dressed in our flying suits and have arrived at our aircraft. We hear [someone] bombarded the French navy bases six hours previously. We take off on patrol but do not see any enemy aircraft.

22nd March 1940

Today we are told by our Czech military attaché that as the Czech NCOs were promoted one rank higher, this will also apply to pilot officers, with an equivalent rise in pay.

Our Czech pilot, Popelka, who had a problem with his engine during a patrol yesterday, luckily managed to land safely at Nancy aerodrome. Later, however, we learn that it was not engine trouble, but he simply got himself lost, because we have no maps at all, and we fly so high. He was thanked by our CO that with so little petrol left he did not parachute down, thus losing a valuable fighter aircraft. We also found that some fifth column soul has exchanged an oxygen bottle with one containing arsenic gas. Possibly it was a French reservist from Alsace where there are still a lot of people who prefer to live under the Germans rather than the French.

1st April 1940
Dreadful news still coming from Paris regarding our legion pay. What gratitude for those of us who marched through the Algerian desert for them, but must remain patient, but for how many more days or months, in order to receive officer's pay, whilst those who were never sent to the legion, are now laughing with all their money bulging out of their pockets. With this lack of money we cannot even buy lunch or supper in the village, so all we can afford is some onion soup, bread and an apple. All this we have to accept and while we are flying on our high patrols there is a risk of fainting from a lack of proper nutrition.

3rd April 1940
I have become so angry that I moved myself into a village. The lack of food, unknown to me, was becoming a serious issue for my body. But I was very fortunate indeed and cannot believe my luck in finding accommodation with Madame Clément. She is 54 years old and in no time she has become my second mother. Her heart is so generous and her affection for a hungry Czech pilot is increasing daily. She has told me that she considers me as a son. The other day I lost a purse somewhere on the aerodrome with 30 francs in it, and if you are only paid two francs a day, that is a lot of money. I was so depressed that I finally admitted my loss of money to her. She at once gave me the money which I was very reluctant to accept. I will never forget her! I only eat the military meal at lunchtime.

My colleague Janouch is concerned as much as I am about our miserable pay and the promotion which is useless without money in our pockets. But he is not like me and has written to General Janousek, in Paris. He asked how any pilot is expected to fly so high with only onion soup for supper?

The result of his letter is astounding, as within three days we receive a banker's draft for 3,000 francs each, as a deposit for our future pay. We could not believe it, or that so many banknotes exist. [Once they cashed the draft and shared out the money] I looked into my hands to examine the pretty picture on a thousand-franc banknote, and there were three of them! I went out at once and bought an alarm clock first and other things I desperately needed. I felt like a demented spendthrift or a legionnaire who had run out of water. I also bought a present for Madame Clément and she is well pleased with it.

10th April 1940

At 5 am an alarm can be heard from the aerodrome, even before Madame Clément arrives at my door. At the airfield we are instructed by our commanding officer himself that we shall be leaving as soon as possible and we have to pack our belongings. I return to Madame Clément and she helps me to pack. Naturally I have acquired many more things and all this has got be squeezed into my cockpit somewhere.

Our orders are to be ready no later than 9 am at the latest because every pilot must prepare and supervise his Morane before departure on a long journey north. At 11 am the whole escadrille takes off, circles the aerodrome we all liked, and I am also leaving somebody who will never forget me – nor I her!

Our course is set at 330 degrees and we fly at 25,000 feet until we reach the French side of the English Channel. As soon as we land at our new base at Berck-sur-Mer at 1 pm, we immediately notice the luxurious hotels and wide boulevards with their large department stores and other rich-looking shops. As soon as we become free we leave the base to make an inspection of this wonderful seaside place where only the rich can stay and play. We suspect that perhaps our task is to defend this part of the French coast.

Berck-sur-Mer aerodrome, later to become a German fighter airfield, was just north of the seaside resort of Berck-Plage. A short distance further north was Etaples, while further south was the Bay of the Somme and St Valéry, the Somme canal leading to Abbeville.

On 24 April GC I/6 suffered a loss due to mechanical trouble. Sergeant B Bertrand was killed as he crashed near Chissey-sur-Loue shortly before 1 pm.

30th April 1940

At long last we receive our first officer's pay of 1,700 francs a month, but still remain in our legion sergeant's uniforms. We are also given ten days leave and a free railway warrant to go anywhere we please. We are asked by the orderly room clerk where we want to go, and we shout: 'Why not the French Riviera?' My friend Frank Bieberle comes with me and we stop off in Paris in order to obtain an address which was some private accommodation property. The name we are given is Lady Hatfield, an Englishwoman who lives in a villa 'La Soun Jarello', at St Jean Cap Ferrat. It takes two days to reach this place, even by express train, and upon our arrival we take a taxi. The address is not a villa but a Spa building. We are received by a secretary and taken upstairs where we are shown our rooms, and take a shower and have a shave.

We are then received by Lady Hatfield for the traditional English afternoon tea. She is a lady of 74 maybe, and very charming towards us.

She informs us that for the Czech pilots she has reserved five bedrooms so that we can relax after our recent flying duties with the utmost leisure. What a wonderful gesture from such a terrific lady to we foreigners who cannot speak a word of English. Later on our former commanding officer in Paris base staff, Captain Duda, arrives. At first our conversation is strained but soon after exchanging our flying experiences we soon become good friends and begin to discuss how we shall spend our holiday here.

We soon get into a routine of waking up at 7.30 in order to play a game of tennis. Immediately afterwards we have a full English breakfast which is served in our room. It is brought up on a silver tray by an English butler who wears white gloves. Meanwhile, our uniforms are taken away and pressed, and our shoes are polished. Quite frankly, this style of living is unbelievable. Alternatively, after we awake we go swimming, using the private beach belonging to the villa. Lunch is always served at 1 pm precisely.

During the afternoon we are allowed to take the motorboat and sail off over the horizon. Some of the afternoons are spent sight-seeing at Monte Carlo and Monaco. Dinner is served at 8 pm exactly and we all have to dress for it. Lady Hatfield has so many jewels on her that we are astounded how she can walk without falling over. Our dinner table is lit by candles and we are not served by butlers but by men dressed in military uniforms. One in British army, and one in British navy. We are not allowed to pour our own wine, this is done by these chaps, but you can drink as much as you want.

After dinner we retire to the lounge, where for the first time we see the traditional English fireplace lit. We sit around the fire and later go to a nearby music room where the most modern dance records are played. Lady Hatfield is an extremely good dancer, and it is such a pity she is so old that out of respect I do not dare to ask her for a dance.

One day we were taken to Nice and saw a cabaret and afterwards we went to the casino. Life here is so wonderful and we do not go to bed sometimes until 4 o'clock in the morning when the sun is starting to rise. Thus our nine days pass very quickly and on our last day we are taken to the castle owned by an Italian contessa for dinner, which is only four kilometres from the Italian frontier, perched on top of a 900-foot cliff.

The furniture and pictures are all in the style of the Middle Ages. Also invited to this dinner are the British ambassador and the minister of foreign affairs from Roumania. You can probably now imagine what type of meal we had here. This was the upper class at its best. We finally leave on 7th May and take the evening train via Marseilles, Lyon, Reims and Abbeville. Here we sleep in a hotel near the station and the next morning take a bus to our aerodrome, where we are met by an air-raid siren.

Chapter Three

Blitzkrieg

Fejfar's pleasant break in the south of France came at just the right moment, for unknown to him and many others the German offensive in the west was about to begin. Safe in his hotel in Abbeville prior to his planned return to the aerodrome after some breakfast, he had no inkling that France, Britain, Belgium and Holland were about to be plunged in a real fighting war.

Not that there had been no combat at all over France. The French and British air forces had often been in contact with German aircraft and had had frequent air battles since war was declared. The Germans had also been busy invading Norway, but now Hitler's attention turned to France and his old enemy of WW1 days. The date set for the opening of his *Blitzkrieg* – Lightning War – was Friday the 10th of May.

The day dawned with German aircraft flying in numbers into France, bombing airfields and front line positions, while its airborne assault troops parachuted into the Netherlands, aiming to capture airfields at Rotterdam and Den Haag. Once captured further troops would be flown in by Ju52 transport aircraft. Important bridges too were targeted while others struck at Amsterdam and The Hague. Defenders were quickly in disarray and being either captured or pushed back. While the Allies had expected some kind of assault in the spring, the magnitude and ferocity when it began completely overwhelmed everyone. Still luxuriating over his wonderful ten days holiday, Fejfar told his own story in his next diary entry.

10th May 1940

We are awoken at 4 am by the air raid sirens going full blast and we have no idea as to why. We sit waiting for an explanation and are told that three Heinkel 111 bombers flew over from [the direction of] Belgium where they had bombed their targets. We quickly board a train and at 6 am we are back at our Berck aerodrome only to find our aircraft gone. We are told the airfield was bombed by the Germans at

4.30 am, and some nearby houses have been destroyed. Apparently the planes flew back and forth over the town spraying the streets with bullets. Two of our escadrille pilots were killed and two more suffered serious wounds, one very seriously. Our unit had taken off during the raid and engaged the enemy machines but were unsuccessful in damaging any. They were then ordered to fly back to Marignane.

We pack what is left of our clothes at the aerodrome and re-board the train. It takes two days to reach our unit and when we finally arrive we are ordered to fly to Belgium, but this is subsequently cancelled.

14-16th May 1940
It is rumoured that the Fascist Italian government will declare war on France soon. Some other escadrilles fly down to Marseilles and beyond, to protect the borders. First thing next morning we have an order to stand-by for flying duties but this order is later cancelled. Again on the morning of the 16th we are on stand-by to fly somewhere but are not told where. Due to unfavourable weather conditions this is also cancelled. The Germans have been advancing into Holland these last few days and we hear too on the news that Holland has finally capitulated. Belgium will no doubt follow.

17th May 1940
We take off at 5 am, via Lyon which was bombed. We land later near Paris, at Lognes/Emerainville, at 11.45 am. We are continuing full readiness and are pitched in our tents on the aerodrome itself and await the next order. In the meantime we sleep like logs.

18th May 1940
Some of us move into the building which used to be a bar but now has a lot of broken glass windows and furniture. Nevertheless it is good enough for shelter to sleep in at night. Reveille is at 4 am and we are on a state of readiness but I am excused flying because of the long flight yesterday. It is very strange to be asleep on the aerodrome but quite suddenly at about 5.30 am I'm awoken by huge explosions. Remaining glass window panels vanish as the bombs fall. One bomb hit the hangar and injured three airmen of our ground staff, one seriously. The ammunitions stores caught fire and some 12 bombs exploded. It has been decided that everyone must move into a concrete bunker near the aerodrome.

At 2.30 pm we have an order to fly towards the Belgian frontier because the Germans are now advancing quickly with their infantry and panzer units, whilst the Luftwaffe is bombarding various towns and north-eastern aerodromes. We take off to catch some of the elusive bombers. At 4.30 four enemy bombers pass over our own aerodrome and drop bombs on the grass runway. The anti-aircraft batteries so far have not scored a hit. At 7 pm we take off and shoot down two Dornier 17s. On landing we learn that our wonderful commanding officer, Mauvier, is missing, whilst Captain Bruneau, although shot down, has fortunately survived. Unfortunately our own anti-aircraft gunners bring down S/Lt Paturle.

Twelve of us take off and are ordered to patrol at 18,000 feet to look for any straggling aircraft. With great pleasure I spot a bomber fly past me with the familiar cross markings in black on the [wings and] rudder. I [attack] and press at once my firing button although not exactly in my sights, but he had then completely disappeared somewhere. We are now returning to land and consider that this was a successful day. Unfortunately still no news of our commander.

It is sometimes difficult to reconcile Fejfar's diary entries with known facts, but this is no doubt understandable considering the pressure of daily actions. Also, by the time he finds a moment to write up his diary, hours if not a day or two may have passed, and so times and exact dates become blurred.

Captain F Mauvier was shot down by a Messerschmitt 110 of 4./ZG76 whilst attacking some Dornier 17s on his own. He baled out after being wounded north-east of Cambrai at 2.45 pm, and taken prisoner.

Captain G Bruneau's Morane was damaged in an attack on a Dornier but was then shot down as he dived to attack a German AA gun north-east of Verdun. He crashed near Pontru at 7.45 pm and did not survive.

Sous-lieutenant J Paturle was also hit by return fire from a Dornier and wounded in the shoulder. He got down safely and was taken to hospital. His aircraft, although damaged, was repairable. Dornier gunners also damaged the Morane flown by Adjutant Conte west of St Quentin at 7.15, and although he got down safely was taken to hospital suffering from severe shock.

The Dorniers were from Kampfgeschwader (KG) Nr.2. One returned damaged after the attack by Bruneau, assisted by Commandant G Tricaud, the GC 6 group commander, and Lieutenant Jolicoeur over St Quentin at 3 pm, while another crashed after the attentions of Mauvier and Sergeant Popelka. It went down near Ognes, west of Chauny, with the loss of its four-man crew.

20th May 1940

Our escadrille was ordered to fly towards Amiens to attack some German bombers reported in the vicinity. We only take off with ten aircraft following our losses yesterday. We are led by Commandant Tricaud. We climb to 14,000 feet and suddenly observe nine aircraft off to our right. As they are very fast they must be British and they quickly disappear.

I join our section of five, the other five having flown off somewhere else. Suddenly six Messerschmitts are diving at us from the clouds above. In addition some other Me109s appear on our left. I feel hot and uncomfortable because after all these weeks of no action and dreary waiting, I now have more aircraft than I can cope with. One of my colleagues opens fire and I notice one Me109 go past me in flames. The pilot has managed to bale out and open his parachute. I now have two Me109s behind me but my friend Jicha is assisting me whilst I go into a steep dive. I try to shake off these two German swine and I finally recover from my dive, and find another Me109 just in front of me, right in my gun-sight, bless him. I press the firing button again and again. Then I am out of ammunition and dive once more and finally land.

The result of today's fight is that three Me109s were shot down. One by myself, one by Jicha and the third by Commandant Tricaud. Unfortunately we lose Sous-lieutenant Duchène, Sous-lieutenant Raphenne and Sergeant Pagès.

After a short lunch we are back in the air and whilst I am flying beside Czech Sergeant Kučera, he shoots down a Dornier 215 bomber, so today the Czechs in our escadrille have done better than their French comrades.

Fejfar's unit was in combat with the Messerschmitts of Jagdgeschwader (JG) 21 north of Villers-Brettonneux at around 5.20 pm. Sous lieutenant Duchène-Marulez was shot down by Leutnant Ostermann, and he was badly burned on the face and baled out, landing at Franvillers. For Max-Hellmuth Ostermann, this was his first victory. Before his death on the Russian front in August 1942, he would amass 102 victories flying with JG54, and receive the Knight's Cross, with Oak Leaves and Swords.

Sous-lieutenant Henri Raphenne was probably shot down by Unteroffizier Marcks of the same unit, he and his Morane making a forced-landing at Ailly-sur-Noye. Raphenne was not hurt and his aircraft was repairable. He had, however, damaged a Dornier 17 from 3./KG3 that had attacked Amiens-Glissy, but it got home.

Sergeant Pagès' Morane crashed by the River Luce, between Demuin and Hangard after he had taken to his parachute. He was wounded and admitted to hospital, probably the victim of Oberleutnant Scholz, the Staffelkapitän.

It seems that 109s of JG1 were also involved in this combat, for Leutnant H Braxator baled out but did not survive. Five other 109s of this unit had to force land due to lack of fuel.

Two pilots of GC 1/6, Sous-lieutenant Janis and Sous-lieutenant J Halgrin, attacked a reconnaissance Dornier 17P from 2.(F)/123, over Ham at around 5 pm and damaged it. The German crew got home with one crewman wounded on board.

21st May 1940

Out of the 22 aircraft we originally had on strength in our escadrille, only ten remain serviceable this morning. Ten of our pilots have gone to

Marignane to collect replacements. Our remaining ten pilots take off at 2 pm as we have been allocated a task by the French army who are counter-attacking German infantry positions. My section consists of myself, Bieberle and Kučera. Then the order changes to escort some Curtiss fighters on an attack in Belgium. The German ack-ack guns are deadly accurate and we are obliged to zig-zag to avoid being hit while carrying out our task. Then Bieberle's Morane becomes uncontrollable after an AA shell explodes beside him. It made level flight almost impossible but luckily he was able to cope with it.

The other section of ours disappeared and we landed at 3.30 pm. We are not pleased that only eight aircraft have returned, for Commandant Tricaud and Capitaine de Sacy are missing. Pilot Senet was also hit by enemy AA fire but he managed to land safely despite his damaged aircraft. During our evening meal we learn that Sergeant Pagès and Sous-lieutenant Duchène both parachuted out and are safe. Of the others, no news yet.

This other section of GC I/6 had run into Me109s from JG3 over Cantin, near Arras, just after 3 pm. Tricaud had been shot down by Hautpmann Müller, Staffelkapitän of this group's 4th Staffel. Tricaud baled out unhurt. Capitaine Silvestre de Sacy had just shot down a Fieseler Fi156 of 3.(H)/21, but attached to JG3, and had been making a landing approach when attacked. De Sacy did not survive.

Adjutant E Senet's Morane was badly damaged by a 109 east of Arras, and claimed shot down by Feldwebel Hessel. Sous-lieutenant Raphenne was also shot up in this action by Oberleutnant Keller, Staffelkapitän of the 1st Staffel, but he got down unhurt. Both French fighters were repairable.

The French credit Raphenne, de Sacy, Senat and Tricaud with a Dornier 17 destroyed between them.

24th May 1940

Depressing news received today about my Czech friend Kulhánek, who is reported as missing.[1] We hope that he has landed on the French side, which is important to us Czechs because of the Gestapo actions if they ever catch one of our countrymen. With so many flying now it is logical to assume that some will have 'bought it'. We rejoiced when he telephoned us later, saying that he had shot down a Dornier 17 bomber, but that the rear gunner had damaged his ailerons so had to make a forced landing on our side.

---

[1] Captain Kulhánek, together with Sous-lieutenant Raphenne and Sergeant Jicha had been attacking a Dornier from the staffel of II Gruppe KG2 near Clermont, south of Montdidier at 11 am. The bomber, however, managed to make it back home carrying one wounded crewman. Jaroslav Kulhánek turned up safely later. He was lost in combat in March 1942 flying Spitfires with the RAF.

25th May 1940

Most tragic day for me because my best friend Frank Bieberle, not so long ago with me at Lady Hatfield's house on the Riviera, is dead. We were flying today in escadrille strength in an attack on a formation of Heinkel 111 bombers. My section attacked three of them and one, detached from the others, was our first target. He flew towards his earthly grave. Then along came 22 Messerschmitts that were escorting them yet we coped, but soon began to run low on petrol. I managed to land at an unknown aerodrome, then after refuelling and flying back to base, learnt that Frank wasn't there. Nobody saw him again after such a fracas. I just cannot believe it. Frank my dear friend, where are you?

The Me109s were again those of JG21 and in the air fight Leutnant Bob of 3./JG21 shot down the Morane flown by Adjutant R Vantillard. He was wounded in the right arm and leg but managed to crash land south of Arras, but inside enemy territory. However he was able to evade capture and eventually got back in July. His victor, Hans-Ekkehard Bob, would survive the war with 59 victories and the Knight's Cross.

Bieberle was shot down by Oberleutnant Schneider, the Staffelkapitän of 3./JG21 while the Czech was making an attack on a 109 of 9./JG2 between Noyen and Péronne at 6.45 pm. He crashed by the road to Trescault in the Bois d'Havrincourt. He was 28 years old and came from Zhoř.

Fejfar was credited with a He111 shared destroyed.

28th May 1940

And so it goes on. We fly every day and never know when the enemy may catch us by surprise. The favourite trick of the Germans is to come at you from behind from out of the sun or they dive from very high altitude. We have now received another sad piece of news of our escadrille pilot Halgrin.[2] He was attacked the day before yesterday by three Messerschmitts and was shot down, going down on fire like a torch. We shall avenge you one day!!

29th May 1940

Today nine of us fly to do battle with the master race. We encounter a severe buffeting from the German ack-ack fire and in the end decide against orders and climb one thousand feet higher. My Morane received a near miss. It jumped up and then went sideways, obviously the exploding shell missing me and preventing my disintegration by a

---

[2] Sous-lieutenant J Halgrin was making a lone attack on some enemy bombers north-west of Crépy-en-Valois just after 1 pm but was himself attacked by a Me110 of 9./ZG26 and went down on fire. Halgrin managed a belly-landing at Auger-Saint-Vincent, but his Morane exploded in flames and burned out, and he did not survive.

millimetre. I did not think that I would get back safely today and I discover one cannot control one's destiny since it is rarely in your hands.

Fejfar makes no reference on this date about shooting down a Heinkel 111 bomber, but he was credited with one. Nor does he mention an action on 3 June. The escadrille claimed two Me109s destroyed, one probably so but lost a pilot. The victorious Frenchman was again Henri Raphenne, who badly damaged one north of Lagany which was finished off by ground fire. The German, Oberfeldwebel Ernst Vollmer apparently baled out and it is reported he was killed on his parachute, shot by French territorial troops.

Raphenne then hit another 109 whose pilot, Leutnant H Fleitz, was forced to belly land at Dammartin-en-Goële. He was badly wounded and died on 8 June. Both pilots were from JG53.

Further to the north, the British and French forces were being hemmed in along the English Channel, around the port of Dunkirk. Thanks to the miracle of the 'little ships' it became a historical event, with the evacuation of over 338,000 Allied soldiers to England between 26 May and 3 June. GC I/6 were, of course, operating further south, and along with other French and British units were gradually pulling back to the north-west of France.

3rd June 1940

Today was not our lucky day because we had lost another Czech pilot – Popelka. 400 German bombers were flying over Paris and everybody was ordered up. Unfortunately for me my engine began to splutter so I had to return and was quite furious about it. I assisted my ground crew to find the problem and discovered the malfunction. I waited for an hour before I saw three aircraft coming back to land. I searched the sky for others to turn up but no more did. I do not see either Janouch or Hranicka either. I am hungry but depart at once to the escadrille wireless room.

The first news is that Janouch was shot down by three Messerschmitts but before coming down he took one with him. The message is that he is returning to base with no mention of hospital either. Hranicka was also in the same predicament in being attacked by three Huns and one of them hit his wing, taking the tip off. Fortunately the ailerons were, by some miracle, still functioning, and although he obviously went into a spin he was able to correct it enough to crash land. He only did so because he would have made it if German bombers were not in the process of bombing his chosen airfield.

Finally the sad news of Popelka. He managed to fight with two Me109s but eventually they shot him down. At least he did not go down in flames.

Fejfar's diary becomes a little confusing at this time. Although he rightly records that Popelka was shot down on the 3rd, Janouch went down on the 5th.

Hranička was to be killed on the 5th too, but his combat and forced landing was on the 4th.

Sergeant Stanislav Popelka was 22 years old and came from Františky. He was shot down by Hauptmann Werner Mölders, Gruppenkommandeur of III./JG53. He fell over Ozoir-la-Ferrière, crashed and burned. By this date Mölders had over 20 victories and just a few days earlier he had been the first German fighter pilot to receive the coveted Knight's Cross of the Iron Cross. Two days after his success over Popelka, the German ace was himself shot down by a French fighter pilot and taken prisoner. When France surrendered, he was released from captivity and by mid-1941 had 115 victories, scored in Spain, in the west and over Russia. He died in a flying accident in November 1941.

As well as Popelka, GC I/6 had Sergeant J de Lestapis severely wounded in the chest during combat with 109s, and although he got down, he died while undergoing surgery for his injuries. Mölders also accounted for Sergeant Jost, who baled out badly wounded in the same action. He took to his parachute but hit the tail of his Morane as he did so, landed heavily and broke his thigh.

On the 5th the escadrille, having lost Hranička between Creil and Montdidier at 11.40, also had Adjutant Gaudry slightly wounded by ground fire whilst attacking German armour at around 3.10 pm, and Captain J Kulhánek was similarly wounded in this ground attack mission. At 7 pm, Adjutant Senet was forced to bale out over Marchélepot, whilst attacking tanks north-east of Chaulnes. He was burned about the face and after being admitted to hospital in Marcoing, was captured by advancing German troops.

Fejfar's next entry is dated 6th June, although he seems to be recording events that occurred on the 5th.

6th June 1940

Today we paid the German bastards back for the loss of our pilots. Two escadrilles took off and engaged at least 35 dive-bombers.[3] These were flying quite happily along in a tight formation seemingly oblivious of our presence and with no fighter cover anywhere to be seen. With typical German disdain they simply tried to show that they were masters of this particular part of France. When we joyously attacked, knowing that they could not effect dog-fighting manoeuvres like acrobatic school aircraft, they began falling down like ripe fruit. We shot them down from a distance of a few feet hoping that the master race this time stopped being so, and they will never again drop their whistling bombs on the civilian population.

More sad news when we land and hear we have lost our 'granddad' (he had so few hairs on his head) Hranička. Only yesterday he managed to land after being shot in the wing and getting out of a spin at low level.

---

[3] The dive-bombers referred to were in fact Henschel Hs123 biplanes from II./(S)LG2. GC I/6 found them at about 10.30, and Fejfar, Janis, Janouch each made claims. The German unit in fact lost one shot down at Mennessis, another near Hallu, south of Chaulnes, and one force-landed damaged near Mons-en-Chaussée.

Now he is reported 'missing' and that sounds as sad as it always is.

7th June 1940

And so one after another of us is dying in the unequal battle of superior machines and organisation. Somewhat in despair and most certainly over-ruling a pilot's advice, the French high command has ordered suicide attacks on German panzer tanks. With their two-inch steel armour you can imagine what little damage an ordinary bullet will do to such a monster.

Today, so laughingly late, the French air ministry has given the Czech air force permission to form their own units and supply even their experienced ground staff. Like everything else it is tragic to comprehend the situation which now seems insoluble. I mention this only since I was to be included in our escadrille programme and the leader of this purely Czech unit was to be Captain Kulhánek, with pilots and others already mentioned in my diary.

But the desperate French have ordered our C-in-C to commence this idiotic spraying of bullets on tanks by we foreigners who are as expendable as the French Foreign Legion itself.

We have therefore become the Czech escadrille and are unable, as regular airmen, to disobey this sub-human order which only confirms what we often felt and recently discussed, that France is at its end as an independent and free country.

Our task is therefore to attack the relentless German panzers that are speeding towards Paris. Today we lost a corporal pilot, Bendl, and a French pilot, Major Paturle. Our own Janouch was shot up by the tank machine guns but he managed to land safely somewhere. Adjutant Senet who served with us in Africa was also hit and his Morane caught fire. A parachute was observed but no one saw him land. We think that the bastard German tank crews shot him to death when he landed nearby. Comrade Jicha and I had so many holes in our aircraft that they were considered write-offs.

Although written as of the 7th, these actions are recorded above after the entry for the 5th. Somewhere it is recorded that Fejfar was credited with six tanks during these attacks on German panzers, but exactly what category of damage is unclear.

Losses within the escadrille on the 7th were as follows: Sous-lieutenant J Paterle killed, shot down by ground fire whilst attacking German armour near Formerie at 6.30 pm; Sergeant J Bendl also lost in the action, while Lieutenant S Janouch was wounded in the leg and his Morane so heavily damaged it was a write-off. As already mentioned, Adjutant Senet had been wounded and captured as his hospital was over-run.

8th June 1940

Sergeant Jicha lost consciousness today at 25,000 feet but recovered when in a dive and not very far from mother earth. He told me later that he thought that he had not had enough food and sleep lately. We are now taking off five times a day and my flying log-book records eight hours, 25 minutes of flying time today, and you can multiply this every day.[4]

9th June 1940

The doctor at our base has ordered both myself and Jicha to a French convalescent home for four days rest. We are sent to a château in a small adjoining village, along with another fifteen pilots, and all we have to do is to eat and sleep. It is so quiet and nobody talks about aeroplanes or the war. Next day we are told that the Italian air force will be flying alongside the Luftwaffe and we are given a lecture with illustrations about the current Italian aircraft we are likely to encounter.

11th June 1940

At 5 am we are woken up at the convalescent home and taken back to our escadrille. What a state the French air force is in when they are forced to bring back pilots resting and who only arrived here two days ago. The automobile takes us to Lognes, an airfield not far from Paris. When we arrive there is not a soul about, so we continue our journey to Connântre where we meet with the rest of our Czech unit. As soon as we arrive I discover that my friend Standera has been wounded during the recent dog-fighting with an overwhelming number of Messerschmitts. He was the only one to escape and the two French fighter pilots were killed.

During the afternoon we hear from the wireless that German panzers are approaching Reims and that all surrounding airfields have been heavily bombed. It does not surprise me because I think that the Luftwaffe had at least 3,000 aircraft now of which there must be a good 1,500 fighters. We are now so disorganised (were we ever organised in this country?) and so unprepared that without warning, twelve Dornier bombers approach our aerodrome. The bombs rain down on us as we take off in our Moranes individually, whilst the bombers are still releasing yet more bombs. Their air gunners, as usual with the Luftwaffe, are shooting up anything military on the ground, moving or not. Finally we land and find that three of our ground staff are wounded, one seriously.

---

[4] On the 8th the escadrille lost Capitaine Xavar Poilloue de Saint-Mars, who was killed during another low-level strafing attack on German tanks south-east of Forges-les-Eaux.

We could never have caught up with our invaders and were not prepared to pursue them too far, simply because we know that our aerodrome was still serviceable for landing. One Morane was destroyed on the ground and the surrounding villages were also strafed by machine-gun-happy air gunners. We are happy that not one of us is missing or killed, because we cannot take any more personal tragedies.

Escadrille losses on the 11th, as Fejfar records, included Sergeant Standera, shot down by Leutnant Claus of JG53. He came down between Guignacourt and Berry-au-Bac where he overturned, thus being injured. One of the two French pilots was Capitaine Lefoyer, shot down by Hautpmann Rolf Pingel, Gruppenkommandeur of III./JG53, who also shot down Capitaine Guillaume de Rivals-Mazères, near Épernay. Both pilots were wounded. Guillaume de Rivals-Mazères was a test pilot with the Centre d'Expérimentations Aériennes Militaire, at Orléans-Bricy, and was attached to GC I/6 for flying trials with a modified anti-tank version of the Dewoitine D520, with a 13mm cannon. Sgt J Kučera got his Morane back to base badly shot-up, but repairable, its pilot wounded also. Another casualty was Sergeant V Horsky, also wounded in the fight with these Me109s, but his machine too was repairable.

Rolf Pingel was another early Luftwaffe ace. Indeed, he had scored four victories in the Spanish Civil War. He would receive the Knight's Cross in September 1940 but be taken prisoner in July 1941, having achieved 26 victories.

12th June 1940

At 9 am this morning we receive an order to fly to a deserted bomber airfield at Girmene. When we land we can still see around the airfield perimeter hundreds of French refugees and local inhabitants fleeing in panic and distress. Most of the nearby barns and houses are still burning.

This is the result (speaking as a Czech of course) of the ridiculous appeasement of the Munich agreement leading to a situation whereby a totalitarian power can do anything to anybody. It is difficult to remember now or recollect our happy days after our arrival from Poland to Paris. The abundance of everything and the philosophy that nothing can happen while defended by the Maginot Line and the glorious French empire, was not helpful. We hear that France is expecting Russia and even America to help her but we do not think so.

Suddenly it is deathly quiet and we are just completely and utterly exhausted. Once more we feel deserted. We receive no more orders, no more aeroplanes. There is no organisation left of any kind and so we are packing our suitcases to leave! It is quite simply that the master race has accomplished another conquest but we do not think that this is the end, and ignore remarks by some French pilots not to leave them to the Nazis.

On the 16th the escadrille made its final claim in combat, probably destroying a Dornier 17, although the French pilots of GC I/6 remained in action until late June. Its final combat loss would occur on the 24th, with Sous-Lieutenant Henri Raphenne being shot down and killed by anti-aircraft fire during a last-ditch stand against German armour.

Henri Raphenne came from Tavey (Haute-Saône), born in 1906. He had entered the French air force in 1925, and had joined GC I/6 on 13 March 1940. Although some French records list him with a couple of different German types, they credit him with five victories (including two shared) and a probable.

20th June 1940

We are now informed today that France is going to negotiate an armistice and cessation of hostilities. It is a most bitter pill for us to swallow. To have to negotiate with the Nazi swine rankles in our souls. For us Czechs especially, who escaped from the Nazi-occupied homeland, and after all these sacrifices here. We think of our dead comrades who only a few days ago flew on these suicidal missions against German tanks and armour, many paying with their lives, it is almost impossible to believe. We also find it difficult to comprehend that such a technically and industrially advanced country with their latest Dewoitine fighter planes, have arrived far too late, mainly due, we are told, to communist-inspired trade unions prohibiting overtime in the aircraft factories. How dare these former French comrades in the air condemn us for not continuing in this crazy fashion. We knew, of course, that we as Czechs were far more keen to take off and kill Nazi pilots whilst in many instances we recollect that many French pilots were invariably 'fatiguée', ie: poor tired men.

We finally manage to find an old Renault 12-seater aeroplane used by the civilians on this aerodrome and we do not hesitate, without asking, to fly to the French government town of Vichy. They left Paris a long time ago. Inside the government building there must be a Ministère de l'Air, but when we land, there is simply nobody to speak to since they are in panic, and abandoning their offices as quickly as they can.

Our problems have ceased to be theirs. It now occurs to us that the Gestapo may not be far behind, with their keen fifth column people, so we abandon further attempts to fly south, without fuel or maps. Thankfully we are accommodated in a small hotel, gratis. However, the manager is already worried, so we leave the next morning to his great relief. We are lucky to obtain a lift in a high-ranking officer's car to Clermont-Ferrand. Here we manage to steal a military jeep, seemingly abandoned in a parking lot and begin to travel instinctively southwards until its fuel tank runs dry. We are still wearing our French air force uniforms, of course, and we notice that we would not be quite so welcome this far south if we were wearing khaki uniforms.

Finally we reach the port of Vendres, the Mediterranean gate to North Africa, but there are no ships going there or anywhere else. By a stroke of good fortune, in a cheap hotel we occupy, we begin to talk to a French navy man. Disappearing upstairs he later returned to say that his captain would take us to Oran on his ship [the *General Chanzy*].

21st June 1940

We sail and arrive at Oran to find almost at once that there are a lot of Czech pilots arriving from all over the place, willing to sail anywhere as directed by our government in exile. There are now 32 pilots here and out of those hundreds of us [that had been operating against the Germans], we are leaving 27 dead Czech pilots here in the French empire [see Appendix C].

Chapter Four

England and the Czechs in Britain

The very rapid fall of France to the invading German army led to around 4,000 Czech soldiers and airmen in France escaping by whatever means they could find to England. The first 30 Czechoslovak pilots were sent to RAF Hendon, in north London, on 17 June and the following day President Beneš, still the Czech president-in-exile, sent a letter from his national committee to the British Secretary of State for Air, Sir Archibald Sinclair, begging him to make every effort to help extract those of his countrymen still in France to Britain. It read:

Czechoslovak national committee   114-116 Park Street.
London, W.1.

18th June 1940.

My dear Sir Archibald,
As you know, we have in France our national army with our own aviation. We have about 800 first class pilots and other aviation specialists. They could be saved for the British army. I have just sent a letter to Mr. Anthony Eden asking his help for the evacuation of our whole army from French territory and I am addressing this letter to you asking your help in order to save for the British army especially all our aviators.

Yesterday in the night the first Czechoslovak crew/30 pilots/arrived at Hendon; they were brought here by a British plane. The chief of our aviation General Janousek has already given instructions to his men to try to save themselves and leave French territory as soon as possible, in order to continue the fight side by side with the British military and aviation authorities; all or, at least, the great majority of these soldiers can be saved for the further fight against our common enemies.

For me it is not easy to be in direct contact, in the present circumstances, with our army in France, but I suppose your military authorities know exactly the camps where our aviation in France are now placed. If further information is needed, I shall be glad to complete this letter or to give them, eventually, by paying a personal visit to your office.

In thanking you sincerely for the help you will give us in this matter,

I am yours very sincerely,
Dr Eduard Beneš

The letter to Anthony Eden was very similar in content.

Eduard Beneš, was 56-years old and had been Czech president at the time of the Munich Agreement in September 1938, which compelled the Czechs to cede fortified Sudetenland to Germany. After this he resigned and left for the west. In 1939, after the German occupation of Czechoslovakia, he formed the Czech National Committee in Paris. After the collapse of France he moved this committee to London where he immediately began to try to persuade the Allies to repudiate the Munich Agreement, and get recognition of his own government. Meantime he arranged for any member of the Czech forces who could manage to escape to England to be accepted into the British armed forces. Beneš and his government in exile were finally accepted by the British in July 1941 and the Munich Agreement was repudiated in August 1942. After the war he returned to his homeland and was elected president of the republic in 1946.

On 21 June 1940 Beneš arrived in person at the British Foreign Office to see Anthony Eden, but found him absent. He was received by Mr W Strang, his private secretary. After their talk, Strang wrote the following minute to the foreign secretary for his information:

Dr Beneš called here this afternoon to discuss the new situation created by the collapse of France and the arrival in this country of the members of the Paris-formed "Czechoslovak National Committee" and of elements of the Czechoslovak Armed Forces.

He expressed his grateful thanks to His Majesty's Government for the efforts they were making to evacuate the Czechoslovak Forces. It appeared that a substantial proportion of 12,000 soldiers and 800 airmen would reach this country at an early date.

He then went on to argue, that this new situation reinforced the case for the recognition of a Provisional Czechoslovak Government. Dr Beneš developed his argument as follows:

In the first case he was convinced that the USA would come into the war whilst the Soviet Union would probably come in as well. In this connection and his view, it would be unfortunate if the Czechoslovak people should come to regard the Soviet Union as their only hope for the future.

Therefore, an increased measure of recognition by His Majesty's Government would bring Western Europe back into the consciousness of the Czechoslovak people.

In the second place, there would be now in this country a large number of Czechoslovak Forces, together with an increased amount of Jewish, and other political refugees, such as Communist, Spanish Civil War military personnel. It would no doubt increase Dr Beneš' authority in dealing with possible discontented persons. At present the Paris-formed National Committee did not possess the requisite authority.

In the third place there was the question of Finance. He had himself a draft from the Funds in America amounting to £20,000,000 for the disposal by the Czechoslovak State. If this government was recognised, they would then be able to keep it for their future needs, and also use it as a security loan for current expenses.

I told Dr Beneš that I would of course report what he had said. The new situation would certainly require discussion of many matters between us. For example, whether any proposals of his carried any implications as to the future external or internal frontiers of the post-war country.

He stated that the recognition of the Provisional Government would not imply any commitment as regards frontiers. In actual fact he thought that after the war the Czechs would be more autonomous than the Slovaks and would therefore be more content to let Slovaks run their own country.

On 2 July, Beneš wrote to the British government, requesting that Czech airmen be allowed to operate against the expected assault upon Britain. Sir Hugh Dowding had no doubt that with an already depleted force under his command, he needed every pilot he could get his hands on. The British government acted swiftly and within a month Czech fighter and bomber squadrons had been formed.

There was no time to table a formal agreement on the status of Czech pilots and airmen, so all Czech personnel were either commissioned or enlisted into the Royal Air Force Volunteer Reserve. At first all junior officers were given the rank of pilot officer, whatever their Czech ranks had been, with the exception of squadron or flight commanders who were confirmed in an appropriate rank.

It was not until October 1940 that the official paperwork was completed and signed by the two foreign ministers, Lord Halifax and Jan Masaryk, confirming the employment of Czech airmen within the ranks of the RAFVR, and being subject to the laws of both air forces.

Over the following months more and more Czech airmen found their way to Britain. By the war's end there were around 1,500 Czechs still serving in the RAF, so with casualties over the interim, there must have been something in the region of 2,000 men within its ranks. The casualties amounted to some 480 killed, more than half whilst serving with 311 Bomber Squadron, which was later part of Coastal Command.

Meantime, Stanislav Fejfar had started his journey to England.

27th June 1940

We arrive at Oran aerodrome and naturally my first visit is to see the girlfriend of Frank Bieberle, killed on 25 May, and to tell her of his heroic death with such an overwhelming number of Messerschmitts around him. This is a very tearful episode for me too because we not only knew each other well for a long time but we were flying side by side before the Nazi mob separated us and he was killed.

Today we are now 51 Czechs assembled here and we take the first express train to Casablanca, hoping to find a ship going to England, because our county's president, Eduard Beneš [of the Czech Republic in exile] has arranged for our entrance into the Royal Air Force. But the language!!?

30th June 1940

We are lucky and secure a place in a small motor vessel, the *Neuralia*, heading for Gibraltar, and we are well looked after on board with the best French food. The ship is British but none of us speak the language because in pre-war days only the neighbouring countries' language was compulsory. Voluntary French was also taught as it was an international language but the importance of English was nil for central European inhabitants.

The ship has already taken a number of Poles to Gibraltar, including the air force people. The captain feels, after our arrival in Gibraltar, that there are too many of us and advises us to find a larger ship. Unfortunately, while this is a large ship it is a coal carrier [with limited accommodation for people]. Suddenly we are no longer so contented. Another reason is soon discovered because Czech army officers have already settled in all the available cabins, and the colonel sends us below the water line. There are no water facilities either, for drinking or washing, and all we have is a semi-dark atmosphere with a low wattage, blinking, bare bulb.

Naturally we complained bitterly but the colonel was not interested, although, after we contacted the captain, we were allowed as a concession – some concession! – to remain on the top deck. A further concession was that if we agreed to serve as waiters we could get better accommodation! We told him to jump overboard. At least we are on board and will soon be heading for England.

2-16th July 1940

We sailed from Gibraltar on 2 July, and our convoy consisted of 36 ships, accompanied by 14 cruisers and destroyers. Our miserable journey took us 14 days, days that I will never forget. Finally, and at long last, we disembark at Liverpool.

* * *

Meanwhile in England, more and more Czechs – and others – were still arriving from various corners of the globe, especially France. On 12 July 1940 the British Air Ministry Directorate wrote to the Department of Personnel.

With reference to our conversation today, it is important to sort out the Czech pilots and other air force personnel, who have arrived in the Country after evacuation from France.

(1.) The probable intention is to form a complete Czech unit, but before this can be done, it is necessary to find out, whether there are sufficient amounts of trained pilots and personnel and the requisite numbers to make up a squadron of air force establishment.

(2.) In order to get this sorting out done quickly, it is essential to have an officer who is acquainted with the Czechs to assist the Czech authorities in this work.

(3.) Group Captain Beaumont would be eminently suitable, since he speaks some Czech, and is known personally to the majority of the Czech senior officers, who are now in this country.

(4.) May this officer therefore, be spared for a period of 10 to 14 days to assist to resolve the Czech situation?

A Wing Commander Gibson at Air Ministry responded:

Director of Personnel has kindly agreed to Group Captain Beaumont, former Air Attaché in Prague, being made available to work out the details and assist in the schemes submitted.

1.) This morning I held a conference at which were present Group Captain Beaumont; the Czech Attaché to this country, Colonel Kalla, and the officers of the Czech Air Force Section, General Janousek and Lt. Colonel Kubita.

2.) We all agreed that every endeavour should be made to ensure that each individual of the Czech Air Force was being employed on some useful work, within 10 days. Their morale and discipline has been reported as excellent, by their Station, and it is vital that this most desirable attribute shall be maintained and stimulated by immediate employ.

3.) It will be seen from the résumé at enclosure 10A, that there are sufficient trained and experienced fighter pilots, and bomber pilots, to be formed at once. One, the fighter squadron and one bomber squadron together with the necessary non-pilot flying personnel and ground maintenance people, and that sufficient number of flying personnel is available for wastage.

It is therefore proposed:

(a) The whole of the Czech air personnel shall be sent at once to a flying station, together with 60 or 100 ground personnel which they will select.

(b) That all officers be commissioned and other ranks enlisted in the Royal Air Force Volunteer Reserve.

(c) That they form one fighter squadron (Hurricane) and one bomber squadron (Wellington).

(d) That a small station Headquarters be formed with a British Commanding Officer and Staff (doubled where appropriate with Czech personnel).

(e) That a few supervisory British Technical Non-Commissioned Officers be attached temporarily to the squadrons together with the flying instructors.

(f) That two Magister and Master aircraft be supplied at once, and the operational aircraft progressively, so that all the pilots may be used to the British type of aircraft.

(g) That unless a Station can immediately be chosen on the south east coast, the units be moved somewhere nearby as soon as possible.

(h) That the Station Commander then submits further pilots, not immediately used for employment on ferrying duties etc, within the RAF.

Remarks: The experience and zeal of the Czechs is such that it is considered that under the guidance of Group Captain Beaumont, they could complete their internal organization efficiently and speedily, for the limited operational work suggested, within 14 days, ie if the equipment and supervisory personnel is at once made available.

* * *

Unfortunately for the Czech fighter pilots, south-east coast stations were already fully established, while the overall shortage of Spitfires and Hurricanes after the losses sustained over France and Dunkirk, contributed to Fighter Command deciding that the Czechs must be sent into 12 Group, rather than 11 Group in the south-east.

The main task of 12 Group was to protect the Midlands, and be ready to support 11 Group as a tactical reserve. The fall of France made 11 Group, and 10 Group to the south-west, more likely to see enemy aircraft than 12 Group, whose opponents had until now been thought to be more likely to come from Germany direct, across the North Sea.

On 10 July, Colonel (Group Captain) Josef Berounský arrived from the London Czech Inspectorate. It was a newly created establishment and had all the records of French aircrew since their escapes from Czechoslovakia, and the information gathered was very helpful to the RAF. Berounský, who was nearing his 45th birthday, was held to be the father of the Czech air force, and would be made an OBE for his work. Sadly he was killed in April 1942, aboard the cruiser HMS *Edinburgh* sailing from Murmansk. His help in creating personnel movements was invaluable to the forming squadrons. There would also be an excess of fighter pilots, therefore some would have to be posted to RAF squadrons.

* * *

With the fall of France, and following Winston Churchill's inspiring speech telling the nation that Britain and her empire would not surrender and would fight on, it was obvious that Britain, and her air force which would be taking the initial brunt of resistance, needed all the help they could get.

There were any number of Czechs, Poles and French military personnel managing to escape to England by any number of routes and all needed to be sorted out into various fighting forces. One very immediate problem of course, was that most of these men from continental Europe had little or no English. Probably more Frenchmen had a smattering, but men from Poland and Czechoslovakia had virtually none. They had already gone through the trial of learning enough French to get by in training and then operational flying, so they would now need to overcome a new language barrier.

With the number of men involved, there was easily room to form a squadron or two of both Czech and Polish personnel. The one man that helped in this area, as already noted, was 44-year-old Group Captain F Beaumont, mentioned above. Frank Beaumont, amongst other things, had a good knowledge of languages, indeed, he was a qualified interpreter.

He had received his education at Cranleigh, Lille and Leipzig. He had also been the pre-war air attaché at the British embassy in Prague, Czechoslovakia (as well as in Vienna and Belgrade between the years 1934-38), so had an intimate knowledge of how the Czech airmen thought and felt. He had married Baroness Emilia Konitz-Vaněk and they had a daughter, who later married James MacKenzie, a British diplomat, in 1953.

Beaumont had learned to fly in 1916, during World War One, as a second lieutenant in the Royal Flying Corps. He had become a fighter pilot with the famed 56 Squadron but on the day the Royal Air Force was formed, by the amalgamation of the RFC and Royal Naval Air Service, 1 April 1918, he had been shot down by the German ace Otto Könnecke (his 16th victory of an eventual 35) and taken prisoner. He had been on the squadron for less than a week.

After the war he remained with the RAF and by the start of 1938 held the rank of wing commander. In the initial years of WW2 he would be with RAF Bomber Command and then Director of Allied Air Co-operation and foreign liaison between 1942-45. After the second war he was again air attaché in Belgrade till 1948. He retired from the RAF in 1948 having been made a CB the previous year. His last years were spent living in Bavaria, where he died in December 1969.

* * *

The first Polish-manned squadron, No.302, was formed on 13 July 1940, with

301 just over a week later. 303 Squadron followed on 22 July. 310 Czech-manned Squadron was officially formed on 10 July, 311 on the 29th and 312 on 29 August.

Group Captain Beaumont, because of his work with Bomber Command, knew of the numbers of Czech-trained bomber men in France that earlier had been sitting around waiting for a job. He had urged the use of these pilots and other airmen. A report he produced, shown below, is mainly in reference to trained Czech bomber aircrew, but could equally be referred to fully-trained fighter pilots. Unfortunately undated, it must have been written shortly before the French campaign came to its sad conclusion. It reads:

USE OF CZECH AIR FORCE PERSONNEL IN THE R.A.F.

(1)   With the advent of Polish Units in the RAF it is thought that something similar should be done in the use of Czech Air Force personnel with the help of the RAF to which it is submitted, as a great substantial advantage to the present common cause.

(2)   In this case it is suggested that only much trained existing personnel should be used for bomber, reconnaissance and similar duties.

(3)   It is understood the French Air Force have first call on all Czech Air Force personnel, it is believed there are approximately 700 trained and qualified Czech pilots in France, of these there are at least 100 fully trained bomber pilots, who for the present moment there is no prospect of using, owing no doubt to the lack of suitable aircraft.

(4)   The French have offered to give them a conversion course on to fighter aircraft. It would seem a waste to misuse this already highly trained personnel.

(5)   The Czech Air Force training in bomber duties was very efficient and intensive. It is considered they rank with the best that exist. It is further estimated that at least 70 fully trained crews could be easily acquired, and with the present high standard could in a short time be trained in handling our service British bomber aircraft.

(6)   The subject has been discussed with the present Czech Air Attaché in London and senior Czech Air Force officers in France. Apart from their great keenness in being usefully employed and especially with the RAF in particular, they have submitted the work they consider they could be put to with effectiveness, and which from personal knowledge it is submitted they could perform with the greatest advantage and efficiency. The duties with which these crews could be employed and the advantages they have in their favour are as follows: it being borne in mind that such personnel are fully acquainted with the country (Czechoslovakia and important targets in neighbouring countries) they could easily locate objectives under difficult circumstances (weather conditions, night flying, etc.)

    (a)   To attack military and air bases in Czechoslovakia: Most Air Force Stations are located in outlying districts where civil population is scarce, the risk therefore of casualties amongst them, is practically non-existent. It is known that at least three of the important air bases are being used as German training centres i.e. Hradec, Kralove and the bombing ranges at Milovice in Bohemia and Vyskov in Moravia.

(b) To land agents, sabotage and liaison material, W/T equipment for weather reports, information regarding air and military activities and results of attacks etc. Parachutists of Czech nationality could easily and safely be absorbed without fear of detection in the already 100% nationalist population, the latter are known for their bitter anti German feelings.

(c) In this connection the moral support and influence both of the crews and the population would have far reaching effects in keeping the high spirit and antagonistic feeling of the peoples.

(d) The shadow arrangement and the duplicate factories of such well known Armament Establishments as Skoda, C.K.D., Brünn Arms Factory, Poldi Steel Co. were kept a close secret, they are located in outlying districts, as far as Slovakia. These are known to the Czech Air Force and could be attacked with considerable results.

(e) It is suggested that with the co-operation of selected workers in these establishments, including those in the known localities of Pilsen, Prague, Brünn etc., efficient sabotage could be effectively carried out during such attacks, thus covering up such acts and minimising the casualties which normally would be suffered by the employees.

(7) It would be ideal and would be possible to find sufficient personnel to form at least 5 Bomber Squadrons from the existing Czech troops at present in France. Should however, this not be possible owing to the present circumstances and commitments of the RAF, it is suggested that these already trained crews mentioned above could be absorbed at once in RAF units, doing their normal duties and could further carry out any of the special duties outlined above when the occasion arose.

(8) It is further pointed out that there are a great number of partially trained personnel serving in the Czech army and that with further training they could be used as reserves. It is thought the French authorities may be willing to co-operate in releasing such useful personnel for Air Force purposes.

(9) If the Air Ministry could see their way clear to proceed with the above or similar proposals, it would have a far reaching moral effect. It should be kept in mind that Norway, Denmark, Holland, who were not prepared to meet the German onslaught are now considered fully pledged allies, whereas the Czech army which was prepared in 1938 and was equipped in a manner unsurpassed on the continent, had to give up its armaments under the urgent advice of the Allies.

(10) By giving these proven gallant people a chance to fight for the common cause and in the service of the RAF, a great impetus would be given to the Czech people, who up to date have shown wholeheartedly and without exception they support us.

(11) The seriousness of the present situation is all in support of the above

suggestions. No doubts need ever be feared as to the results and achievements of such units, especially by those who know the fibre, efficiency and indomitable spirit of the Czech people.

F. Beaumont.
G.C. R.A.F.

*   *   *

When World War Two began, Group Captain L N Hollinghurst OBE DFC, was working in the Department of the Air Member for Supply and Organisation at the Air Ministry. Leslie 'Holly' Hollinghurst was another WW1 fighter pilot, although luckier than Frank Beaumont in that he survived the last eight months of that war on the Western Front, shot down a dozen enemy aircraft and received the Distinguished Flying Cross.

Holly was a no-nonsense and well respected back-room-boy within the RAF who was to rise eventually to Air Chief Marshal Sir Leslie Hollinghurst GBE KCB DFC. In the mid-war years he worked with the British airborne forces, and despite his rank (also making his own interpretation to specific orders not to 'pilot' a Dakota), flew on troop-dropping missions on D-Day and at Arnhem! [Co-author Norman Franks knew him fairly well during the last years of his life.] As Deputy Director of Organisation (Personnel), the question of foreign airmen and squadrons came under his remit, no doubt through such reports as Frank Beaumont's. On 6 July 1940, just before the Battle of Britain was about to begin, he had written:

POLISH AND CZECH FIGHTER SQUADRONS

It has been decided that one Polish (Fighter) squadron (16 I.E. Hurricanes) and one Czech (Fighter) squadron (16 I.E. Hurricanes) shall be formed in Fighter Command from the experienced Allied personnel recently evacuated from France. These squadrons will be designated No.303 (Polish) (Fighter) Squadron, Royal Air Force, and No.310 (Czech) (Fighter) Squadron, Royal Air Force, respectively. The personnel will be enlisted in the R.A.F.V.R.

2. The squadrons are to form to Establishment No. WAR/FC/158. at separate stations to be selected by Fighter Command.
3. The establishment is to allow for certain posts being duplicated. The duplicated posts will be filled by British RAF personnel. C.2. in preparing the establishment will please consult Fighter Command, B.M.R. and A.I.1.f. regarding these posts. In addition one British flying instructor should be temporarily attached to each squadron, unless D.W.T.T. considers this unnecessary.
4. Will D.P.S.D. of P. and D. of M., in collaboration with the D.W.T.T., B.M.R. and A.I.1.f. please select the personnel for these squadrons and enlist them as necessary. Although the flying personnel are stated to be experienced it may be considered advisable to put all or some of them through Fighter O.T.U.s. If this is considered necessary, it should not be delayed until the commencement of the formation of the units as it is

desired that they should become operationally efficient as soon as possible. It may also be considered necessary (D. of T.) to give the maintenance personnel a short course on the airframe and engine. Alternatively, this may be overcome by double-banking with British personnel temporarily a larger proportion of the maintenance personnel than in the permanent establishment.

5. Will –
   a. D. of P and D. of M., as a result of their discussion under paragraph 4 please, state the date when the personnel will be available.
   b. depending on (a), O.7. please arrange for the allotment of aircraft including one master to each squadron. Fighter Command should be consulted regarding the rate of allotment of operational type aircraft.
   c. D.D.O. please issue an Organisation Memorandum.

L. N. Hollinghurst
P./ D.D.O.

6th July 1940.

*   *   *

Of interest is Article 1 of a schedule relating to the Czechoslovakia Air Force in England under the heading of Organisation.

1. The Czechoslovak personnel available shall be organised into Czechoslovak units attached to the Royal Air Force. Such units although organised in this way for reasons of practical convenience, shall be recognised as units of the Czechoslovak Air Force, which is part of the Czechoslovak Armed Forces.
2. One Czechoslovak fighter-squadron and one bomber-squadron shall be formed as soon as possible with appropriate reserves. Consideration shall be given to the formation of further squadrons as personnel and facilities become available.
3. Czechoslovak personnel shall be selected for service by a joint board or boards composed of British and Czechoslovak representatives. The personnel shall be required to pass a medical examination according to the normal Royal Air Force standard. This shall be carried out by the usual Royal Air Force Medical boards, assisted by Czechoslovak doctors if available.
4. The officers and men selected and medically approved shall be commissioned and enlisted in the Royal Air Force Volunteer Reserve for the duration of the present war. They shall take an oath of allegiance to the Provisional Czechoslovak Government as well as to His Majesty The King.
5. Czechoslovak personnel who cannot be initially employed in the Czechoslovak squadrons shall be utilised individually or in groups or units in the Royal Air Force until it becomes possible to absorb them in

the Czechoslovak squadrons. Facilities for training in Royal Air Force establishments shall be made available to them as required.

6.   An Inspectorate of the Czechoslovak units attached to the Royal Air Force shall be formed whose duty it shall be to inspect these units and to report on their progress to the Czechoslovak Ministry of National Defence and to the British Air Ministry. The Inspectorate shall also maintain liaison with the Headquarters of the Royal Air Force Commands in which Czechoslovak units attached to the Royal Air Force are placed.

The normal channel of communication between the Inspectorate and formations of the Royal Air Force shall be the Directorate of Allied Air Co-operation in the Air Ministry.

The start of Article 2, under Command and Administration said that:

1.   The Czechoslovak squadrons shall, in principle, be under the command of Czechoslovak officers. The post of squadron commander shall, however, be doubled in the first instance, and there shall be a British as well as a Czechoslovak squadron commander, the former being senior, until such time as the latter is sufficiently familiar with the Royal Air Force procedure to assume sole control. Operational control of Czechoslovak squadrons shall rest entirely with the Royal Air Force Command to which they are attached.

2   The stations at which Czechoslovak units are based shall be commanded by British officers. Where a station is used solely or primarily for accommodation of Czechoslovak units there shall be a Czechoslovak commanding officer, who shall act with the British Station Commander, the latter being senior.

3.   The Czechoslovak units shall be equipped with the ordinary scale of Royal Air Force equipment. Their supply, maintenance and training shall be organised through the normal Royal Air Force channels.

4.   The numbers and grading of the officers and men to be authorised for Czechoslovak units shall be those which would be allowed in accordance with normal Royal Air Force practise, and Royal Air Force regulations as to the qualifications of the personnel shall be applied.

In point of fact 302 Squadron was the first Polish unit formed, at RAF Leconfield, on 13 July, while 303 Squadron was formed at Northolt on 2 August. However, it was 303 that first saw action during the Battle of Britain.

The Czech-manned 310 Squadron, formed at RAF Duxford, part of 12 Group, on 10 July, became operational on 17 August. In due time the squadron had, in keeping with most RAF squadrons, its own badge. The wording in the language of the Royal College of Heralds was: *In front of a sword erect, a lion rampant queue fourches. With the squadron motto being: We fight to rebuild.*

Czech pilots began arriving in mid-July, and Squadron Leader G D M Blackwood took his place as CO on the 18th. Sinclair and Jefferies were the two flight commanders with Jaroslav Malý and František Rypl as their Czech deputies. English lessons also began, the Czechs attending three classes a week. By 25 July the squadron could muster 16 Hurricanes.

Although commanded by an Englishman, the squadron also had a Czech CO, Major (Squadron Leader) Alexander 'Sacha' Hess. A well known, distinguished and capable pilot in Czech circles, he was 42 years of age.

A further aid to the problem of overcoming the language barrier was helped by the station commander, Woody Woodhall. He called the BBC with the problem and they had Woody and an interpreter visit Broadcasting House in London where they recorded a series of the more common orders, firstly in English, then followed by the Czech equivalent. Words such as break, scramble, bandits, angels, pancake, vector, and so on. Records were made and within a few days these were received by the squadron and played to all the pilots. It did not take long for them to understand these orders in English alone.

The scene was just about set for the arrival of Stanislav Fejfar, and the beginning of his fight in English skies, and eventually the equally dangerous sky above northern France.

* * *

On 18 July, Squadron Leader Hess wrote the following missive, which was pinned to the notice boards about the aerodrome:

Soldiers – Friends:-

After waiting for such a long time our common dream is finally happening. The first Czechoslovak Air Force Fighter Squadron No.310 is starting here. You have the honour of being part of it. I know you all know how important this job is. I will remind you then of the military codes of our army and to be friendly to your colleagues.

Some of the Czechoslovak pilots and mechanics have already shown in France their hard fighting spirit and strong will for victory.

It is very important for us to show that we are as good as our colleagues already fighting in the air, and help to keep the name of our air squadron in amongst the best ones.

That will be the best way to preserve the names of our air friends killed in France, and contribute to the final victory.

So you all have to behave well, because by your behaviour others will judge our country.

With your good behaviour all of the time, you will get sympathy from the citizens of Great Britain, and by that also get sympathy from our country.

Do not forget that, and always live by this rule.

The best of luck to you all.

CZECHOSLOVAK 310 SQUADRON – HURRAH!

Signed: S/Ldr A Hess.

* * *

By the time 310 Squadron became fully operational the Battle of Britain had just begun. It started at the beginning of July, with the Luftwaffe testing Britain's defences with attacks on Channel shipping, and small raids by fighters over the southern coast of England.

Radar, then known as RDF – Radio Direction Finding – was still in its infancy but Hugh Dowding had understood the advantages of the early experiments into this system of locating aircraft and had been supporting its advancement since the late 1930s. As Germany and its Luftwaffe would soon discover, RDF gave Fighter Command a distinct advantage in the Battle.

Knowing where the enemy were approaching from, the height at which the raiders were flying, and the approximate number, gave the fighter controllers on the ground good time to get squadrons airborne and on most occasions, in the best place to intercept and engage.

Historians now split the Battle into distinct phases. The first was attacks on ships found in the English Channel and its south coastal ports, and against RDF stations along the south coast. The second phase, which began on 8 August, was the assault on Britain's airfields, designed to both knock out these bases and to destroy aircraft. The third phase was the assault upon London which began on 7 September, and finally the mainly nuisance fighter sweeps and fighter-bomber attacks that continued till the end of October and into November.

Fighter Command's 11 Group in the south-east of England took the brunt of the fighting, and could be supported by 12 Group to the north of London, to either reinforce 11 Group or to intercept raiders entering its own territory from the east. 10 Group in the south-west was mainly concerned with covering that part of the country from approximately Southampton to Land's End, and as far north as Bristol.

When 310 Squadron was formed at Duxford on 10 July, they brought in the first Hawker Hurricane fighters ever to be based there. It had previously had the Spitfires of 19 Squadron, that had now moved to Duxford's satellite airfield at Fowlmere, and Defiants of 264 Squadron, that had also now departed.

Towards the end of August Duxford would see the formation of the first fighter wing, comprising 242, 19 and 310 Squadrons. It was known as the 12 Group Wing and was led by Squadron Leader D R S Bader, the famous legless pilot and CO of 242 Squadron who favoured the so-called Big Wings.

Chapter Five

The Battle of Britain

16th July 1940

Upon reaching the British shores, there was a heavy sea fog and drizzle, exactly as we imagine English weather to be from books and films we have seen. Within a few hours after our arrival we know that we are not in France because everything here works! From the harbour we take a train to Leamington where we sleep in Czech army tents, as this is a Czech army assembly point. We are assured by the commanding officer that we shall not remain here very long since he has already telephoned the Czech Air Force Inspectorate in London.

1st August 1940

We arrive at RAF Station Cosford.[1] We are now learning that the British Royal Air Force aerodrome is called a station and not a base. Cosford is a school for any RAF employment but also for receiving a technical status. The buildings and class rooms, plus the general organisation, are perfect and obviously the British are the best business organisers. This most certainly could not be mistaken for France.

This station is at present acting as a Czech depot where everybody will be checked, and according to his qualifications, will be despatched to a suitable unit. We only have French francs with us, and as it is war one cannot exchange this money except directly with the Bank of England. The first thing we have is a medical examination and are then told that we shall soon be properly inducted into the Royal Air Force.

---

[1] RAF Cosford, in Staffordshire, had been opened in August 1938 as the home of No.2 School of Technical Training. During WW2 it would see some 70,000 engine and airframe mechanics and armourers attend courses here. In March 1939 No.9 Maintenance Unit was formed at Cosford and it saw its first aeroplanes, Ansons, later Spitfires, Battles and Blenheims.

5/6th August 1940

Things are moving here. We are now a few hundred in number already, and within days, ten of us are informed that we have been chosen to be fighter pilots. I just want to sit in the cockpit of a British fighter plane as soon as this can possibly be arranged. The next day we are sitting in the officer's mess lounge and I am thinking that exactly a year ago I was in Paris, signing my French Foreign Legion contract. Later my thoughts turn to when I sat in the cockpit of a Morane 406, the French fighter plane manufactured in large numbers. I remember my friend Frank Bieberle who perished on 25th May near the town of Arras. Another pilot, although a sergeant who we called Hranička was killed over Compiègne. The later deaths of my dear friends Popelka on 3rd June, and Bendl on 7th June. I remember you all my friends and will avenge you!

We are told that we shall be joining our first Czech fighter squadron (twice the size of a French escadrille), that is being established at Duxford, near Cambridge.

According to the squadron diary (RAF Form 540) the following Czech officers reported for duty from RAF Cosford:

Pilot Officers K Marek, F Weber, J Studený, Stanislav Fejfar, F Fajtl, F Dolezal, O Posluzný, J Bryks, B Kimlička, J Macháček, plus 14 sergeant pilots. A later-timed entry noted:

> At 15.45 hours the Czech personnel of this squadron, with the British Officers, paraded for inspection and address by the President of the Czech Republic, Dr E Beneš. Dr Beneš inspected the squadron and then addressed them at some length after which the squadron marched past. The President then spoke informally to the officers, sergeant pilots, and airmen who were formed up separately for the purpose. The party then adjourned for tea, after which F/Lt. Jefferies and Sgt. Pilots Zima and Hubáček gave an exhibition of formation flying. Dr Beneš was accompanied by several officials of the Czech legation and the Czech Minister of Defence, General Nizorky, and the military secretary. The following RAF Officers also were in the party. Air Marshal Sir William Mitchell, Air Commodore C E H Medhurst DAAC, Wing Commander Sir Louis Greig and Group Captain F Beaumont. Air Vice-Marshal Leigh-Mallory, AOC 12 Group, was also in attendance. Flight Lieutenant G L Sinclair DFC attended the Investiture at Buckingham Palace.
>
> 12 August: B Flight, under F/Lt. Jefferies proceeded to Sutton Bridge and fired guns. The AOC 12 Group,[2] paid the squadron an

---

[2] Air Vice-Marshal Trafford Leigh-Mallory DSO.

Top: Members of 310 Squadron marching past.
Bottom: President Beneš meeting 310's ground personnel. Major Hess far right.

informal visit. Mr Louis De Glehn of Grantchester, gave his first lesson in the English language to the pilots of the squadron. Arrangements have been made for this gentleman to give three lessons a week to Czech pilots.

It is difficult to date exactly the next few entries in Fejfar's diary, but Henry Prokop translated them thus:

August 1940

We are flown up to Duxford and upon landing we are pleased to discover that, by coincidence, President Beneš is coming today for his first visit. We are all officer pilots but still dressed in French uniforms with Czech insignia on our shoulders, but it does not seem to worry the RAF in the least. We are told that private tailors will soon make our British uniforms.

The number our squadron has been given is 310 and it is called 'No.310 (Czechoslovak) Fighter Squadron'. It will be completely manned by Czech personnel, in the air and on the ground. Obviously the technical English personnel will supervise everything until we Czechs learn enough English to take over.

Our commanding officer is Major Hess, in an English uniform of a squadron leader, and his English counterpart is Squadron Leader Blackwood. The squadron has two flight commanders, just like the French escadrille. A Flight is commanded by Flight Lieutenant G L Sinclair DFC, whilst B Flight is in the charge of Flight Lieutenant J Jefferies. The aircraft are Hurricane Mark Is. We are examined in the air by Flying Officer Boulton [in a two-seater] before we can [be allowed to] sit in a Hurricane. In the officer's mess I meet Pilot Officer Mrázek, with whom I not only escaped from my homeland, but served with in the legion and also in France. He is to serve in 312 Czech Squadron, also based here but soon to move.

Our first flights begin at once, in an advanced fighter aerobatics aeroplane called a Master. The throttle movements in the British and American aeroplanes are exactly opposite to the Czech practice. The next day, after passing scrutiny by the instructor, I fly the Hurricane and we are told that tomorrow B Flight will undergo tests for firing at a towed target at RAF Sutton Bridge.

[At Sutton Bridge] I empty my eight machine guns almost in one go, being so-enthusiastic. The machine smells of new paint, not like the old Morane 'laundry baskets'. I have now flown in a Master, a Harvard, a Battle as well as the Hurricane.

Major (Squadron Leader) Alexander Hess, aged 42, was amazingly a World War One veteran infantryman. Having moved into aviation he had become a fighter pilot in Air Regiment 4, pre-WW2. He too escaped into Poland and then France, being commissioned into the French air force in late 1939. He reached England in June 1940 and joined 310 Squadron as a supernumerary at its formation on 10 July. He was one of the oldest fighter pilots to see action in the Battle of Britain.

His counterpart, Squadron Leader George Douglas Morant Blackwood was only a few years younger than Hess, having been commissioned into the RAF Reserve in 1930. An old Etonian, he had entered the RAF on a short service commission in April 1932 and the following year was with 25 Squadron, taking part in the 1934 Hendon Air Display. Later that year he became the personal assistant to the AOC Coastal Area, at Lee-on-Solent. After his return to 25 Squadron he again moved, this time to 600 Squadron, at the start of 1936. He left the RAF in 1938 but was recalled when war broke out and after a period as an instructor he went to 213 Squadron. He was given command of 310 in late June 1940.

Gordon Leonard Sinclair was nearing his 24th birthday and had joined the RAF in 1937, and once he got his 'wings' was posted to 19 Squadron, flying Spitfires. He saw combat over the Dunkirk evacuation and for his actions was awarded the Distinguished Flying Cross. He brought his combat experience to the new Czech squadron in late June as it was forming.

Jerrard Jefferies had joined the RAF in 1936 and had been in France with 85 Squadron in 1940, and had claimed one victory there. On promotion to flight lieutenant he had been sent to command B Flight of 310 Squadron the day before it was officially formed.

*   *   *

As the month of August began to draw to a close, the squadron became officially operational – on the 17th – and a few tentative patrols were flown. On the 20th a Ju88 bomber was spotted but the section on patrol lost it in cloud. A convoy patrol was flown on the 23rd also, while another patrolled over North Weald airfield. A further patrol over the same aerodrome was made the next day.

On the 26th enemy aircraft bombed nearby Debden and the squadron were sent aloft. A formation of 15+ Dornier bombers was spotted and Squadron Leader Blackwood attacked one which began to trail smoke and flame. Then a shot from the rear gunner set Blackwood's Hurricane (P3887) on fire and he had to take to his parachute. Flight Lieutenant Sinclair (R4184) also received a hit, in his glycol tank, but he managed to get down to base without incident.

Pilot Officer Emil Fechtner claimed a Me110 shot down, but Pilot Officer Václav Bergman had also to bale out of a burning Hurricane but he landed without major injury, just a slight flesh wound to his right leg. Sergeant Eduard Prchal shot down another Dornier but a fighter caught him, wounding him in the back with shell fragments, and forcing him to make a crash-landing near Upminster.

On the 31st twelve Hurricanes intercepted Dorniers and 109s, claiming four bombers, two 109s with another probably destroyed. Pilot Officer Miroslav

Kredba baled out of his damaged machine (P8814) following an attack by a 109, landing at Epping. Pilot Officer Jaroslav Štěrbáček was killed, the first loss to 310 Squadron. He was attacking a Dornier but a 109 got him, and his machine (P3159) crashed near Romford. It is assumed he baled out over the Thames estuary and was lost. He was 27.

Pilot Officer Emil Fechtner's Hurricane (P3889) was shot-up but he was not hurt. Pilot Officer Jiroslav Malý's fighter (V6621) was also damaged in this action. Major Hess claimed a 109 and then helped to cripple a Dornier which was forced to make a wheels-up landing in a field. Following it down he had every intention of making certain that none of the crew survived. Three crewmen clambered out of the bomber and seeing the Hurricane diving towards them, they quickly held up their hands in surrender. Hess hesitated and missed the opportunity to open fire so turned to come in again, but this time he could see the men waving something white, so, cursing, gave up the attempt. As he was later to admit to Group Captain Woodhall – 'I am become too bloody British!'

The Czech squadron had been blooded. Unfortunately Fejfar made no diary entries for this exciting period. He began to write again as September arrived.

1st September 1940

Our further training is thorough and consists of 21 tasks and is most certainly not to be compared with the French practice of preparing a pilot to kill his German opponents. During our Sutton Bridge gunnery we have to stop, since two young English pilots collided in the air whilst practising a simulated dog-fight.

Many of us are not affected by subsequent lectures, for without knowledge of English we are unable to understand them. During the evening after our air gunnery flights have ended, our former comrade and CO of our Czech escadrille in France, Captain Kulhánek, visits us in the officer's mess. He is now employed in the Czech Inspectorate in London, and he brought us some news instead of writing. Number one was that he will exchange any unwanted French currency in our possession at once. Second is that we are to be paid £40 per month in cash this month, but thereafter our future money will be through Lloyds Bank, and we will have a cheque book. Third news is that we must pay the tailor directly for our uniforms but will be reimbursed through Lloyds Bank afterwards.

3rd September 1940

Unfortunately another Czech pilot was killed today. It was Sergeant Stibor[3] with whom I practised many aerobatics. My propeller was shattered by him being so close and I was lucky to get down in a nearby

---

[3] Sergeant Karel Stibor was still converting to Hurricanes with No.6 Operational Training Unit (I), was 25 years old and came from Měsetice.

field. Only a few days ago we lost Pilot Officer Štěrbáček who was the first of our pilots killed in the Battle of Britain. What we heard was that whilst a Dornier bomber was being shot down, by a bad stroke of luck the rear gunner managed to hit his aircraft and kill him outright. His fighter dived into the Thames and he was never found. He was 26 years old. We arranged for a funeral without a body in the coffin, but it was an honourable occasion attended by our C-in-C, Air Commodore Janousek, and Air Vice-Marshal T Leigh-Mallory, commander of our 12 Fighter Group.

I now have over 360 flying hours on fighter planes and I hope to reach double that amount in no time. At least, that is my ambition.

On 3 September, the first anniversary of Britain declaring war on Germany, 310 were scrambled mid-morning and engaged enemy aircraft near to RAF North Weald. Emil Fechtner and the others waded into a formation of bombers, but Fechtner then had a Me110 fly right in front of him. Firing a short burst the 110 went down and crashed, the Czech pilot seeing it burning on the ground 10 miles south east of the airfield. He did not see anyone bale out.

Bohumil Fürst followed his flight commander, Gordon Sinclair, into the attack, both going for the same enemy machine. As he broke away he also found himself behind a 110 which he fired at three times, and this too went down, leaving a trail of smoke and flame south of Chelmsford.

Flight Lieutenant Jefferies, who was leading the squadron, had seen Dorniers approaching from the south-east, with 110s as escort, and began to lead his men above them, then ordered the pilots into 'line astern'. He went for some 110s, giving them short deflection bursts as he closed in. He then singled out a 110 and gave it three or four bursts and it nosed over and down. Thinking it was attempting to escape him, he followed, but its dive steepened and he watched as it hit the ground and blew up, about 10 miles to the north of North Weald.

In all five 110s were claimed this day, with a Dornier destroyed and another probably so. The 110s were from I./ZG2. 19 and 46 Squadrons were also involved in this action and altogether this German unit lost five of their aircraft while ZG26 which was also in the escort, lost two more. 310 lost Sergeant Josef Kopřiva who was shot down by a 110 but he managed successfully to bale out.

The squadron was in the thick of the action again on the 7th, during a wing patrol, taking off around 5.30 pm, led by Flight Lieutenants Jefferies (R4089) and Sinclair (R4084). Engaging the enemy the pilots later claimed three Me110s, one Me109 and a He111 as destroyed, three 110s as probables, with another three damaged. This appears later to have been adjusted to three 110s, one 109 and the Heinkel destroyed, with four 110s as probables. Sergeant Josef Koukal (V7437) baled out of his burning Hurricane, causing him burn injuries to face and hands. Pilot Officer Vilem Göth (V6643), who claimed two of the 110s, was hit in the glycol coolant tank, and had to make a forced landing near Purley, Surrey. The 110s were from I and II Gruppen of ZG2, who lost eight of their number. Other claimants were Pilot Officer Janouch a 110, Flying Officer

Boulton, a He111, Sergeant J Koukal a 110, with probable 110s by Sergeant Fürst (who also claimed a 109 of I/LG2), Pilot Officer Zimprich, while the damaged 110s went to Jefferies, Šeda, Fechtner, and Sinclair.

This was the first planned raid on London by the Germans, and it was also the first time the Duxford Wing had gone into action. Fejfar missed all this by one day.

It is interesting to record that the Duxford Wing, as Squadron Leader Blackwood was later to recall, had no formal training in wing tactics. He described it as rather a case of patrolling in strength. So the wing, when it took off, just flew together, with the added problem that the TR9 radios the aircraft carried were so limited that it made contact between squadrons impossible, and that only one unit was able to talk directly to Sector Control.

8th September 1940

I am posted to B Flight from Sinclair's A Flight. Some Czech friends are also flying with 312 Squadron at Aintree, Liverpool, while others are with other British squadrons and will only be posted to a Czech squadron when casualties occur. The exercises we undertook included gunnery and took almost three weeks to complete but Major Hess will only take the best pilots.

9th September 1940

I shot down the first German bastard today in my Hurricane. He was flying a Me110 with twin engines and rudders. It happened like this. We were flying in a squadron formation with just three English pilots, Squadron Leader Blackwood, Flight Lieutenant Sinclair and Flight Lieutenant Jefferies. I was flying next to Sinclair who only received his DFC at Buckingham Palace on 6th September (although its announcement came in June) for his courageous flights during the Dunkirk evacuation from France.

We were flying at 27,000 feet and it was very cold. As we came through some clouds, we could see some Luftwaffe bombers escorted by many fighters. We were given the order to attack but had to be aware of the German fighters since they spotted us and were above us. I found a Me110 to attack and promised myself that this German swine would not sleep in his bed that night. I manoeuvred behind him and fired all my machine guns at him. He tried to escape by climbing steeply and turning but I managed to deliver three more bursts and he began to smoke, then went down. I saw the smoke emerging but my Hurricane began to vibrate strongly, although the engine was running smoothly. However, I was soon looking for an airfield to land at.

Once I had landed the ground crew discovered that the gun panel cover of one machine gun was bent and it was this that had caused such violent turbulence. I was able to refuel here and took off, reaching

Duxford at 8.50 pm in quite an excited state. My first Messerschmitt over England.

But the day ended tragically for our former instructor, Flying Officer Boulton, who collided with Sinclair's Hurricane but whilst going down he took a German bomber with him by crashing into it.

During this battle, which took place over Croydon, south London, at 17.40, Flight Lieutenant Sinclair (R4084) and Flying Officer J E Boulton's aircraft (P3888) did indeed collide. Boulton's Hurricane is reported to have struck a Dornier Do215 bomber before going down to crash at Woodmansterne, thereby killing the 20-year-old pilot. Sinclair baled out of his machine (R4084) which crashed in a wood at Caterham, spraining his ankle in the process. In his combat report, Sinclair recorded:

> I was Yellow Leader of 310 Squadron in a wing attack on bombers. As we turned into the attack in sections line astern, I saw Me109s coming down on us from port; the squadron was turning starboard and I myself turned very slightly to port to see what the Me109s were doing, when without warning I received a hard blow across the shoulders, accompanied by a loud noise, followed by three distinct bangs, quickly. I then found myself in an inverted spin, thrown hard against the roof, and apparently without any starboard plane, but it was very hard to see anything in that position. I then decided to get out. I had considerable difficulty in opening the roof and undoing the straps, owing to the pressure in the cockpit; having done this I just shot out into space without any effort on my part. The parachute descent took almost exactly 13 minutes, and I finally landed in a road just off the Purley Way in Coulsdon. I was picked up by Lieut. G D Cooper (Irish Guards) who saw the whole action through his field glasses.

In fact, when he landed – in Coulsdon High Street – injuring his ankle in the process, the first person Sinclair encountered was not only Lieutenant G D Cooper, leading a detachment of guardsmen from nearby barracks, but Gordon Cooper an old school friend. Cooper greeted his old pal by saying, 'Good God, Gordon, what are you doing lying there?' He then took Sinclair to the Irish Guards officer's mess at Caterham. However, Sinclair was only wearing his flying overalls over his pyjamas, so was not allowed to dine with them because he was improperly dressed!

Some years later Sinclair also stated that he thought he too had struck the Dornier after the collision with Johnnie Boulton.

* * *

Meanwhile, Pilot Officer František Rypl (P3142) ran out of fuel after a prolonged dog-fight with Me109s and had to make a crash-landing at Oxted and was unhurt. Squadron Leader Blackwood also claimed a Me110 destroyed, while Sergeants Řechta and Hubáček claimed probables.

Stanislav Fejfar was able to dictate, or perhaps write out himself, his first RAF combat report to the squadron intelligence officer, which was then typed up and signed. It referred to the combat over south-west London at 17.40, at 22,000 feet. The narrative read:

> I was No.3 in the section led by F/Lt. Sinclair. We approached the formation of enemy bombers from the starboard side, when enemy fighters made a counter attack and tried to get in the rear of us. The leader of the front section gave a sign to dismiss. I made a sharp turn and came in at the rear of the formation of eight Me110s. These aircraft parted when attacked. I followed an Me110, which by turns, steep climbing and diving tried to escape. I delivered three attacks on him and the e/a went into a steep dive. I saw smoke pouring from his port engine. I dived at him and fired one more burst and the port side of the e/a caught fire. In this moment I noticed that [the] starboard leading edge fairings were loosened and my aircraft began to vibrate and went to the ground. I slowly pulled the aeroplane's nose up, and by then I had lost the Me110 from my sight. At the last moment I saw that this burning e/a was followed by another Hurricane. I thought that my a/c was hit by splinter from an A.A. shell, and I left the battle. I landed at Pittesburg (*sic*).

The squadron diary – Form 540 – records the afternoon's events as follows:

> Duxford. 9 Sep. 17.05. The squadron (12 aircraft) led by the CO were ordered to patrol N.Weald at 20,000 ft. They joined up with 19 Squadron and 242 Squadron to form a wing, the latter being in the van. A formation of about 75 Do215s escorted by about 150 Me109s, 110s and He112s were sighted south of the Thames estuary heading N.W. The squadron were ordered to form line astern in preparation for an attack on main enemy formation. The attack was delivered south of London at 17.35 hrs at 22,000 ft, the cloud being about 4/10ths at 7,000 ft. A collision occurred between two Hurricanes which was seen by other pilots of the squadron who thereupon broke formation to avoid further ones and a series of dog-fights ensued. F/Lieut. Sinclair was hit by a cannon shell and forced to bale out: he landed at Purley Way unhurt except for a sprained ankle. F/Lt. Rypl who was engaged by some 10 Me109s ran out of petrol and was forced to land which he did near Oxted in an obstructed field and crashed his aircraft. F/O T E Boulton who had been attached to the squadron as a flying instructor almost since its formation, but who had specially asked to be allowed to serve as an operational pilot was, most unfortunately, one of those involved in the collision mentioned above and went down in a spin.... Our own losses amounted to 1 aircraft crashed, 1 missing and 1 pilot missing

probably killed. It was bad luck to lose an officer of the type of F/O
J E Boulton who had done a great deal to help the squadron in its
early stages of training.

By most accounts the 110 that Fejfar engaged and claimed shot down came
from 15/LG1, and it crashed on the Maori Sports Club ground, Old Malden
Lane, Worcester Park, Surrey. Both crew members were killed, Unteroffiziers
Pfaffelhuber and Kramp, their aircraft coded L1+DL. Remains of this machine
and its engines were later recovered by the London Air Museum.

Hurricanes flown by the pilots involved in this action were: Sinclair R4084,
Göth V6642, Fejfar P3143, Malý V6556, Zima P3056, Bergman V7405,
Blackwood R4085, Rypl P3142, Zimprich V7304, Boulton P3888, Hubáček
R4087 and Řechka L2715.

*   *   *

In the cold light of historical fact one or two items in the diary entry need some
clarification. One concerns the Duxford Wing, which was mentioned earlier.
The famous legless pilot, Squadron Leader Douglas Bader, commanding officer
of 242 Squadron, had been encouraged by 12 Group's AOC, Trafford Leigh-
Mallory, to lead a wing of fighters from the north of London. Bader had argued
that by leading twice or three times as many aircraft than just a single squadron,
two or three times as many German aircraft could be shot down. This 'Big
Wing' theory has had much airing ever since, with pro and anti factions arguing
the merits of the idea.

While in theory Bader had a point in pure mathematical terms, the AOC of
11 Group, Sir Keith Park, always argued that by the time Bader had formed up
his 'wing' the enemy aircraft had come and were on their way home before he
could bring his force to bear. Whatever the final analysis might be, 310
Squadron had become part of this Big Wing and often flew in company with
these other two squadrons (242 and 19). Post-war records also suggest a high
degree of over-claiming by the wing.

Reference to German He112 fighters often appeared in wartime action
reports during the Battle of Britain. While it is true that the Germans had this
type, and also the similar He113, they did not see action over England. These
types were very much publicised by the Luftwaffe in the immediate pre-war
years, so much so that the RAF assumed they would be met in numbers over
home territory. In fact they were all Me109s, being of a not-dissimilar
configuration and design.

While 27-year-old František Rypl is recorded here as a flight lieutenant, his
RAF rank was that of pilot officer. It may be his rank in connection to his Czech
air force status, although he only joined that formation in March 1939, and the
RAF did not give him flight lieutenant rank until 1 March 1941.

*   *   *

15th September 1940

Today the leader of my flight is Squadron Leader Hess. We are ordered to fly over the east part of London and when we come through the clouds we see at once at least 100 Dornier 17 bombers. They had an escort of Me109s. I made an attack on a Dornier that had become detached from its formation and I fired from the right at once and saw petrol coming out of the fuselage. He disappeared into the clouds but I was waiting when he emerged and I fired at him twice more. Later I fired again until my guns were empty. The result was one Dornier that landed on the Isle of Grain.

This was a day of large battles and we accounted for four bombers destroyed. Squadron Leader Hess was lucky to escape from his Hurricane by parachute and Warrant Officer Hubáček escaped with only a wound to his right foot. Some pilots are wounded and require only a brief stay in hospital but nobody is as tired as we were in France because in the RAF you have your days off. Our 310 Squadron has now shot down 37 enemy aircraft in three weeks.

* * *

September 15th is today remembered as being Battle of Britain Day, for it was the high water mark of the battle. It was a day when the RAF claimed a massive number of German aircraft shot down, and although the figure was later much reduced, it proved to be the final big throw of the dice for the Luftwaffe.

Squadron Leader Hess was brought down by a Me109 over the Thames estuary and parachuted down near Billericay, Essex, unhurt. Sergeant Hubáček was similarly hit by a 109 and baled out, landing near Pitsea. The attacking 109s were flown by JG26 and it was its Kommodore, Major Adolf Galland who shot down Hubáček, while his wingman, Oberleutnant Walter Horten, despatched Hess. Galland reported:

> With my Stabstaffel I attacked two Hurricanes which were about 800 metres below us. Maintaining surprise, I closed in on the wingman and opened fire from 120 metres as he was in a gentle turn to the left. The enemy aircraft reeled as my rounds struck the nose from below, and pieces fell from the left wing and fuselage. The left side of the fuselage burst into flame.

It was Galland's 33rd victory, and Horten's 5th. The squadron diary only records:

> 15 Sep. Sgt/P Řechka, Blue 3, shot down a He111 which he saw crash in Foulness Island. F/O Fejfar, Red 2, shot down a Do17 which landed near Grain, two of the crew being taken prisoner. The day's 'Bag' for the Station amounted to a respectable total of 44 enemy

aircraft destroyed, 8 shared and 8 probables, conclusive proof of the efficiency of the wing formation.

Fejfar wrote up his second combat report – in the Czech language – which was then translated and typed out. It covers his action at 14.40 hours over the east of London at 17,000 feet. The narrative reads:

> The section was attacked by a formation of Me109s East of London. I attacked with three Hurricanes and two Spitfires, a formation of 12 Do17s. After the first attack the last section of the formation was dispersed. The aircraft that was attacked by me from the right turn disappeared in cloud. From the fuselage there was pouring a stream of culmus [sic – presumable cumulus, ie: a cloud of] – probably petrol. I made another attack on the formation of Do17s. The second e/a disappeared in the clouds. I waited for him behind the cloud – and after he appeared again, I attacked him twice. When carrying out a second attack, I sighted a Spitfire attacking from below. The e/a then made an emergency landing near Grain. I was flying over the e/a with the Spitfire until the civilians approached him. Then I returned to Duxford aerodrome.

The Dorniers were from 4./KG3 and Fejfar's victim that crash-landed at Grain at 14.45 was a Do17Z-3 (Werk No.2881) coded 5K+CM, which became a write-off. The crew of Unteroffizier Wien, Feldwebel von Goertz (pilot), Gefreiter Schild and Gefreiter Weymar were all taken prisoner. The Spitfire Fejfar saw attacking was thought to have been flown by Flight Sergeant Harry Steere DFM of 19 Squadron. However, Steere says in his combat report that he saw the crew of his bomber bale out. Whether or not the four crewmen from KG3 baled out before the bomber crash-landed – crewless – is unclear.

*   *   *

The squadron were again scrambled on the 16th to patrol over London but failed to make any contact with the enemy. Then the weather deteriorated which curtailed further operations. On the 17th the squadron received the news that Flight Lieutenant Jefferies had been awarded the DFC. A patrol this day also proved fruitless. The next day Fejfar sat in the sun outside dispersal, writing up his diary whilst awaiting the call to action. The scene would have been a typical one re-enacted on dozens of fighter airfields across the country, especially in the south and south east. Pilots would be lounging in a variety of seats and chairs, even the odd metal-framed bed might have been brought out from the flight hut so someone could snooze in the warm sun. Many would be nodding off, others reading newspapers or books. Some might be playing cards or chess. All would be wearing their yellow Mae West life preservers in case they came down in the sea. There would be no time to put these on when the 'scramble' call came, so they had to be worn the whole time while at readiness.

As Fejfar recorded, there was the almost obligatory gramophone grinding out the latest tunes of the day. However unconcerned everyone would appear, a small part of the brain would be anxiously or nervously twitching whilst listening out for the jangle of the telephone, usually manned by an airman in the hut, or perhaps the instrument had been brought out through a window and placed on a stool or small table.

Just a short distance away would stand the Hurricanes, facing the take-off area across the flying field. Sitting or lying close to each one would be the engine fitter and rigger, no doubt in shirt-sleeves, also listening out for the telephone's ring. When it did ring the airmen would be galvanised into action, ready for the yell of 'scramble!' They would then start the aircrafts' engines – one man in the cockpit, the other by the two-wheeled trolley accumulator, already plugged into the Hurricane, and once the propeller was whirling, the one man in the cockpit would climb out onto the wing, as 'his' pilot was now racing towards him. Helped into the aircraft's seat, his mechanic on the wing would help him buckle on parachute and safely harness, then plug in the wireless connection to his headphones, and attach the oxygen supply. With the 'trolley-acc' disconnected and the wheel chocks removed, and perhaps with a final: 'Good luck, Sir,' the fighter would begin its take-off run with others ahead or following.

Grass and dust would be blown back from the prop-wash produced by the powerful Merlin engines. Windows of the flight hut would rattle, while outside it, the quickly vacated chairs, seats and beds would have been left in disarray, with books, papers and chess pieces scattered about on the ground. Peace had been shattered, death and destruction were probably just minutes away.

18th September 1940

It is a beautiful day, very sunny, and somebody inside the dispersal hut is playing the latest hit on the old fashioned portable gramophone. When the scramble is ordered every pilot runs towards his machine. Today we are three squadrons taking off to fight the Luftwaffe.

The combination of three squadrons is called the wing. One squadron is Czech, one Polish and one British. We fly towards London at 26,000 feet. We cannot see anything whilst flying in cloud but these are the orders. When the clouds suddenly disappear right in front of us there is a magnificent sight to us Czechs, a formation of 30 Luftwaffe bombers with that confounded black cross on their fuselages.

We attack at once and I chase one of the bombers. All around me I notice that four bombers are already on fire and are falling down to a deserved rest. I also notice that one of the aircrew who parachuted out has been caught by the harness and cannot detach himself from the Dornier's tail-plane. So he is approaching his death on the soil of hated England. Some mother is losing her son. I do not see his end because of the intervening clouds and I am also running short of petrol.

I land at the aerodrome and later speak to my brother officer, Zimprich, who also witnessed the attack and the demise of a Luftwaffe pilot, or maybe he was a navigator or an air gunner.

No.310 Squadron's diary for this date:

> Duxford. At 16.15 hours they took off again, led by F/Lieut. J
> Jefferies DFC, accompanied by the same squadrons as before, and
> intercepted a formation of 15-20 Dornier 215s east of Hornchurch
> at 22,000 feet. In the ensuing combat one Do.215 fell to F/Lt.
> Jefferies, P/O Bergman, P/O Fechtner and Sgt E Prchal. All our
> aircraft returned safely. In this instance the enemy bombers were not
> escorted by any fighters.

Fejfar's personal, translated, combat report reads:

> I was No.2 in Red Section. In the first attack of our formation I was
> not able to fire, as I came below the formation. I carried out a new
> attack on the enemy formation and one e/a that broke away. Jointly
> with me were attacking two Hurricanes, one from 310 Squadron
> and one from another Squadron. The e/a made aerobatics and of the
> crew two baled out. The e/a, probably without a pilot, disappeared
> in cloud. The e/a made turns [like] an uncontrolled aircraft. I cannot
> say where exactly the e/a crashed, as I had not enough petrol and
> had to return to the aerodrome. It was on the right bank of the
> Thames before the estuary. The attack was seen by P/O Zimprich (he
> saw aircraft 'J' – mine), and P/O Fechtner saw the crew bale out
> from a Do215, which made aerobatics. The e/a was not in flames.

This report timed the action at 17.00 hours at about 20,000 feet, and he
claimed one aircraft destroyed, shared with P/O Janouch and another
Hurricane. There is no Dornier loss that fits this action and most probably the
aircraft encountered were in fact Junkers 88 bombers. Many 11 Group fighters
engaged this raid by III/KG77, and the Duxford Wing also got in amongst them.
The wing claimed an amazing 30 shot down, although in fact their total was no
more than four.

As mentioned above, the one problem with the 18th claims is that there were
no Dornier bombers shot down this day and if 310 were claiming bombers they
must have been Ju88s. On occasion pilots have misidentified Me110s for
Dorniers, simply because of the twin rudders, but the Ju88s had a single, central
fin and rudder. KG77 were involved in this action and had several of their
machines shot down (but there were no Me110s lost). All the lost Ju88s fell
over Kent or near Tilbury and as they had been engaged by upwards of 100
Spitfires and Hurricanes, it is little wonder the claiming was difficult.

It has been suggested that Fejfar had attacked the Ju88 from the 9th Staffel
that fell in flames near Vange Creek, Pitsea Marshes, near Basildon, Essex. If so
the aircraft was coded 3Z+FT and it was piloted by Feldwebel Wahl, who along
with Gefreiters Buschbeck and Lesker were killed, only Feldwebel Graf
surviving as a prisoner.

However, it is more likely to have been another Ju88 from the 9th Staffel (3Z+DT), that crashed at Cooling Court, Cooling, Kent following an attack on Tilbury Docks. Unteroffizier Kurz and Gefr Koehn were killed, Unteroffizier Burkart missing, and Unteroffizier Glaeseker captured. In 1979 pieces of this aircraft were recovered by the Wealdon Aviation Group.

The problem is that Fejfar says his victim did not go down in flames and that the crew were seen to bale out by Emil Fechtner. Not all the 88s went down on fire, and some did have crew members bale out, so the interpretation of 'crew baling out' may not necessarily mean all four crewmen.

Emil Fechtner certainly wrote about attacking a Dornier 215 in his report. He had closed in to 200 yards before opening fire and he followed the bomber into cloud. On the other side he met the bomber again over the Thames estuary and fired again. This time he saw its left petrol tank erupt in flame and then the port engine began burning. After another attack the starboard engine also caught fire and the bomber fell into the sea. The German gunner had opened up on Fechtner's Hurricane and upon landing he found one bullet had struck a propeller blade while three more had gone through one of his elevators.

Svatopluk Janouch, who was leading A Flight on this occasion, found himself and his two sections in an awkward position as the attack began, being too close whilst effecting a turn, following the squadron leader. Climbing, he and two other Hurricanes attacked a bomber – again recorded as a Do215 – and he picked out one that had started to lag behind. With this attack he saw the crew bale out. He continued to chase the raiders out to sea but was unable to close, but did see several Spitfires going after them.

Miroslav Jiroudek, Red 3, also attacked a 'Do215' that attempted to dodge into some cloud. He followed it through and attacked again, noting that the rear gunner ceased his return fire. Smoke was beginning to stream from both engines and then the bomber crashed. Two other Hurricanes were also attacking this machine, one of whom he identified as Půda, who also confirms this machine crashed and burned.

No doubt 310 Squadron and the wing were more than pleased with their air fight, it is just a pity that the claiming was not what they thought it was. One has to wonder too if Fighter Command HQ truly believed that their fighters were indeed taking such a heavy toll on the enemy, or did they perhaps feel that it was good for morale if the pilots thought they were? Wrecks on the ground could be counted, but of course, there was no guarantee that aircraft did not fall into the sea off the English coast, or whilst struggling back across the Channel. The important thing surely was that the fighter pilots believed they were winning.

Chapter Six

After the Battle

While it is generally accepted that 15th September saw the Luftwaffe seriously blooded, the fighting continued during the latter half of September, and with just as much vehemence. The Luftwaffe were putting up more fighters in an attempt to stave off the Spitfire and Hurricane pilots who continued to get in amongst the bombers, but AVM Keith Park was now ordering his fighters not to mix it with pure fighter sweeps and confine their aggression to only those times when bombers were in evidence. The Germans, having received a bloody nose in attacking London in daylight, were now switching their raids upon the capital during the hours of darkness.

However, before we leave the mid-September battles, and especially those on the 15th, 310 Squadron, along with other fighter squadrons had received a copy of a message from the prime minister, Winston Churchill, to Sir Hugh Dowding, AOC-in-C of Fighter Command, and Sir Archibald Sinclair, the air minister, which read:

> 'Yesterday eclipsed all previous records of Fighter Command. Aided by squadrons of Czech and Polish comrades using only a small proportion of their total strength and under cloud conditions of some difficulty, they cut to rags and tatters three separate waves of murderous assaults upon the civil population of their native land, inflicting a certain loss of 125 bombers and 53 fighters upon the enemy, to say nothing of "probables" and "damaged" aircraft, whilst themselves sustaining a loss of 12 pilots and 25 machines. These results exceed all expectations and give just and sober confidence in the approaching struggle.'

It is interesting that Churchill used the phrase '...using only a small proportion of their total strength, for during the 15th, Churchill had visited Fighter Command headquarters at Bentley Priory, and had watched as squadron after squadron had been committed to the air battle. He had then asked Keith Park, OC 11 Group, what reserves he had? Park had replied, soberly, 'There are none'.

Meanwhile, the OC 12 Group, Air Vice-Marshal Trafford Leigh-Mallory, also took the opportunity of congratulating his squadrons on their efforts on the 15th. 310 Squadron, therefore received this signal:

> 'The Germans have made a great effort today and you have played
> a notable part in frustrating it. Heartiest congratulations.'

While we know today the reported damage inflicted upon the Luftwaffe on the
15th was somewhat inflated, nevertheless the Germans had been severely
mauled, and it marked the high water mark of their effort against Britain and
her Royal Air Force. While daylight activity continued, the enemy were now
putting much more effort into night raids against London and other British cities.

* * *

26th September 1940
The weather is not very good and we fly only twice a day locally. The
nights are very busy with Luftwaffe bombers continuously bombing
London. Some bombers flew towards the Midlands over our station. We
heard them but luckily they didn't see Duxford through thick cloud.
　　I receive two days leave, but where can I go? I have no English friends
but I am feeling rich with my French francs having at last been changed
into pounds sterling. I hear that somebody is selling an English
automobile – an Austin 10 – so I do not hesitate to buy it at once. I
cannot believe I have advanced from a Czech military refugee to the
French Foreign Legion sergeant and am now an RAF officer who can
afford to buy his own car [BXH 628].

The next day, the 27th, Flight Lieutenant 'Rusty' Sinclair (the Czechs called him
Rusty due to his hair colouring) was shot down by an Me109 over Thanet at
12.20 and parachuted down over Chilham (V6608), unhurt. Pilot Officer
Fechtner claimed a Dornier as a probable and Sergeant Kominek a 9/JG3
Me109 destroyed. These were the final claims by 310 Squadron in the battle,
and in these latter stages of the Battle of Britain the main air fighting was
concentrated much further south in 11 Group's territory.
　　Sinclair's ailerons were destroyed in the 109's first attack, and a second burst
set his Hurricane on fire. Without ailerons he was unable to turn his machine
over to bale (drop) out and so he had difficulty in extracting himself from the
now diving machine. However, he finally succeeded and he and his parachute
landed in the branches of a fir tree, from which farm labourers helped him to
the ground.

10th October 1940
In our Duxford sector there is not much to do nowadays. Most of the
flying is towards London and we rarely encounter any enemy aircraft
[north of the River Thames]. What there is of the fighting is mopped up
by 11 Group with our Polish friends at RAF Northolt. The exception is

our Czech bomber squadron, No.311, which is flying to Germany every night. My friend from pre-war academy days was shot-up during a raid over Berlin but although the Wellington was hit he managed, as a first-rate pilot and captain, to land in Holland. He hid for three days but finally the Gestapo found his complete crew. One Czech Wellington flying next to him caught fire and only two of the crew were seen to save themselves. All this news came from a radio transmission to England. They will now be interned in a PoW camp.[1] The operational training units are very busy replenishing our lost Czech aircrew.

20th October 1940

We have a rest for a few days because of the low clouds and some continuous heavy rain. More pilots arrived directly from [No.6] OTU Sutton Bridge [15 October]. Flight Lieutenant Hanuš, Flying Officer Hýbler, Flying Officer Foit, Pilot Officer Burda and Sergeants Dvořák, Střihavka, Mlejnecký, Březovský and Chalupa[2]. This latter poor devil lasted a day, because his first flight resulted in the explosion of his Hurricane, probably due to leaking petrol.

25th October 1940

After all those strenuous days during the Battle of Britain, Fighter Command HQ have decided to rest some pilots by making them instructors. 310 Squadron despatched therefore, the following pilots: Flying Officer Göth, Pilot Officer Zaoral, Warrant Officer Fürst [Bohumír Fiřt] and Warrant Officer Půda.

I do not feel happy that I was excluded from this action and [obviously] somebody in the Czech Inspectorate feels that I am more suited to continue my fighter pilot career. Today someone arrived from RAF Honington, where our 311 Squadron resides, and reported that unfortunately last week two more Wellingtons never returned and that

---

[1] This was probably the crew of Flight Lieutenant Karl Josef Trojáček, raiding Berlin on the night of 23-24 September. He was 29 at the time, but survived the war in Stalag Luft III. He died in 1966. This was Bomber Command's answer to Hitler following the first raids upon London in early September, although the Germans reported that their bomber crews had not meant to hit the city, only the Thames-side docks.

[2] Sergeant Jan Chalupa, from Brno, had only just arrived and was killed on a training flight near Ely in P3143 NN-D on the 16th. He was 21 years old. According to the aircraft movement card, the engine cut out and although he managed to bale out, did so too low. The Hurricane dived into a river near Ely Station. Chalupa is buried at Brookwood.

was two more dead crews.[3] I am instructed to go to London HQ of the Czech Red Cross to collect a hand-embroidered Czech national flag. This will be hung in the officer's mess. I enjoyed enormously a day off amongst the charming Czech and English ladies, with the luxury of a private lunch.

28th October 1940

A sacred anniversary of the liberation of Czechoslovakia in 1918 but today it became a double celebration since Fighter Command has awarded the Distinguished Flying Cross to Squadron Leader Hess, and also to Pilot Officer Fechtner. This arrangement was achieved by my countrymen organising some Czech entertainment in the largest hangar at Duxford in the presence of our C-in-C, Air Commodore Janousek, and our well loved Group Captain Beaumont. In addition, Czech pilots were promoted to a higher Czech officer rank.

After the festive evening with the hangar absolutely full of every officer and other ranks, plus the beautiful English WAAFs in their uniforms, the officers were then invited by the C-in-C to the University Arms Hotel in Cambridge, which was also attended by the Czech foreign minister, His Excellency Jan Masařýk, a son of our liberator-president of 1918.

The DFC citations for Hess and Fechtner, the first for 310, read as follows:

> Squadron Leader Hess has displayed outstanding keenness and courage and has set a fine example to his squadron. Since the squadron became operational he has destroyed two enemy aircraft and severely damaged a third. In one engagement his aircraft was set on fire but, in order to clear a populated area, he did not abandon it until it had descended to an altitude of 400 feet, although this barely allowed his parachute time to open.

> Since joining this squadron from the French Air Force, Pilot Officer Fechtner has displayed great keenness to engage the enemy on every possible occasion and has at all times set an outstanding example by the way he has led his section. He has destroyed four enemy aircraft and severely damaged a fifth.

---

[3] 311 Squadron lost Pilot Officer B Landa and crew on 16/17 October, during a raid on Kiel. Bohumil Landa was 33 years old. Two of his crew survived as prisoners. Two other Wellingtons came down, one due to icing (S/L J Veselý and crew), and it actually crashed at Bentley Priory. The other, (F/L J Šnajdr and crew) had to abandon their bomber near Nottingham due to technical problems. Šnajdr rose to become a wing commander and win the DFC.

Hess was presented with his DFC by King George VI during a visit to Duxford on 15 January 1941.

The 28th had started with a scramble, which saw the last air action for the squadron within the now accepted official dates of the Battle of Britain. Squadron Leader Blackwood (V6579), with Malý (V7436) and Bergman (P3143), intercepted a Dornier 17 soon after 8 am, and although several hits were scored, they eventually lost it in cloud.

Red Section had been scrambled at 07.55 with orders to intercept the intruder. After gaining height to 3,000 feet over base they were vectored to course 190° and after about five minutes, Red 3 (Bergman) spotted the enemy aircraft flying south-east some 2,000 feet above them. The German crew must have seen the three Hurricanes too for the Dornier was soon climbing steeply towards some cloud cover. Bergman, in the best position, made the first attack from the starboard quarter while Blackwood came in from the port quarter, but he was only able to loose off a short burst before the bomber went into the clouds. Malý also made an attacking pass before the bomber gained sanctuary.

Hits were observed on the Dornier but they could only claim a 'damaged'. This may have been a machine of 8./KG3 that was attacked by fighters, and which returned from its mission with two of its crew wounded.

29th October 1940

Today we were up for a whole hour searching for reported Luftwaffe aircraft but never found the bastards, and it was extremely cold. I was glad when we landed at 3 pm. As soon as I touched down on the grass airfield I fainted and the ground crew had to take me out of the aircraft and put me in an ambulance, which took me to Ely hospital. I was barely settled when they brought in Flight Lieutenant Malý [P3707] who had collided with Pilot Officer Fechtner [P3889], during a formation flight across the airfield, cutting his tail off. Malý was in a state of shock. His propeller was so heavily damaged in the collision that his machine was vibrating severely but he managed to get it down in a field. Fechtner of course went in and was killed.

This is a big shock for everyone in 310 Squadron and in fact the whole station. It was well known that Fechtner was a favourite of the WAAFs section. One WAAF especially, a singer called Betty. He was handsome, tall and with curly hair.

Emil Fechtner came from Prague, where he was born in September 1916. Originally working as a clerk he was called for military service in 1935 and served with the artillery. The following year he entered the military academy as a second-lieutenant but in 1937 transferred to aviation. A pilot by 1938 he flew B-534s and after the German take-over he escaped to Poland and then to France. Joining the French air force he failed to see active duty before France fell and after the armistice he managed to get to England by ship where he joined the RAF and was posted to 310 Squadron. Apart from the British DFC, he received the Czech Military Cross and the Medal for Bravery. He was buried at Royston cemetery, Hertfordshire, just south-west of Duxford, on 2 November.

According to the squadron diary, 310 were part of a wing patrol from 13.30 to 15.15 hours. The collision occurred about a mile from the aerodrome. It is recorded that he was the best and most efficient officer on the squadron and his loss was keenly felt by everyone.

The 5th of November also proved a bad day for 310 Squadron, but luckily nobody was killed. The squadron was engaged with Me109s over Kent. Flight Lieutenant Jefferies was hit and had to make a belly-landing at Hornchurch. Sergeant Raimond Půda had to take to his parachute, Sergeant Alois Dvořák crash-landed near Fowlmere, Sergeant Miroslav Jiroudek was hit by British AA fire over Sittingbourne and his Hurricane was wrecked in a crash-landing, while Sergeant František Mlejnecy's aircraft was also damaged by fire from a 109, and crash-landed at base, turning right over, but he was only slightly injured.

On 8 November, Fejfar heard the news that another 310 pilot has lost his life. Twenty-eight-year-old František Hradil, from Těšetice. After a very brief stay he had moved to 19 Squadron to fly Spitfires and was shot down in combat with Me109s south of Canterbury on 5 November, falling into the sea. His body was recovered a week later. Earlier in the month, Pilot Officer František Vindiš had crashed his machine coming back from a patrol on the 1st but fortunately he was not seriously injured.

19th November 1940

The doctors at Ely hospital have decided to move me to a place called Littleport [Suffolk] since the hospital was far too busy with bomber squadron casualties. Littleport is run by the Canadian Red Cross and I arrived without ambulance, they being so scarce, reporting to reception. They were surprised to see a pilot officer just walk in to a ward whilst most other flyers they see, are brought in upon stretchers.

Later on I sat on several beds with wounded pilots but my insufficient language and the traditional reserve of the Anglo-Saxons, plus my thick Czech accent, discouraged most of them from telling me what ailed them. Among all these patients, some were suffering from third degree burns; the Canadian Sisters of Mercy moved caringly amongst them. Most we called sisters. They seemingly had renounced their private lives to take care of us and I cannot as yet understand the automatic call of womanhood in this purist form. They continue to smile at all those who will not be too long with us and they are indeed angels.

10th December 1940

Time passed and finally I had an operation and was told not to worry, but I would like to know what had happened to me exactly. Alas nobody told me and all I had to do was to take three tablets a day in order to keep me asleep. In no time I felt so drugged it was as if I was under the influence of 20 glasses of whisky. I am thinking maybe the excessive high flying in France plus the lack of proper food there might have finally caught up with me.

22nd December 1940
At long last I am declared fit enough to be discharged and to be a suitable candidate to be moved to another convalescent home somewhere in Torquay, Devon. I say goodbye to all the sisters, nurses and the friends I have made here and it is a very foggy day when I depart from Ely railway station at 6.30. We head south and then the train goes very slowly along the south coast of England, especially during the night. In the distance we can see from our compartment, by lifting a corner of the blackout curtain, that areas along the south coast are being bombed. Because of this my journey is delayed for five hours but we finally arrive at Torquay at 11.30 pm.

26th December 1940
It does not feel like Christmas at all, so I spent the whole evening in the bar of the Hotel Imperial. I feel understandably very lonely here on my own in a foreign land, and think of my family and friends in my homeland. I also recall my last Christmas, spent in Marseilles, where six of us pilots had that tiny tree lit in that small restaurant. There are now only four of us left.

I hold my glass so strongly that it shatters in my hand and other officers in the bar ask me what is wrong but I cannot even explain it to myself. Thus ends Christmas 1940.

29th December 1940
Today I am delighted that at least somebody remembers me. In a parcel I receive some perfume, soap, a handkerchief and 20 cigarettes. It is a gift from my Czech countrymen in the USA.

There are no air raids here in Torquay and life is very peaceful. I wish this feeling of peace could last forever! Two days later is what in England is called New Year's Eve, but in my homeland it is the last Christian name in the RC calendar, so it is Sylvester Day. As I am alone, the only thing to do is to get drunk and I succeed in this admirably because later I have no recollection of time or falling into bed.

31st January 1941
A month has elapsed and I am still not in good enough health to be allowed to resume flying. I await every day for the doctor to say something to me but it is not to be. I am lucky though because I have acquired a girlfriend here in Torquay. Nanette calls every afternoon and tries to cheer me up. I have been told though, that I must undergo a

second operation and I am not looking forward to it because it means more delay before I will be allowed to fly.

Today I received a letter from Duxford informing me that President Beneš visited the station officially as our president. Subsequently another, more important, visit took place, when their majesties King George and his Queen Elizabeth honoured this Battle of Britain station.

24th February 1941

At long last after all this time the doctors have pronounced me fit enough to be discharged from the hospital, although they would not consider me yet fit enough for flying duties, at least, not for another two months. I am fervently hoping that the two months will pass quickly and that I shall be sitting once more in the cockpit of an aeroplane. Thus ends my peaceful time in Torquay and I say goodbye to everyone who has been kind to me – a foreigner!

I return to Duxford and find the whole squadron has changed considerably. To begin with the Czech pilots have enough knowledge of the English language that they can now command A and B Flights themselves. Squadron Leader Hess has been promoted to wing commander, and will leave shortly. The new squadron commander is Weber, whilst the A Flight commander is Dolezal and B Flight is to be led by Janouch.

The squadron is in perfect order and completely harmonised in every aspect. I am made liaison officer with the Czech Inspectorate in London. The reason for this clerical job is that I am still not considered totally fit for operational flying. Sadly I decide to sell my Austin 10 car that has been standing all this time at Duxford. It was bought by my colleague [Rudolf] Holeček. The first day after my arrival here the Luftwaffe prepared a surprise visit by bombing the airfield. They dropped an assorted 15 to 20 bombs, including anti-personnel ones which killed two of our Czech ground staff who were both on the point of entering an aircraft shelter bay. Before my posting to London I ask for some leave. The orderly room clerk asks me where I would like to go? I say quickly, Torquay, and why not?

Squadron Leader František Weber was approaching his 33rd birthday. He came from Podivín. He too had arrived via France and the French air force, and flown in combat with GC I/2. Once in England and having passed through No.6 OTU, he had been posted to 145 Squadron in September 1940 but had been shot down by a Me109 on 27 October. He baled out over the sea but was rescued. He took command of 310 on 28 February and would lead it till April 1942. He had arrived as 1941 began, initially taking over Jefferies' Flight.

František Dolezal, from Ceska Trebova, was 31, and had joined the Czech air force in 1937. Escaping to France he had seen action during the Blitzkrieg

Fejfar on leave with Yvonne.

with GC II/2 and had scored victories. Once in England he had gone to 310 Squadron but immediately moved across to 19 Squadron, were he added a few scalps to his score, despite being wounded in one leg on 11 September. He came back to 310 in January 1941, and was destined to command it in 1942 and receive the DFC.

Fejfar's old comrade, Svatopluk Janouch was now 27 years old. His victories in France and over England now totalled three and two more shared destroyed. He was to remain with 310 until rested in May 1941.

12th March 1941

Ten days leave, and what a pleasant occasion to spend it in England! I am told that Torquay is known by the British as the 'English Riviera' but of course, when one has lived or stayed in the French one, there can be no comparison. For one thing the weather, and the architecture is different, but it does have tall palm trees.

I meet Yvonne again and she now owns an MG sports car, so takes me daily to other parts of the Devonshire coast. Finally my leave is over and I have to return to Duxford. Before I go I wonder if I shall ever see Nanette again.[4]

---

[4] Fejfar does not make it clear who some of his lady friends were, and other names occasionally pop up in his diary.

Two days after my return from leave I receive a posting order. I feel very sad because the squadron is to be issued with new, more powerful machines, powerful especially in the climb. [The Hurricane Mark II that Fejfar would have loved to fly.]

1st April 1941

Once again I am in London but for work, not leave. I can now see the damage rendered by the Luftwaffe during the Blitz, especially in the East End of the city and the dock areas. The city itself also shows damage, but not St Paul's Cathedral, which has survived so far, and is an encouraging sight.

I am posted to an office at 19-26 Woburn Place, WC1, where a desk awaits me for my new job. I soon find out it is a heavy responsibility in this inspectorate office because I have to fill the posts of killed or missing pilots with replacements.

10th April 1941

I was examined five days ago by a specialist doctor and I expressed my anxiety about the fact that I am still not allowed to fly, but I am only told that he will see me again next month before making any decision. I am very upset sitting in the office which is rather dark and has the atmosphere of a village church.

The biggest air raid by the Luftwaffe since I have been here was carried out the day before yesterday. I am billeted in a small hotel, the Hotel Cora, where for £5 per week I share a room with Stefan. I find it difficult to sleep because there is bombing every night and we often have to leave the hotel for the air-raid shelters after 11 pm, and from where we are we can see the glare from the burning docks.

Tonight our turn came because the German planners decided on bombing the centre of London and that is our district. When the Luftwaffe began to unload their bombs, Stefan and I ran out of the building and found the nearest bomb-shelter. We were dressed only in pyjamas with our RAF greatcoats around our shoulders. We hear the bombs exploding for the next seven hours and are lucky that our improvised shelter was not hit or buried by masonry from adjacent buildings. When it finally became quiet we hurry back to our hotel but part of it is on fire and burning quite fiercely. Therefore we walk around for a while until the firemen have put out the blaze and we can get into the part where our room is. We find it and try to salvage some of our clothing and other belongings in our suitcases. Although we are not in a joking mood, Stefan makes a comment about Rome burning.

We observe a lot of dead bodies whilst crossing the street, mainly of people taken from burning houses for collection. Typical of the English population and their character, there is no panic or emotional scenes. What a wonderful country. How does the Führer hope to subjugate Britain to the will of his master race?

We are allocated about one third of the Hotel Cora that is still standing, and soon we have to return to our work. We have to accept this experience of night bombing as part of the London scene. [Fejfar's official starting date at the inspectorate was 15 April 1941.]

5th May 1941

Life goes on in this city and after a few weeks I am called back to the medical commission today, but once more, they say, I have to wait another month. So I am back in the office which bores me because I would rather sit in the cockpit of a fighter than this rickety chair of mine. The work is very depressing, planning the various postings of pilots and crews who have barely recovered from burns or broken bones after emergency landings and the like, be they in fighters or Wellington bombers. Some crews manage to extend their time away from operations and their destiny, but they must eventually return to their task sooner or later. Many marriages between them and British girls take place and our office has to give permission to those who are single since life must go on.

15th May 1941

Because of the continued bombing we decide that every night we will go out to the shelter in order to try and sleep and be fit for our work. Remembering back to the 10th of May, we had a beautiful clear moon over London but it must have also appeared beautiful to the German navigators up above us. Such was the intensity of the bombing that nobody could carry on a normal conversation. A telephone call the next morning confirmed that one night fighter squadron is being equipped with a more advanced radar and our sergeant pilot Dygryn[5] shot down at least one bomber during the night since they were clearly observed. The newspapers specified 30 enemy raiders destroyed but seeing these pre-1918 anti-aircraft guns in Hyde Park I doubt it. The night fighter action is only in its infancy.

---

[5] Josef Dygryn (actually Dygryn-Ligoticky) came from Prague, and he was 23 years old. He too had been in France before escaping to England where he flew with 85 Squadron and then 1 Squadron. In three separate sorties over south London he shot down two Heinkel 111s and a Ju88 on the night of 10/11 May 1941. During the summer of 1941 he claimed two enemy fighters and damaged another in operations over northern France, for which he received the British DFM and the Czech Military Cross and Medal for Gallantry. He was lost during a night intruder sortie off Le Havre on 4 June 1942.

Night fighting in single-engined Hurricanes and Spitfires was far from easy above a blacked-out Britain. While a pilot could be guided by a ground controller, it was actually luck if the pilot then spotted the raider in the dark, let alone shoot it down. Depending on the visibility, either a fighter pilot spotted the raider by its exhaust flames, or saw it in a searchlight beam, or silhouetted over a burning target or cloud. The RAF's night-fighting strength was limited in the early stages of the war, although airborne radar (AI) was now being used. This enabled a radar operator in a two-man Beaufighter aircraft, to locate and follow a 'blip' on his radar screen, and guide his pilot into an attacking position, but the pilot had still to spot it in a darkened sky.

20th May 1941

A splendid occasion for our Czech air force boss, Air Commodore Janoušek, who has been made a Knight Commander of the [Order of the] Bath [KCB] at an investiture at Buckingham Palace[6]. The notice of this honour was not kindly received by our Czech armoured brigade and infantry because they have yet to be sent to an overseas theatre of war. However, the medical commission made me happy enough, allowing me to fly, but only in two-seater training planes. I disappeared from my office at once and went to RAF Hendon aerodrome where our Czech instructor pilot Altman[7] gave me a solo training flight. Afterwards I did six circuits of the airfield, each with perfect landings, so that I can now hope that Fighter Command will finally relent and I can resume the job I was trained for – a fighter pilot!

3rd June 1941

It is two years since I escaped from my homeland and the world has gradually changed over this time. Two years mostly of depressing news in France, but the entries in my diary are now improving. I am thinking of my mother and stepfather often, as well as my stepsister.

I feel strongly that all these dear ones of mine are thinking of me at the same time today. I ask myself what will happen within the next year or two? Will I even live in order to write some more sentences in this diary?

---

[6] Karel Janoušek was born in 1893 and came from Přerov, so he was now 47 years old. A pre-war pilot, he became Inspector-General of the CzAF in England. It has been written the Janoušek was distrusted by President Beneš, but the British thought he was the most able Czech officer associated with their RAF. Certainly Czech airmen liked and trusted him, and they knew that he fought many diplomatic battles on their behalf. He later rose to air vice-marshal and also received the Distinguished Service Order from the British.

[7] František Altman was 37 and as well as serving in 311 Squadron was a good flying instructor, for which he was to receive the Air Force Cross.

6th June 1941

I received a telephone call and am instructed to proceed at once to our Czechoslovakian embassy at 3 Grosvenor Square, London, to identify the body of a Czech pilot, Jaroslav Malý,[8] who has shot himself in the Cumberland Hotel. I am distressed, somehow, because cutting the tail off Emil Fechtner's Hurricane [back on 29 October] could not entirely be attributed to him but rather to a sudden turbulence of air or buffeting. He was a unique man and prior to our occupation, he was our Czech air force military attaché in Berlin. The death of Fechtner must have affected him deeply and we all think that he was not of sound mind to end such a promising career here in England. This is very sad!

18th June 1941

At long last excellent news arrives. I am allowed to return to operational squadron duties. I am also told that Malý's job of chief planner is to be taken over by my very good friend and the former military attaché in Paris, Major Perníkář.

I feel very sorry also for Malý's mother who is living in England, and I think she must have had a lot of correspondence about her son's tragic departure, and also a lot of visits. She was well known in pre-war diplomatic circles and spoke English before their arrival here.

I have been impatient to receive my posting and when at last it arrives, it is to the newly formed Czech fighter squadron number 313. Its commanding officer is Squadron Leader Jaške, a famous fighter pilot during his time at Chartres with the French air force. He later flew with our 312 Squadron in Liverpool. Other arrivals whom I know from France, Africa and the legion are Karel Mrázak, Jícha and Kučera.

After all this excitement I was given ten days leave and told to report for operational duty on 15th July. I now begin to wonder whether this posting to 313 will be my last. Enough of speculation, I am to be a free man from any future stress and will definitely go to the seaside.

4th July 1941

Ten days leave is here and I travel by train to Torquay, and I also spend some happy days in Lyme Regis, a most picturesque little place on top of some cliffs. It looks utterly unspoilt and I have reserved a room in a small family inn with my new girlfriend Yvonne. Nobody seems to know anything about the war here, perhaps only the news heard over

---

[8] Jaroslav Malý was 35 years old and came from Prague. He was one of those who escaped into Poland where he rejoined the Czech air force, but when Poland fell he went to France, then after arriving in England was posted to 310 Squadron. When he died on 5 June he held a wing commander's rank for his work with the Czech air force inspectorate. He is buried at Brookwood cemetery.

the wireless, and I notice there are no newspapers in the lounge. We do not listen to the radio anyway. We only exist for each other and this is the first day of our holiday.

10th July 1941

We spend heavenly days just swimming and lazing about on the beach. We take long walks inland during the evenings, stopping occasionally at a country pub. Then we carry on walking, admiring this beautiful land, as I am beginning to appreciate it now. We return to the lounge later and listen to dance music on the radio. On other days we hire a car and drive to observe different parts of this charming south Dorset coast. Even in wartime you can hire a boat and go out to sea. This reminds me of the French Riviera days and sentimentally of the days spent with my late friend Frank Bieberle. Life goes on and during this charming idyll of a young man and a young, very appropriately, English woman.

The last two days we dance together and are oblivious of all other people. During this holiday I became a man, and an admirer of everything English.

19th July 1941

I return to London, which is rather dirty-looking after the freshness of the seaside. I sit in my office recollecting the happy days, but also now awaiting further details of my posting. The work of such an unpleasant nature such as collecting the possessions and pitiful belongings of a dead pilot or airman is especially harrowing, particularly when I think that the parents, wives or fiancées will only be able to guess at an indistinct picture of what life this son, husband, fiancée, led without his vivid personal commentary.

21st July 1941

At long last the posting comes and it is for me to go to RAF Leconfield, where 313 Czech Squadron is being established. I am promoted to flight commander which will be unwelcome news for some pilots who will probably think that I arranged this posting and position whilst working in the inspectorate. This jealousy is completely unfounded and later I found that apart from Jaške, the supernumerary squadron commander, nobody else flew in the Battle of France. Only time will resolve this sad state of affairs.

I fly the first day on an old Mark I Spitfire and I must admit that after eight months without a flight [except for that one training session at Hendon] my flying is a little bit rusty, so that I have to take the tight turns and aerobatics easily. The atmosphere after a few days with the other pilots is improving, even when Jaške mentions how we flew in

France. Friendship among pilots is essential for the utmost co-operation during battle when each pilot is dependent on others and at times quite desperately when two or three Messerschmitts are diving down on you.

Our newly-formed squadron has for the first time, English ground crews and this is due to the fact that so many former ground personnel, even in technical grades, have volunteered for aircrew training.

[The best news of course is that] our squadron commander is Squadron Leader Sinclair DFC, with whom I flew on many occasions in his A Flight in 310 Squadron. Jaške will take command when he is considered good enough with his English language, and knowledge of RAF regulations. Fighter Command is very happy with this state of affairs because experienced officers like Sinclair are desperately wanted for other newly formed squadrons, as well as operations rooms, and administrative commands, etc. We are not as yet fully operational since we are to have a minimum of 26 pilots, but this should be achieved within a few days.

* * *

Some time before Sinclair was given command of 313 Squadron, probably while he was still with 12 Group HQ on staff duties, he wrote an article for an aviation magazine about his time with the Czechs in 1940. He sent a copy to the authors and we reproduce it here:

I Lived and Fought with the Czechoslovaks
One day early in July 1940, I was having a pre-lunch glass of beer when the station commander walked in and announced that a Czechoslovak fighter squadron was to form on the station. The news did not really impress me anymore than it did anyone else – we were all busy preparing ourselves for the future – doing practise attacks, air firing and all those things which train a pilot for action. Squadrons came and went pretty quickly in those days; what was another one more or less, even if it were a Czechoslovak one?

A few days later I was summoned by the AOC and informed that I was to be a flight commander in this Czech Squadron. This was going to be quite different – here was something tangible – I was going to work with Czechs. I, whose knowledge of foreign languages was confined to the approximate position of 'the watering-can of my aunt' in French. Feverishly I searched my brain for anything I knew about Czechs. Yes, they had a world-famous leader, the great Dr. Beneš; they had been overrun by the Nazis in March 1939.

I had heard about these people, who escaped from their own country because they would not knuckle under to the Nazis and had fought in France. And now that the French had collapsed they must have come over to England to continue the fight against the common enemy. Was I really to have the honour of being one of the first Englishmen to work with these pilots in England, perhaps to lead them to battle? What sort of people were they who refused to be beaten; they must be very stout-hearted. But how would they take to us – would they speak any English? – would they understand that Englishmen always raise their voices in a vain attempt to make themselves understood? Above all, would they drink beer or would we have to increase our stocks of vodka and prune gin?

A few days later news came that the fist 'batch' of officer pilots were to arrive at the local station at 11.10pm – hardly the time of night one would choose to meet a lot of people who probably couldn't speak any English. After some hasty last-minute preparations and instructions to the mess staff regarding rooms, tents and food for our guests, off we went to the railway station. Of course, the train was late, but eventually it arrived, the engine puffing steam rather importantly as though conscious of the unusual passengers. Out of the train stepped some 30 dark figures dimly outlined on the half-lit platform. I stepped forward but was stopped short by a clear grave voice, 'Good evening, Sir, I am....; I have come from... with the Czech pilots'. I was in luck – a Czech who could speak English.

Into the bus, a 2 mile drive and we were in the mess, and able to see each other for the first time. Pretty tough-looking crowd – broad shouldered, well-built, with a courteous bow when shaking hands. All wearing French uniforms, some with medal ribbons – what stories of daring and skill lay behind those ribbons?

Yes – a glass of beer seemed to be all right – but perhaps they were only being polite. Now a meal – this time there was no mistaking the feelings. They appeared to look on bacon and eggs with as much favour as a tired Englishman would – my heart warmed to them at once.

There followed several days of bustling activity – new arrivals to be met and accommodated – officers, NCOs, troops, technicians – and some English technicians to help the Czechs learn our methods. Measurements and fittings for RAF uniforms, lectures in England about English methods, English lessons, English salutes, English food, English beer, English reserve – English everything, and no language in common. The trials might have been insuperable, but no – they seemed to fade away into insignificance before the quiet and unassuming determination to overcome trouble and to fit into our way; charm of manner smoothed many a difficulty, eased many a worried mind. Led and inspired by that gallant officer and sincere personality, Major H[ess], whom I am privileged to call a friend, these men from Central Europe showed a spirit and courage under the most trying circumstances from which many of us were proud to take lesson.

A week after the first arrivals the aircraft began to arrive. A few trainers to get their hands in again, and Hurricanes, big, cheerful-looking fighters they are, for the war business. Parachutes to be tried on and fitted. As the pilots buckled the straps, faces seemed to assure a look of grim satisfaction, a look that seemed to say – yes, this is what we came for, where are the Huns?

Almost at once, it seemed, after a brief exploration of knobs and taps, a Hurricane opened up, streaked across the flying field, and 'the major' became the first Czech to be airborne in a Hurricane. We seemed to have accomplished something then, seemed to have passed from the tuning-up stage to the opening bars of the full orchestra. Quickly, one after the other, one from the other, these pilots learned the cockpit drill, the workings of the dials, away and back again, and yet another had done his first Hurricane flip. It seemed almost that there were not enough hours in the days for these boys to fly, so keen and anxious were they to become proficient enough to be termed 'operational'.

Meanwhile, as well as flying, other things were going on. Budding acquaintance had blossomed into friendship, that friendship which is so essential to teamwork in the squadron's activities; pilot with pilot, technician with technician, orderly-room staff, all were working in harmony, a harmony born of a keenness and enthusiasm which overcame trouble and difficulty. Miraculous it seemed that these Czech fitters and 'riggers', who had never before seen a Merlin engine or an English airframe, were able to keep the aircraft serviceable, but they did it. I knew now and recognised how great was the honour and privilege to be working with such people as these – how much I could learn of courage and determination.

One hot August afternoon, just when Göring had started to unload his fury and to launch his much-vaunted Luftwaffe against this country, we took off on our first operational flight, the first of many that were to be filled with the excitement of battle. How happy were those days, in spite of the grimness of the task that was before us. Hot, cloudless days spent almost entirely in the air it seemed, with breaks at dispersal point. A gramophone playing, tea on the make, Czech voices – a telephone bell – 'Off we go' – landing in ones and twos, all the excitement of combat reports, comparing notes, talking it all over and over again. We didn't need a common language then to find out the results of combat – a look of very grim satisfaction gave the answer.

How could these fellows fight, far from their own homes, far from their own kith and kin, fight with gallantry in defence of our island home? Were they just fighting for the love of the thing? No – it was something far deeper – they fought remembering their own country – their fathers, mothers, wives, lovers, homes – all that was and is Czechoslovakia. Fought with the will to regain what the barbarous invader had taken from them, with the certain knowledge that all would be theirs again. That was the will with which they fought – fought the enemy in the air in combat, fought the enemy on the ground by keeping the aircraft serviceable, fought him in their very hearts. That was the will that had helped them to carry the fight from country to country undaunted through danger and hardships undreamed of, helped them in battle, in their lives lived among strangers. How great was the lesson that we, as Englishmen, could learn from these gallant, purposeful men.

Time passed, the battles over London and the south coast were over, we were proud to claim a fine record in the squadron. The long days of August and September were gone, old faces were going, new ones coming to take their places. Eventually there arrived the day which I knew would come, a day which I feared because it meant losing so much – the day when the English personnel of the squadron would hand over to the Czechs – the day when I would have to leave the squadron. I was to leave behind my friends whom I knew would be my friends for ever, whom I never could forget; men who had enriched my life, shown me that sheer determination can overcome everything in its path.

Theirs was an example never to be forgotten.

Today I look back on my months of service with and for the Czechs and Czechoslovakia, look back with regret at the end of those months, but with pride that the privilege and honour was mine of working with so fine a people. People whose courage, I know, will carry them through to their ultimate goal of return to their mother country.

It is of course a great pity that the Czechoslovakia that these courageous Czech airmen had fought for, and indeed died for, was not the welcoming homeland when the war was eventually won. The new regime saw them not as returning heroes. Many were put into prison, others demoted or sacked from the air force. It was many years before anything resembling the halcyon days of the mid-1930s began to emerge once more.

In 1991, Wing Commander Gordon Sinclair was honoured by the Czech President, V Havel, in Prague Castle, with the Most Ancient Order of the Bohemian King George of Podebrad. For post-war services to the steel industry in England, he was later made an OBE, to add to his Battle of Britain DFC and his Czech War Cross.

* * *

Fejfar's new squadron had been formed at RAF Catterick on 10 May 1941, and equipped with Supermarine Spitfire Mark Is, there beginning its working-up period which continued until it moved to Leconfield in July.

Since being wounded during the Battle of Britain, Gordon Sinclair had been on staff duties with 12 Group HQ at RAF Hucknall, but he had been awarded the Czech Military Cross for his work with 310 Squadron.

Josef Antonin Jaške came from Nymburk, and was 28. He had been in the Czech air force since 1933 and escaped to France in 1939, serving with GC II/5, making a couple of claims flying Curtiss Hawks, before France fell. Getting to North Africa he sailed on a British cruiser to Gibraltar, then to Cardiff, where he arrived on 5 August. One month later he was with 312 Squadron, and in 1941 had become a flight commander.

* * *

When 313 Squadron was formed, it drew its first batch of pilots from all over Fighter Command. As always in these situations, there were more national pilots than could be accommodated in the available squadrons, so that Czechs, Poles, Norwegian, French, Australian, New Zealand, Canadians, etc, were liberally distributed throughout the RAF. With 313 now being formed, Czech pilots began to receive postings to man the new squadron.

This began on 18 May with the arrival of Sergeant Jiří Kučera, in from 501 Squadron. The next day Sergeants Prokop Brázda and Jaroslav Šika came from 43 Squadron while Flying Officers Josef Čermák and Karel Mrázek came in from 312 and 257 Squadrons. Four more new arrivals came on the 20th, Pilot Officers Alois Hochmal and Jaroslav Muzika from 501 Squadron, Pilot Officer

Karel Kasal from 607 and Sergeant Josef Gutvald from 3 Squadron. The 20th also saw in the first Spitfire I, from 452 Squadron RAAF.

Two more Spitfire Is from 452 were delivered on the 21st, the same day that Sergeant Bohumil Dubec was posted from 32 Squadron. Four more of 452's old Spitfires came in on the 22nd. On the 27th Sergeants Václav Fogler and Jiří Rezníček arrived from 17 Squadron, but this day also saw the squadron's first loss. Sergeant Gutvald was killed in a flying accident near Scorton, Yorkshire. Josef Gutvald was 29 and came from Třest. On the 28th three more officers arrived, Flying Officers Frank Fajtl, Karel Vykoukal and Pilot Officer Václav Jicha, all old friends of Fejfar's, the three having been with 175 Squadron.

On the 30th Mrázek became a flight lieutenant with effect from the 17th, leading A Flight, while Flying Officer Čermák remained in command of B Flight. However, on 3 June Flight Lieutenant T W Gillen arrived, posted in from 403 Canadian Squadron, to take over B Flight. Tom Gillen was a pre-war pilot, and had been with 247 Squadron in 1940. Although a Battle of Britain squadron, it had been equipped with Gloster Gladiator biplane fighters and based near Plymouth, with night readiness at St Eval. It began to convert to Hurricanes just before Christmas 1940.

The next day another new flight commander arrived to take over A Flight. This was Flight Lieutenant I J Kilmartin DFC, a veteran of the Battle of France. He came from a flight commander's position with 602 Squadron. His main job was to give the pilots the benefit of his operational experience.

Two more NCOs arrived on the 6th, Sergeants Karel Čáp and Rudolf Ptáček. Then came a lull in new arrivals until the 18th, on which day Sergeants Otto Špaček came in from 615 Squadron, while Sergeants Jan Truhlář and Josef Valenta were both former 312 Squadron men. Pilot Officers Karel Drbohlav and Vladimír Michálek came from 601 Squadron on the 23rd, but two days later 'Killy' Kilmartin left for overseas, where he would join 128 Squadron as CO, in West Africa.

Top brass arrived on the 27th, in the shape of Air Vice-Marshal Janoušek, Group Captain Alois Kubita (Czech HQ, London), accompanied by Squadron Leader Berridge. Janoušek had come to see the new squadron and to present medals to several pilots: Mrázek, Čermák, Jicha, and Sergeants Rezníček, Šika, Ptáček and Kučera. Also present was Catterick's station commander, Group Captain G F Wood. Another VIP in attendance was Air Vice-Marshal J O Andrews DSO MC, the AOC of 13 Group, Fighter Command, and he was presented to the visiting officers.[9] Andrews was a veteran fighter ace from World War One, having achieved a dozen victories in that conflict.

On the 28th Sergeant Arnošt Mrtvý arrived from 65 Squadron but two days later, Jiří Kučera was posted to the Czech Inspectorate in London, where Fejfar had spent time, for staff duties.

The squadron managed to get in some operations during the first part of August, Fejfar himself flying two convoy patrols on the 1st and 2nd, a scramble over base on the 5th, then two patrols on the 8th and 9th. Hopefully things would get more exciting before too long.

---

[9] Leigh-Mallory was now commanding 11 Group of Fighter Command.

Chapter Seven

313 Squadron

At the end of July 1941, 313 (Czech) Squadron comprised the following pilots:

Commanding officers: S/Ldr G M Sinclair DFC and S/Ldr J A Jaške

A Flight:	F/Lt K Mrázek		
	F/O F Vancl	F/O F Fajtl	P/O V Michálek
	P/O K Drbohlav	P/O V Jícha	Sgt F Vavřínek
	Sgt F Pokorný	Sgt O Špaček	Sgt J Řezníček
	Sgt F Bönisch	Sgt P Brázda	Sgt J Truhlář
	Sgt M Zauf	Sgt K Pavlík	Sgt K Valášek
	Sgt B Konvalina		
B Flight	F/Lt S Fejfar		
	F/O K Vykoukal	F/O V Hájek	F/O J Muzika
	F/O K Kasal	F/Lt T W Gillen (Br)	P/O A Hochmal
	P/O J Kučera	P/O J Příhoda	F/Sgt V Foglar
	Sgt K Čáp	Sgt B Dubec	Sgt V Horák
	Sgt J Dohnal	Sgt J Valenta	Sgt M Borkovec
	Sgt J Hloužek	Sgt K Stočes	Sgt P Kocfelda
	Sgt O Kresta		

At this time the squadron was flying the Spitfire Mark I, which still only had eight .303 machine guns. Hopefully the arrival of the faster Mark IIa would not be long in coming. The 20 mm cannon were installed in the even better Spitfire Mark V.

1st August 1941

We are now recognised as a fully operational unit and after waiting the whole day we finally take off for our first task, a convoy patrol. We land back at dusk and our duty ends by 11 pm. The individual sections flew in perfect formation and I am very pleased as to how good we must have looked from the ground.

6th August 1941

Today we are caught by a single Junkers 88 which suddenly appeared in our sector. We took off at once but we are already late, then one of our Spitfires gets hit by the air gunner of the 88, which results in our pilot barely able to land. Upon inspection the machine is in fact Category 'C' – ie: severely damaged. Later we [sic] manage to catch the Junkers on its way back to France and shoot it down.[1]

All of us are also furious the next day when another Luftwaffe group is recorded above us but the clouds are so thick that nothing is found. Tonight we have a very good social evening in order for everyone in the squadron to get acquainted. Squadron Leader Jaške recounts the true story of a recent 312 Squadron 'Rodeo' operation over the Pas de Calais.[2]

13th August 1941

Nothing new to report except that President Beneš has awarded a Czech flying wing badge to our English pilot, Flight Lieutenant Gillen, with full authority to wear it. Sergeant Kučera, who flew with me in France, has so many hours on fighters that he was commissioned to the rank of pilot officer. I am delighted, and quite agree with the RAF, which allows non-commissioned officers to be thus promoted. Czechs do not allow this but owing to the pressure of the RAF, the practice will probably be adopted in more cases in future.

If one accepts that a British fighter pilot with 20 flying hours or slightly more, can be an officer, it would be impossible to find a Czech sergeant-pilot with less than 400 hours. This also confirms my view of the fact that although this country is a monarchy, it is acting far more flexibly in war-time where true heroism and the amount of dangerous

---

[1] Despite the inference, this Ju88 was not shot down by the squadron but was presumably the one shot down by 129 Squadron, although the rear gunner was again able to hit his attacker. The RAF pilot got home but had to crash land on reaching base.

[2] A Rodeo was the code-word for an operation involving RAF fighters. Very much like the coded Sweep operation, although the latter was often in conjunction with light bombers, whereas a Rodeo had no involvement with bombers. Other operations were code-named Circus, which was a small number of light bombers escorted by several wings of Spitfires, the object being to entice enemy fighters into combat. A Ramrod was a similar operation but where the main objective was to destroy a specific target. Rhubarb sorties were those carried out by perhaps two or four fighters, generally in poor weather conditions and at low level. Their object was to shoot-up anything Germanic that could be found, such as trucks, locomotives, gun positions, troops and so on. A Roadstead involved fighters escorting light bombers against shipping in the English Channel, or off the Dutch coast.

flying hours during combat, are properly rewarded. We drink at once to George Kučera and commiserate with him since he cannot enter the officer's mess until the tailor makes him an appropriate uniform.[3]

Bad news from Duxford about a well-known fighter pilot, Plzak, who is reported missing over the English Channel.[4] He was the first Czech pilot to be attached to 19 Squadron RAF, and was to be commissioned shortly. According to his Number Two [wingman], W/O Smith, his machine for no apparent reason just exploded in mid-air. I personally believe that if you are in the middle of the English Channel it is the better way to go than sitting for hours in a small dinghy awaiting rescue.

So there goes another Czech airman who, I was informed in our pre-war flying control school, was able to fly solo after just two hours, as if he had been born a bird.

20th August 1941

Today, fantastic news for our squadron. We are to be equipped with brand new Spitfire Mark IIs, which are faster than the ones we fly now. Our commanding officer was told by our English CO, that everyone must stop chattering whilst flying and in future it will not be tolerated for anyone using the radio unless absolutely necessary to do so. Luckily we are not like the Poles in this respect, who cannot be controlled, and no English CO will fly with them. So all that is missing now is the appearance of the Luftwaffe.

Two days ago we received a new posting and we are told to go to RAF Portreath, in Cornwall. It is quite a flight from northern England to reach this place but we make it safely. Naturally our last night at Leconfield the station CO gave us a goodbye party and wished us 'Good Hunting'. These English are always horse minded and that is the same as when an attack is about to be made on German aircraft, with the [hunting] call of 'Tally-Ho!'[5]

---

[3] Jiří Kučera was 27 years of age and came from Roudnice nad Labem. He was with Fejfar with GC I/6 in France (three victories). Getting to England via North Africa and Gibraltar, he fought with 238 Squadron in 1940 (two victories and two damaged). Later he became a staff officer at RAF Air Ministry. His final war posting was to 544 Squadron flying PR Mosquito aircraft. He would survive the war and died in Plzeň in 1980.

[4] Stanislav Plzak was born in Plzeň in November 1914 and was another escapee to France pre-war. He fought with GC II/2 and shared in four victories during the French campaign. He came to England and served with 310 Squadron until he moved to 19 Squadron on Spitfires, towards the end of August 1940. With this unit he claimed three more victories, and damaged another in June 1941. He was lost on Circus 66, on 7 August and has no known grave.

[5] Of interest from this remark is that later on Fejfar would have the words *Tally Ho!* painted on the fuselage of his Spitfire, along with the Disney cartoon dog character Pluto.]

At this new station we will be flying on convoy patrols. The station is brand new and not quite finished. The food is lousy and so is the billeting which is even worse. It should not be called an RAF station but a field emergency station. True enough so far we have been spoiled by flying from pre-war RAF stations, but this place is awful. The only alleviating feature for us is the sea. That we can never have enough of. It is like those miles of orange tree orchards in Algeria.

RAF Portreath was opened in March 1941, within 10 Group of Fighter Command. There had already been a number of squadrons based there, including visiting light bombers of 2 Group, Bomber Command, who used it as a staging point for raids on Brest or St Nazaire. It had also seen a couple of sneak attacks by German aircraft, although little damage had been done.

The move to the south-west came on 25 August, with the squadron armourers leaving by train just after 7 pm that evening. It took them 23 hours, not arriving at the new base till the next evening after a stop at Redruth at 5pm. The pilots flew down after lunch on the 26th.

31st August 1941

We have commenced operations and begin convoy patrol escorts over the English Channel, veering towards the port of Bristol. As we fly over the sea for hours the biggest risk is to run out of petrol which will result in ditching in this vast expanse of water. I keep thinking that I am not all that far from Devon. Where is Yvonne now? Is she married?

6th September 1941

An operation today was cancelled due to the weather, and we have returned to convoy patrol duties in spite of this weather. We become bored with sitting in the cockpit for hours and hoping the weather would allow us to return safely. My Flight was the leading one today and suddenly we flew into a thick pea-soup fog. I called out at once for a homing course but it did not come quickly enough, so I had to search desperately for a break in the fog in order to get us down to land. I eventually had to force-land in a field, smashing my Spitfire and injuring my leg as well.

According to the squadron diary, Fejfar isn't correct. His forced landing came after he and Sergeant Horák were scrambled at 06.15 that morning. Poor visibility was the cause but he was only up for a short time before he came down, in Spitfire P8274. Within a few days this Spitfire was sent off to No.33 MU for repair and to be converted to an air sea rescue Mark IIC. This would be fitted with life-saving equipment that a searching pilot could drop to an airman in the water.

7th September 1941

Owing to my injured leg, the medical officer has given me eight days leave to recuperate but where can I go? No relations and I don't know anyone in this part of England. So, I do what most other Czechs do – I proceed to London. After my arrival I visit my old office at the Czech Inspectorate and run into Major Rypl, my successor there. With him I meet Captain Veselý. All too soon my leave is over and I return to Portreath.[6]

18th September 1941

At first light we are at readiness, but no orders come for us to take off until after lunch. Our task today is to escort bombers to France. We are ordered to fly to another aerodrome and await further orders. However, thick cloud prevents further planning and we have to return to Portreath. The weather continues to close in, which results in two of our Spitfires crashing into each other.[7] Both aircraft are destroyed but thankfully the pilots survive.

19th September 1941

Yesterday's cancelled operation is back on today, and the whole squadron took off, although two machines had to return immediately due to engine trouble. We make rendezvous with some Whirlwinds – special aircraft with four large cannons. I dream that we will encounter the Luftwaffe, but no such luck. We reached the French coast and after 12 minutes the Whirlwinds could not locate their target because of ground fog, so they reverted to a secondary target by shooting-up a small barge. The operation lasted one hour 45 minutes and we landed at base without mishap.

28th September 1941

Today we took on a harder task. Once more we flew with the Whirlwinds but our orders are for an attack on the German aerodrome at Morlaix, near Brest. We are told that this base holds many Luftwaffe bombers that are parked on the airfield itself.

We took off at 2.45 pm and my section consisted of Kasal, Muzika and Dohnel. This time we flew only three metres above the sea and you could almost touch the white tops of the waves below. This endless

---

[6] František Rypl ended the war as a wing commander. Antonín Veselý became the chaplain at 123 Wing Headquarters.
[7] The two pilots were Flying Officer Fajtl and Sergeant Bönisch. Again the squadron diary is slightly clearer about what happened. The two aircraft had collided on the ground after landing, but '...nothing too serious'.

flying produces eye strain. At 2.50 we could see the enemy coast and later observe French people running out to wave at us because they know we are here to shoot at the Germans and their aircraft.

Anti-aircraft batteries began to fire at us and we could clearly see the black streamers coming towards us. At such a low height you cannot shoot at anything as everything flashes past too fast. Now we saw that the Whirlwinds had completed their task and are on their way back to England. We followed them but suddenly a Messerschmitt 110 was coming towards me. I pressed the firing button immediately but I am unable to turn and follow it because I am not allowed to do so while flying escort, and our orders are to return to Cornwall.

As we came back over the south coast of England a radio message blurted out from one of the other aircraft: 'Sorry boys, I have to land quickly. Give my regards to my wife.' I unfortunately discover this is Sergeant Mrtvý, who was only married last week. I cannot understand this. It must be his engine I think. I finally landed at 3.35 pm at our base and see one result of our operation. One of the Whirlwinds was heavily damaged and the pilot had been seriously wounded. One of our Spitfires is also badly damaged, and the pilot, Kasal, is one of my B Flight pilots.

We had, however, one pleasant surprise when Sergeant Mrtvý telephoned us to say he was safe. His aircraft was damaged because he hit a telegraph post over France and the vibrations got worse and worse until he had to land quickly on reaching England. We are all pleased he made it.

The squadron diary entry for this operation reads:

Weather conditions improved and were excellent for flying. At 14.20 hours, 11 Spitfire IIA of the squadron took off from Predannack as escort for 4 Whirlwinds of 263 Squadron to attack Morlaix aerodrome. Course was set and English coast crossed at 14.27 hours and aircraft passed over Channel at sea level. French coast crossed at Plouexat at 15.00 hours. Spitfires followed Whirlwinds, one Flight at either side and both experienced difficulty in keeping pace. The Whirlwinds gained height to 500 feet on sighting aerodrome on their left, and attacked. One Me109 was seen and attacked. Whirlwinds attacked various targets and experienced heavy fire from ground defences.

The 11 Spitfires crossed the French coast a few seconds after the Whirlwinds. 'A' Flight passed north of Morlaix aerodrome from west to east and 'B' Flight in similar directions actually over the aerodrome at 15.03 hours. White 1 fired a one-second burst at a 4-machine-gun nest in north-west corner; also a short burst at a single-engined plane in the building and saw bullets hitting.

On return journey F/Lt Mrásek and F/Lt Fejfar both saw a black Me110 heading towards Morlaix aerodrome at 1,000 feet. The former fired two short bursts and it dived away. F/Lt Fejfar saw the e/a at 300 feet, climbed and attacked, firing a two-second burst. E/a took violent evasive action. No claim was made. P/O Jicha saw a Me109 taking off from the aerodrome to the south. All pilots reported M/G and gun fire Roscoff; also friendly reception and much waving of civilians. Eight Spitfires landed at Predannack at 16.04 and three Spitfires at Portreath at 16.04. Weather fine 2/10ths cloud at 10,000 feet.

Our Casualties:
       1 Whirlwind Cat II (W/Commander Donaldson slightly wounded).
       1 Whirlwind Cat I (probably)
       1 Spitfire Cat II

Enemy casualties:
       1 Me109 damaged on ground.

On return from this operation, Sgt Mrtvý's aircraft hit a telegraph pole whilst he was flying in formation to avoid ground defences, but despite damage to aircraft he returned and landed safely at Predannack. F/O Kasel's aircraft suffered slight damage, the extreme section of one wing being shattered by flak.

Arnošt Mrtvý was not a lucky pilot. On 12th November he overshot on landing in Spitfire AD192, overturned and crashed into a lorry, killing a civilian and injuring another. His luck finally ran out on 19 April 1944, by which time he was a warrant officer. Still operating with 313 Squadron he was shot down by a FW190 of JG26 during an escort mission to B.26 Marauders. He is buried at Antwerp and was 28 years old.

The wounded Whirlwind pilot was none other than the commanding officer of that squadron, Wing Commander A H Donaldson DFC AFC, who was hit in both arms. 263 was one of only two RAF squadrons equipped with the Westland Whirlwind, the other being 137. Donaldson was one of three brothers in the RAF, each having distinguished war records.

During the attack, a shell exploded in the fuselage of his machine, and as well as wounding him, another shell fragment ripped open the top of his flying helmet. His aircraft had over 100 holes in it and had its tail wheel shot off as well. He was temporarily knocked unconscious, but luckily he did not dive into the ground, for when he came to his senses he was some ten miles from Morlaix, so must have flown by some unconscious instinct. He was later to report: 'It gave me a bit of a headache for about six weeks.' He had only recently been awarded the DFC, to which he later added a Bar (for operations on Malta), having by then received the DSO.

The Westland Whirlwind was a twin-engined fighter-bomber used extensively for ground-attack missions over enemy territory and against shipping. 263 Squadron generally operated over the western approaches and over the Cherbourg/Brest areas of France, while 137's hunting ground was the North Sea and over Holland.

29th September 1941

We are again at a state of readiness and within a few minutes of being so, we are ordered to fly to another aerodrome – Predannack – where

Above left: The world before him; Stanislav Fejfar, 24 July 1932, aged 19.

Above: Fejfar in his leathers.

Left: New recruit into the Czech air force, 1932.

Above: Drill at the academy, 1933.

Left: Fejfar in full military dress.

Below: A fine body of men at the military academy. Fejfar and Fajtl are 3rd and from the left, middle row.

Top: Tug of war at the academy. Fejfar is on the left team, 5th from the centre.

Left: Daily exercise at the Prostejov academy. Fajtl is on top at the front, Fejfar two behind him.

Below: Swordsmanship was part of the training of air force officers. Here Fejfar (left) takes his 'guard' with the instructor. His friend Fajtl stands dead centre at the back, 12th from the left.

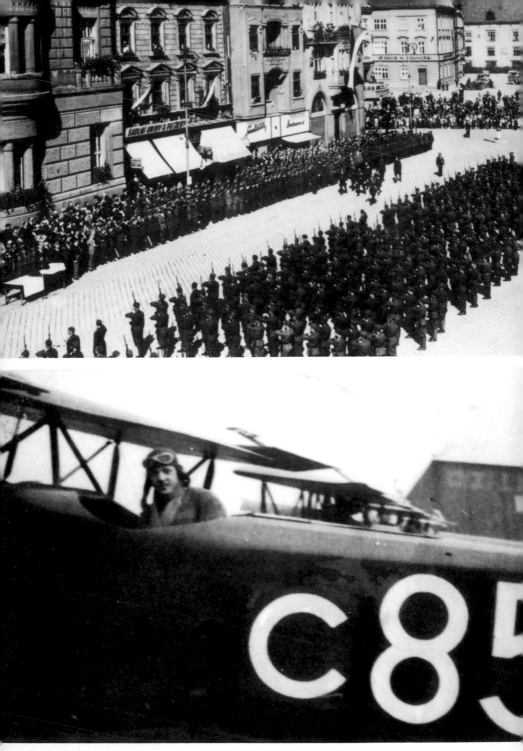

Top: Passing-out parade, Prostejov, 1935.   *Bottom:* Fejfar seated in a training ma[...]

Left: Fejfar's official portrait at the academy in 1935.

Below: Members of Fejfar's Czech squadron in 1938, standing in front of an Avia B-534. NCOs stand at the rear, pilots seated with Fejfar second from the left. Next to him in the middle is the CO, Josef Duda who later flew with 312 Squadron in England. Front row are the mechanics and ground crew.

LETECKÉ ODDĚLENÍ VOJENSKÉ AKADEMIE

II. ROČNÍK

1935

Top: The class of 1935. Fejfar's picture is at the right end of the small portraits under the word Akademie.

Above: Escaping Czech pilots in civilian clothes, 1939. From the left: Hugo Hrabáček, František Fanta, -?-, Krajina, Rudolf Holocek, Emil Foit, František Bieberle, Miroslav Liškutín, Buhuslav Tobyška, -?-, František Altman.

Right: In the French Foreign Legion, 1939. Fejfar stands on the left, Karel Mrázek, second from the right.

ejfar in France 1940.

Some of Fejfar's comrades in France,
...ber 1939. Rear: Tomáš Kruml,
...ochmal, František Vancl, Hajsk,
...Hrbáček, B Tobyška. Middle:
...av Zimprich, Rudolf Holocek,
...ek Fanta, František Bieberle. Front:
...ek Fajtl, Emil Foit, Karel Mrázek.

Typical scene in France, 1940, with
pilots of GC II/2, Chissey, in June.
...ng L to R: Lt Josef Hýbler, Adj
...ek Bernard, Sous/Lt Karel Šeda,
...t Bohimir Fürst at rear of the table.
...ground crew seated in front. All
...ots later saw service with 310
...on in England.

Left: Flying for Fran
1940. L to R: Sgt
Sgt F Bieberle. Sgt
Sgt F Vancl, Otma
Kučera, Václav Jich
František Adam, Vi
Popelka.

Middle: Captain Jar
Kulhánek by his M
406. He later serve
the RAF but was k
action on 13 Marcl
with 124 Squadron
flight lieutenant.

Bottom: Squadron L
G D M Blackwood,
310 Squadron, Gro
Captain Frank Bea
who helped Czech
in England to beco
operational, and M
Alexandre Hess, the
second-in-comman

Above: At the formation of 310 Squadron at RAF Duxford in July 1940. The Czech pilots are in their dark uniforms. The four pilots in RAF uniforms in the front row are, Flying Officer John Boulton, S/Ldr Blackwood, Group Captain A B Woodhall (Station CO), (with Hess on his left) and Flight Lieutenant Gordon Sinclair.

Left: Squadron Leader Blackwood and Flight Lieutenant Sinclair 'ham it up' for the press. Rear: P/O Stanislav Janouch, Sgt Bohumir Fürst, Sgt Rudolf Zima; Front: Sgt Rudolf Zima, P/O Vaclav Bergmann, F/L Jiroslav Malý and Sgt Josef Kaucký.

Bottom: F/O John Boulton and Flight Lieutenant Jerrard Jefferies.

Top: Stanislav Zimprich, Viktor Bergmann, Emil Fechtner, P/O Vilém Göth and John Boulton.

Bottom: Hurricane of 310 Squadron (W9323). It had a long service life in England and India with various units finally struck off charge in 1946.

*: Vaclav Jicha was with
_r in France and briefly with
_in August 1940. KIFA in
_uary 1945 as a flight
_enant DFC AFC.

Left: Stanislav Fejfar climbing
into a Hurricane.

Top: Czech pilots chatting to the Czech president, Eduard Beneš.

Above: Henry Prokop, in work coat, and some of his ground crew team. It was Henry who translated Fejfar's diary into English.

Above right: Fejfar in 1941 with his Czech 'wings' on his right breast pocket. Note the Czechoslovakia shoulder flash.

Fejfar's Austin 10 car, BXH 628,
1.

Fejfar had another car too, this
ng MG.

Flight Lieutenant Fejfar receiving
his several decorations, from
ent Eduard Beneš, RAF
hurch, 1942.

Above: Back on the job, with 313 Squadron, 1942, with F/L Václav Hájek.

Below: Pilots of 313 Squadron talk ove[r] mission. L to R: Sgt J Řezníček, Sgt [V] Truhlář, I/O, Sgt P Brázda, P/O V Ji[ ] S/L G Sinclair DFC, F/O F Fajtl.

eft: Fejfar in 1942.

ight: Fajtl, who was allowed to kccp his

Below: Fejfar by his Spitfire Vb (BL973 RY-S). Note the 'Tally-Ho!' coming from Pluto's mouth and the victory marks below. Fejfar was shot down by Pips Priller in this machine on 17 May 1942.

Above: Sergeant Miroslav Borkovec, Fejfar's wingman on the fateful 17 May 1942, who was also shot down and killed by JG26.

Right: Hauptmann Josef 'Pips' Priller, leader of JG26's III Gruppe in 1942. His victory over Fejfar was his 72nd combat claim, of an eventual 101 by the war's end.

we land to refuel. We are to fly another mission the same as yesterday, although the target airfield is Lannion. We take off at 6.25 pm and set our compasses on course 152 degrees, the same as yesterday also, and once again fly just above the waves.

We reach the French coast at 7.05 pm and it is getting dark. The German anti-aircraft batteries produce an unusual concentration of fire which resemble fireworks coming up at you. Suddenly our CO, Sinclair, warns that enemy aircraft are behind us. We change course to 327 degrees, hoping to reach England in one piece. With visibility rapidly deteriorating we head out to sea at full throttle.

We reach Cornwall and it is now completely dark but we manage to land safely at 8 pm. We never saw any of the Whirlwinds because they were attacking another aerodrome. That is, they were flying without fighter escort, and it resulted in one Whirlwind being shot down, another missing, and a third only just making it back. Only one aircraft landed at Predannack.

Therefore we are the only ones without mishap but we expect to be back in France since those aerodromes are a continuous danger to our shipping lifeline to England and must be destroyed.

In the event, 263 Squadron only lost one aircraft, so the missing pilot must later have turned up. Sergeant T Hunter was forced to bale out over the sea off Plymouth when he ran out of fuel and was not found.

The raid as recorded in the squadron diary is as follows:

Weather again favourable. At 18.20 hours, 9 Spitfire IIs of the squadron took off from Predannack as escort for 4 Whirlwind IIs of No.263 Squadron to attack Lannion aerodrome. The English coast was crossed at 18.37 hours and aircraft passed over the Channel on course 150° at sea level, making landfall at Sept Iles 19.05 hours. The coast was followed to east of Ile Grande and aircraft turned south-east to Aval Bay, then dived towards Lannion aerodrome, approaching from the north-west. The Spitfires left the Whirlwinds 3 miles north-west of the aerodrome and circled. The Whirlwinds carried out the attack on the aerodrome in the face of heavy fire from ground defences; no enemy aircraft seen in the air by the Whirlwinds. Weather was hazy.

F/O Coghlan, leader of the Whirlwinds and P/O Warnes[8] reported the

---

[8] Flying Officer H St. J Coghlan was a pre-war auxiliary air force pilot who had joined 263 in May 1941. He received the DFC soon after this operation, which is mentioned in his citation. He later commanded the squadron and rose to wing commander. Geoff Warnes gained fame for being the only known officer to fly operationally with an early example of contact lenses, having managed to keep his secret from the medical people. He too rose to lead 263, but was killed in action, having received the DFC, in 1943.

escort was satisfactory. Red 1, of 313 Squadron, escorted the Whirlwinds over the target and saw attack by 3 Whirlwinds but results not observed. The Spitfires escorted 2 Whirlwinds on the return and landed at Portreath at 20.10 hours. 4 Hurricanes IIa's of 247 Squadron took off to follow the Whirlwinds. All 9 Spitfires landed safely. Enemy casualties: 1 Ju88 destroyed on the ground.

The four Hurricanes of 247 Squadron that were part of this evening sortie, were briefed to strafe Lannion shortly after the Whirlwinds had flown off. Leading 247 was Flying Officer K W Mackenzie DFC, a Battle of Britain veteran. Ken Mackenzie was not at all happy about his part in the operation for he argued that with the Whirlwinds having stirred up the German defences at Lannion, they would run into an alert bunch of German AA gunners when they arrived. And so it transpired. Mackenzie was hit and although he made the coast had to ditch in the sea, then paddled ashore to become a prisoner. A second Hurricane was also hit and the pilot wounded, but he managed to get back to England. What also annoyed Mackenzie was that he was convinced they would find no aircraft on Lannion airfield.

The Whirlwind pilots likewise thought the attack foolish, especially so late in the day. 263 Squadron had been harassing this part of the Cherbourg area recently, looking for the Ju88 fighters of KG40 that constantly attacked transport and Coastal Command aircraft out over the Atlantic. Although they kept receiving intelligence reports that Ju88s were lined up on the airfields, they always seemed to have vanished by the time the Whirlwinds arrived.

Upon their return to Predannack the pilots could not see any airfield lighting and Coghlan's port engine failed as his fuel gauges read zero. For a moment this engine picked up but as he made his final approach both engines stopped and he had to force land 200 yards short of the runway. Warnes was in a similar spot and was preparing to bale out but was saved by the sudden appearance of Predannack's Chance light. He got down with just three gallons of fuel remaining.

13th October 1941

Today we patrol over Land's End at 25,000 feet. It is so cloudy that the order is changed and we go down to 10,000 feet. Our operations room insists that according to their radar there are enemy aircraft in the vicinity. I search the sky until my eyes drop out of their sockets but finally I spot a Ju88 on my right side. At once I remove the safety catch on my firing button, but this bastard must have seen our 12 Spitfires and quickly disappears into the cloud. In addition we have to worry about the amount of petrol we have used during our climb and search, so we immediately return to the aerodrome.

Next day we were angry with our English CO, as he grounded the complete squadron because one Czech pilot failed to lower his landing gear, and consequently severely damaged his machine.

15th October 1941

Sinclair's order to stop flying is rescinded and we are now at a state of readiness once more and take off at 6.30 am in order to fly to RAF Merston [near Chichester]. This is about 300 kilometres from us and after landing, we refuel and are told that we shall be acting as escort to 24 bombers to Le Havre in a wing formation. The wing is enlarged and contains five squadrons of fighters.

We take off at 11.45 am and rendezvous with the bombers at 12.00 when some 100 kilometres from the port of Le Havre. We observe burning ships hit by our bombers, and the German anti-aircraft batteries are formidable, resulting in one bomber falling in flames. The bombing continues and we see other ships being hit. Then the bombers are turning round and vanish in some clouds. We are unlucky that nothing happens on our side of the bombers because on the far side, they are busy repulsing Messerschmitts from attacking the bombers.

We land at RAF Woodford aerodrome at 13.25 and report to the intelligence officer. The result of the mission was that one bomber was shot down by enemy ack-ack and a second one by a Me109. The other RAF squadrons claim to have shot down three Me109s.

This operation was Ramrod 69 (10 Group's Ramrod 12), going for an oil tanker in the harbour. 226 Squadron's Blenheim bombers were involved and they did in fact lose two, although they were thought to have both been shot down by German fighters. The Germans also claimed to have shot down six Spitfires, but only one was lost. In turn the RAF claimed eight Me109s destroyed and four damaged.

The squadron diary reveals:

> Twelve aircraft (Spitfire Mk.IIA) of the squadron left RAF Station Portreath at 08.10 hours for Merston. Merston was left at 11.50 hours and together with 10 aircraft of 130 Squadron, acted as close escort to twelve Blenheims of Bomber Command in an attack on the docks at Le Havre. Rendezvous was made at 8,000 feet over Tangmere and course set at 12.00 hours. Bombers were in two boxes of six each, escort being 100 yards on either side, 313 Squadron on the port side and 130 Squadron on the starboard, weaving in pairs astern. Channel was crossed at 8/9,000 feet, landfall being made near Le Havre at 12.20 hours at 8,000 feet. Owing to Blenheims having arranged to keep Le Havre on port side and actually making landfall from due north, escort became detached. Contact was not regained and Spitfires, after weaving up the coast, returned independently, still at 8,000 feet, making landfall over the Isle of Wight at 13.00 hours.
>
> All aircraft of 313 Squadron landed at Warmwell at 13.00 hours.

No enemy aircraft seen. Flak was heavy over target but inaccurate and well below. Weather – cloud 2/10th to 3/10ths at 5,000 feet and then layer at 15,000 feet. Visibility very good up to 20 miles. Squadron landed at Portreath at 16.30 hours. Pilots participating in this operation were as follows:

A Flight	B Flight
F/L Mrázek	F/L Fejfar
Sgt Rezníček	Sgt Ptáček
F/O Vancl	F/O Vykoukal
Sgt Bönisch	F/O Kasal
P/O Jicha	F/S Foglar
Sgt Špaček	Sgt Valenta

Two days after this operation the squadron was notified that Spitfire Mark Vb's would soon be arriving.

23rd October 1941
A few days ago I filled up the second exercise book that I use for my diary, and frankly, I am not as busy as I would like to be....

Today at 12.30 pm we once again returned to France. Our task was to escort six Blenheim light bombers who will attack the aerodrome at Morlaix.[9] We are ordered to fly at 12,000 feet but the bombers go right down to 2,000 feet, whilst we are acting as top cover. Our second mission is exactly the same, at 2.20 pm and we rendezvous with the bombers at 15,000 feet. We escort them across the Channel and after crossing the French coast we have to descend to 10,000 feet, as we are unable to see the ground. Visibility does not improve and we finally have to abandon the mission when down to 6,000 feet. We land back at 4 pm, having flown almost continually in cloud, but at least there was no anti-aircraft activity to annoy us.

28th October 1941
This is the second year in exile that we celebrate the birth of our Czechoslovakian nation of 1918. It is usual to promote military personnel and by order of President Beneš, I am promoted to captain, which will prove very useful in post-war days.

The meal in the officer's mess was our normal fare as this is an RAF station and not a Czech one. I am furious that George Kučera, who has been commissioned as a pilot officer, but is still not with us as the tailors appear to be too busy with so many Czech personnel also being commissioned by His Majesty. Why is it not possible for all pilots to eat

---

[9] This mission was a 10 Group Ramrod, R-13, but to Lannion, and not Morlaix. The six Blenheims came from 114 Squadron.

in the same mess? [On this special day, Squadron Leader Sinclair sent a telegram of congratulations to everyone in his old squadron. No one was missing from the festivities because flying was impossible, due to southern England being struck by a violent gale.]

29th October 1941

I am given 48 hours leave and borrow a car in order to visit the town of Barnstaple in north Devon. I find a reasonably priced hotel, but have the shock of my wartime life to discover how many people are just sitting about the whole day reading newspapers and consuming continual cups of tea. During the evening, a big fire is lit in the fireplace and the gentlemen arrive in their dinner-jackets, while the ladies appear in long evening gowns. Many of these ladies wear so much gold and jewellery that they can hardly lift themselves out of the lounge armchairs and settees. Limousines then start to arrive outside and I begin to wonder where all the petrol is coming from.

During October, Fejfar had flown two convoy patrols on the 1st, and others on the 3rd, 9th, 10th, 19th, 21st and 26th. Along with 26-year-old Pilot Officer Alois Hochmal, he had been scrambled over Land's End on the morning of the 13th but found nothing. On the 15th came the Le Havre operation, while on the 23rd he was on that Ramrod mission.

1st November 1941

A year ago I was sent to hospital and hopefully, since my return to operational flying, the RAF, with our Czech help, has sent some Germans to hospital, or better still, to a cemetery.

We take off and head for Morlaix aerodrome. Intelligence reports indicate that two German bombers, responsible for bombing the town of Southampton last night, are there, so we are in a suitable mood today to catch some of their brethren and repay them for their visit.

We escort six bombers on this raid and such is their success, that the Germans will not be able to land here, or use the aerodrome facilities, for some time.[10] We reached the French coast at 1.20 pm. The ack-ack was heavy and it is interesting to observe that due to the weather, every exploding shell is visible as white frozen vapour, measuring some two feet across. Whilst looking back we cannot see Morlaix which was totally obscured by smoke and white dust. We did not receive any more orders, so we returned home and landed around 2.45 pm.

---

[10] This operation, 10 Group Ramrod R-15, while directed against Morlaix, attacked Lannion airfield in error. There were in fact 12 RAF bombers, three from 82 Squadron and nine from 114. At this time 313 Squadron's strength is given as 13 officer pilots, 15 NCO pilots, 9 officer ground crew and 114 airmen.

7th November 1941

No flying today because we are moving from one side of the aerodrome to the other. Within two hours we are in new billets, and we have a new ping-pong table, something we use every day. Everything looks first class.

17th November 1941

I am given a full seven days leave and with £21 in my pocket I feel very rich. Obviously London is my destination, like 99% of Czechoslovak airmen. I also want to find out at the inspectorate, what happened to my request for the money I spent during my convalescent period, whereby I was very weak and needed extra food to rebuild my strength. Altogether I spent the sum of £18, which is a lot, considering my monthly flying pay.

I found London completely changed from the days when I worked here and the Luftwaffe was raiding every night. No one seems to care about the state of the war and are all enjoying themselves. With parental and environmental control of the ladies in uniform gone, romances flower easily and the atmosphere reminds me a little of our Paris days in 1939, before the German swine invaded France.

On this leave I am revising my opinion of the British opposite sex, and am enjoying myself tremendously. All that confounded reserved behaviour seems to be disappearing – and I hope it's gone forever.

There is no question that Fejfar was upset with the RAF and the Ministry of Defence, for he took the following letter with him which one assumes he left with whoever he spoke with:

Kpt.Let. S. Fejfar   London, 17 November 1941.
   313 Czech Squadron, RAF.
   PORTREATH, Redruth, Cornwall.
--   Ministry of National Defence
                                                      Czech Inspectorate.

I have sent a request to the Ministry of National Defence requesting payment of £11.10 shillings which has been taken from my salary in order to pay for food during my treatment at Ely and Torquay hospitals.

With reference to this request to the MND, I even have to pay for my food when I am attached to my squadron.

Today I am asking you again about paying me the amount of £11.10 shillings for the following reasons:-

1. I was taken to Ely hospital after operational flying on 30.10.40, when I blacked out during an air attack against a group of enemy

      bombers, diving from a height of 24,000 ft to 18,000 ft.

2. After having two operations and staying in hospital for 4½ months I have been suspended from flying for the next 6 months, which shows how bad my injury was.

3. True, during my treatment and recovery I spent more than £11.10 shillings on my food, but I am trying to speed up my recovery and return to the fight as soon as possible. British food at the hospital wasn't adequate, that was the reason I spent more money on my food and that is why I am asking for you to pay me back.

4. The hospital management took the money from my salary, which after my tax deduction leaves me £18.10 shillings. Now my salary is so low I haven't got enough money even to exist on the minimum.

5. Because my injury didn't happen to me due to my own mistake, I hope that after a further examination of my request, the MND will give me the £11.10 shillings which will help me.

S Fejfar.

Unfortunately we do not know if he was successful in his request for these funds.

22nd-29th November 1941

The squadron is temporarily relieved of operational duties because we are to undergo a course of gunnery. We have been transferred to RAF Warmwell [Dorset] where we will undertake daily shooting at ground targets. The aerodrome as such, is closed for normal landings, and at one stage the station was on the Luftwaffe's list of bases to be destroyed.

We are billeted in the town of Dorchester, a place close to the sea, and I am housed with a lady whose hobby is collecting antiques. It is also her business. I have never seen so many china figurines, including some made by the German Meissen company. Her house is very cosy and the rooms extremely comfortable. Not being British-born I do not share her enthusiasm but I love her home.

Firing cannon at ground targets from a Spitfire is a marvellous experience because it will be ascertained afterwards just how good one is. The two pilots that ended up with the best results are Flight Lieutenant Fajtl and Flying Officer Hajek. My own score was 22 hits out of 120 cannon shells fired and 142 hits out of 200 with my machine-guns bullets.

We are told by the commanding officer of the gunnery course that we as Czechs are above average in our gunnery, with the most favourable results. I could not tell him about the sad French equipment we had in the Morane 406, which had six machine guns, and I still shudder to think of when the French ordered us to attack advancing German tanks with those pitiful guns.

Although Warmwell airfield had been built to fulfil a minor, secondary role, it was located in exactly the right place to help defend the south-west coast during the Battle of Britain, and was a perfect stepping off place for early operations over France in 1941. It had been around for several years and an armament practise camp had been set up there pre-war. The gunnery ranges were on Chesil Bank, and pilots would regularly go through armament courses there.

When war came the gunnery side was upgraded and it became the home of The Central Gunnery School. Meanwhile, by 1940 it was able to help defend nearby Portland naval base, and a number of squadrons used it as an advanced base, especially units based at Middle Wallop.

November saw Fejfar flying very few sorties. That Ramrod on the 1st and convoy patrols on the 3rd, 8th (twice), 19th and 30th.

12th December 1941

A date to remember for all of us. The famous 11 Group of Fighter Command has requested our help with immediate effect. We are hundreds of kilometres from RAF Hornchurch [Essex] but RAF Transport Command has undertaken to move our ground personnel in their aircraft. We pilots have to await the more favourable weather in order to fly there, because it is December in England. Everybody is delighted with the move because access to London can easily be had when having a day off, as one can quickly get into town on the underground railway system. Hurrah! We shout!!!

Three days later we are finally able to fly off with our Spitfires, leaving the strange Cornish folk behind us and we land at Hornchurch at 1 pm. After we land, additional Harrow aircraft of Transport Command deliver much of our ground equipment.

The latest news for us is that Squadron Leader Jaske is leaving us for a rest, whilst my former colleague from the French campaign, Squadron Leader Mrázek, is taking his place as CO. From being a sergeant in the foreign legion, to the leader of a Czech fighter squadron in a civilised England is good news.

Karel Mrázek was born in Nachod on 29 November 1910, one of five railwayman's children. He joined the Czechoslovak army in 1932, attended the Flying School for Reserve Officers, and then was sent to Air Regiment 3 as an observer. Over the next couple of years he trained to become a pilot, first with an observation unit and then going on to fighters. He also followed the route of Poland, then France, and finally Oran, where he was retained as an instructor. Finally making his way to England via Gibraltar, he flew Hurricanes in the Battle of Britain.

After a period with another British Hurricane squadron in early 1941, he became A Flight commander in 313 Squadron, from which position he gained command after Jaške was rested. One of his actions, on 11 November 1940, was to be against Italian biplane CR42 fighters, in one of their rare appearances over England in late 1940.

Mrázek would see much action with his squadron in 1942, and even became the leader of the Exeter Wing that summer. He ended the war as a group captain with the Czech War Cross, three Medals for Bravery and the Medal for Merit, 1st Class, as well as the British DFC, awarded to him in 1942. The communists arrested him in 1948 but could prove nothing against him but he was discharged from the air force. He was reinstated in 1990 with the rank of a retired brigadier-general. He died in 1998, aged 88.

16th December 1941
We are settling down and fly sector patrols in order to familiarise ourselves with our new surroundings and locality, and to find exactly where our aerodrome is, especially in times of fog. I learn more of the London geography and everything seems to work here. The officer's mess is a dream and the food is excellent. The underground [railway] station is not that far away after all that distance we had to travel from Cornwall, even to reach a village pub. Flying is also very different because after you take off you can often see suburbia in a haze of fog. In December this is entirely caused by coal fires, and this sort of fog is called smog.

The River Thames, which is a vital landmark for a pilot's orientation, is always dirty-looking and also sad-looking when the sun does not reflect on its surfaces. Our grassy airfield is so green, and so near to the centre of London. All this is simply unbelievable!

Although he does not record it, Fejfar was on operations on the 18th, flying with his flight on a sortie led by Wing Commander H L Dawson, a morning sweep of the French coast. Dawson had taken over as wingco flying on the 4th. He soon went to the Middle East, his place taken in early 1942 by Wing Commander Peter Powell DFC.

24th December 1941
Although the 24th is traditionally a date for continental Christmases, for British crews and staff it is just another ordinary working day. But flying today is prevented by a sudden change in the weather and so we have time to remember our Czech Christmases.

Tomorrow is the 25th and the British Christmas can be celebrated properly. With British forces it is customary for Christmas dinner to be served by officers to the other ranks, and this includes the station commander. We Czechs received parcels which have been prepared by the Czech ladies of the Red Cross organisation but additional gifts come from Group Captain Beaumont, along with his wife. A man mostly responsible for all of us being accepted into the RAF so speedily last year. It does not seem like our Christmas at home since there is no snow on the ground and there is always plenty of that at my home in northern Bohemia.

There are now 24 officers serving at the tables and I am wondering whether this is going to be the last Christmas here on foreign soil. We drink to that and begin (as all Czechs usually do) singing our sentimental Czech songs, old and new. The British officers are pleased because apart from the occasional organised sing-songs, ours are always spontaneous and we are ready to sing at any time. So our Hornchurch friends, the RAF boys, enjoy themselves especially when we sing *Roll out the Barrel*, which they adapted with their own words but which, in fact, is an old Bohemian polka song, about lovers.

Personally I am a little depressed because I think of my beloved mountain town family in Nova Paka. Squadron Leader Mrázek then informed us that more parcels have arrived from the USA and our Czech countrymen living in England. When the weather brightens we are placed on a readiness state, but fortunately nothing occurs.

31st December 1941

Today sees the end of another year in exile and I am delighted that I am not in hospital like last year. Our squadron received an invitation from the Bata Czech shoe factory in Tilbury, Essex. The company itself provided the transport. All Czech RAF personnel were invited and we were joined by other Czechs from other squadrons as well as from our inspectorate in London, along with Air Commodore Janoušek. All in all we amounted to about sixty persons.

The managing director, Mr John Tusa [whose son, also John, was later with BBC TV], also provided a big band which, as an exception and honour, played Czech polkas and waltzes for us. He wanted us to feel at home and our enjoyment was his too, he told us later.

This was the best party I have had since I left home. The surroundings are luxurious, and the food, despite wartime shortages, is abundant. Especially welcome are a number of Czech ladies, imported from all over England it seems, and they certainly admire their countrymen pilots. After midnight we all sang in the New Year of 1942.

Chapter Eight

Hornchurch 1942

The pilots of 313 Squadron were anticipating an upsurge in operations now that they were part of 11 Group, Fighter Command, and part of the well-established Hornchurch Fighter Wing. Added to this, they had started to receive the Spitfire Mark V, with two 20-mm cannon, which reduced their eight .303 machine guns to just four.

Fighter wings had become firmly established during operations over northern France in 1941, operating within all those Circus, Ramrod and Rodeo Ops. Hornchurch was among the elite of 11 Group along with the wings of Kenley, Biggin Hill, Tangmere, North Weald and Northolt.

At the start of 1942, Hornchurch Wing comprised 411 Canadian Squadron, 64 Squadron and 313 Squadron. The Canadians were led by Squadron Leader P S Turner DFC, who had been one of Douglas Bader's pilots in 242 Squadron during 1940. He had taken over in December, as 313 arrived but would leave in February, at which time Squadron Leader R B Newton would take over.

The British 64 Squadron had Squadron Leader B J Wicks DFC in command, another December promotion. Bryan Wicks had gained fame during the 1940 Dunkirk evacuation, being shot down over Belgium, but managing to get back to England, after evading dressed like a French civilian, aboard a navy motor torpedo boat, from Dunkirk itself.

The wing leader was in fact the station commander, the charismatic Group Captain Harry Broadhurst DSO DFC AFC. 'Broady' was a young 35-year-old! He had joined the RAF in 1926 and commanded a Hurricane squadron when war came in 1939. In early 1940 he was in charge of RAF Coltishall. He had commands in France during the French campaign, and in December 1940 took over Hornchurch. Being the station 'boss' never precluded him from flying on operations, though!

1st January 1942
I am in a philosophical mood today and believe implicitly that a change is coming for the good of us all, especially the severely rationed British populace. The absence of the German Luftwaffe is evident. It would appear that the reason for this is possibly the Russian front, with many machines and pilots having been posted there. The war situation is

completely different since our arrival from France in July 1940. Our present strength in 313 Squadron is 12 officer pilots and 15 non-commissioned officers, along with 18 Spitfire Mark Vb.

6th January 1942

Our task today was as top cover, 'Jim Crow', for bombers and we took off in our wing formation at 2.10 pm. We reached our assigned operational height of 24,000 feet over Manston and were joined by another wing. My section was Alois Hochmal, Jaroslav Muzika and Jaraslav Hloužek. I felt safe and proud that the Royal Air Force, after initial manufacturing problems associated with war shortages, can muster all these Spitfires that fly around me. We soon reached the French coast and the anti-aircraft batteries begin their firing, but we were too high for them to be effective.

When the bombing is completed we are returning when suddenly a warning is received that a group of Messerschmitts is not too far southwards of us. We anticipate an encounter keenly but because of the amount of petrol we have consumed, we are not allowed to fly deeper into France today. At the same time as the warning, we discovered the Messerschmitt group had in any event turned around and were flying away to the south. We were despondent that no action took place, and land back at base by 3.30 pm.

8th January 1942

At 8 am this morning we were assigned a new task, that of escorting ships mine-sweeping the Channel, because German mines were deposited during the night. From a state of readiness we are ordered to fly down to RAF Manston first where we refuel. Not so long ago the concrete runway there was damaged and we hope that it has been repaired.

From Manston we take off and set a course of 62 degrees and fly below 2,000 feet. We are in two sections and keep one eye on our compasses and the other on the time. After 18 minutes we reach the minesweepers and fire off colours of the day so they can recognise us as friendly. After 30 minutes our task is completed and another section arrives to relieve us. All the time we keep our eyes open in worsening visibility, watching for any German aircraft which might fly lower than us and be undetected by radar. We head for home and in no time the English coast is visible and we land with the cloud base down to 2,000 feet.

Our neighbouring squadrons had the same task last week and also must have been wondering why maintaining course is so important. In their case they were unable to locate the minesweepers which proved fatal because they began edging towards the Belgian coast. German patrols spotted them and three were shot down.[1]

We fly in two sections because in that way we keep the Luftwaffe from coming in at sea level and surprising us from below. This precision flying is nerve-racking and even more so in adverse weather conditions. When we land we are greeted by the air officer commanding (AOC) Fighter Command, who comes later to our dispersal area to talk to us. We are greatly honoured because he visits only our squadron and makes sure he speaks to each one of us.[2]

10th January 1942

At 8.10 am we are alerted for an offensive patrol over France. During the mission, operations report that ten Me109s are coming into our sector but no such luck, and the bastards soon vanish when seeing 12 Spitfires I suppose.

Our flying, however, is not over today because we have some night flying this evening. The Spitfire, unlike the Hurricane, is not a good machine for night flying. You cannot see much from the cockpit because when the engine runs on slow revolutions prior to landing, the exhaust sparks are flying all over the place and all but blind you. In addition the landing lights are not all that good but night flying is ordered.

The first pilot not to be able to see the landing lights properly is Muzika, who smashes his Spitfire upon landing and is unable to get out of the wreckage without assistance from ground crews. Two minutes later Hajek takes off but manages to rip some tiles off a nearby roof before his undercarriage is fully retracted. This results in a bad landing later, but luckily he gets down in one piece. After these two incidents, all night flying is cancelled.

11th January 1942

Our good friend and pilot Sergeant Valenta[3] was killed today. His engine failed as he took off, just as he had reached a critical height and he died instantly in the crash. We are very depressed because in addition three other Spitfires were extensively damaged near to where he came down.

---

[1] In fact only two were lost, one each from 134 and 616 Squadrons, on 6 January.
[2] The AOC of RAF Fighter Command at this point was Air Marshal Sir William Sholto Douglas KCB MC DFC, who had succeeded Air Marshal Sir Hugh Dowding GCVO KCB CMG, master-mind of Britain's air defence during the Battle of Britain, on 25 November 1940.
[3] Josef Valenta was 24 years of age and came from Hrdlovka.

14th January 1942

Today we attended the funeral of Sergeant Valenta, and we leave Hornchurch to go to the local cemetery, and place another white cross in the ground. Our commanding officer, Squadron Leader Mrzšak said something that sticks in my mind: 'When I leave this earth, nothing will change except the drop of a tear from somebody.'

17th January 1942

Today the squadron is ordered to undertake firing practice, shooting our guns at a towed target. In this country it is easy to do, whereas in Czechoslovakia before the war, we could only do this over a specially selected forested area. Here we can fly over the open sea.

We are able to provide our own pilots to fly the aircraft that tow the 'drogue' and thereby speed up the process. In the evening we officers receive an invitation to a dance, held by members of the Women's Royal Air Force (WRAF). Some of the ladies we recognise from our trip to Torquay and we have a grand evening. I returned to the officer's mess at 2.30 am, so I must have had a good time.

22nd January 1942

The flowers on Sergeant Valenta's grave had not yet faded when we lost another pilot, Sergeant Konvalina.[4] He was practising dog-fighting with his friend but he was far too low above the ground. He hit an obstruction and the Spitfire was wrapped around him. It was lunchtime – 12.15 – and many of us could not face eating afterwards. Such low flying is absolutely prohibited and a pilot, if seen doing so, could be discharged from further flying duties.

25th-31st January 1942

Nothing much is happening so I obtained a six-day leave of absence. I went to London and during my time there the weather got even worse. The squadron flew down to Manston in order to escort a convoy while I was away, but that was about all that happened. On the day I return, Sergeant Pavlik forgot to lower his landing gear and his machine was severely damaged. This will inevitably lead to some disciplinary action.

Apart from those already mentioned in his diary, Fejfar flew a further three convoy patrols during January.

---

[4] Sergeant Blažej Konvalina was 18 days past his 23rd birthday. He came from Blížkovice.

7th February 1942

The weather is unbelievably foul and with heavy snow storms as well. Even the newspapers are not being delivered. Our Squadron is ordered to fly to Southend aerodrome. It is in fact a detachment of 13 Spitfires and 20 pilots but no ground staff. The aerodrome is not in good order and the officer's mess is five kilometres away. We remain indoors for hours just playing ping-pong mostly, or pool. Next day, the weather improves slightly today and we are supposed to do more target-towing and air firing, but instead of this we are ordered to fly an offensive patrol over France in the Dunkirk-Calais areas at 14.40. We do not see any Germans because they are not interested in being killed in such weather, either by us in the air or landing back on snow-covered airfields. We are back by 16.20. After our return we finally get some air-firing practice in and also have some simulated dog-fights.

11th February 1942

We are ordered to participate in a Circus operation in a wing formation. We take off at 14.25 pm and rendezvous at 6,000 feet five minutes later. Then our squadron is told to climb to 20,000 feet. Snow is on the ground and later, at 24,000 feet, we are joined by another wing, consisting of one Belgian squadron and a Dutch one. Operations order us to 11,000 feet as they report the presence of 30 enemy aircraft, but where the hell are they? We land back at 15.25 bitterly disappointed once more but ops maintain that radar never lies.

*   *   *

On Thursday 12 February 1942, the Germans decided to move three capital ships from their harbour in Brest, where they had been constantly harassed by bombing raids, to the safer area of Norway. They had the choice of two routes, either north and then east around the top of Scotland, or a dash through the English Channel and up the North Sea. While the latter would be the more dangerous in respect of aerial attack from Fighter and Bomber Commands in England, it would be quicker. The longer, northern route would be less hazardous from air attack but they would have to run the gauntlet of the Royal Navy's big ships.

The three German ships, the battle-cruisers *Scharnhorst*, *Gneisenau* and the heavy cruiser *Prinz Eugen*, had been a constant threat to Atlantic convoys ever since they had been in Brest, and both the RAF and the Royal Navy had been keeping a keen eye on them, not only trying to bomb them, but ensuring they did not slip out into the Atlantic unseen, where they would cause havoc amongst the merchant ships bringing vital supplies to Britain.

The Germans chose the Channel/North Sea option and with secret and amazing planning to put the operation underway, and taking into account recent bad weather, it was decided to make what became known as the Channel

Dash, on the evening of the 11th. A warm front was moving down from Iceland which the forecasters predicted would bring low cloud and reduced visibility over and off Brest, and following a bombing raid by the RAF, the three ships slipped out of harbour at 22.45 hours.

Luck was with them and they escaped without being detected by RN submarines which were on constant lookout for just such a move, and the force headed up the Normandy coast. Along the route they would be joined by six destroyers and 15 E-boats (the equivalent of British MTBs), and when daylight came, a massive air cover of German fighters would be ready. By the time dawn broke, the ships were somewhere between Cherbourg and Dieppe. It was not until 10.00 that British radar picked up something that suggested activity off the French coast, and aircraft were sent out to take a look. Therefore, the ships were not spotted until about 10.30.

One radio call to base alerted the RAF of the danger, but nothing was done until other Spitfires had returned to confirm the sighting, wasting even more valuable time. Finally, having realised exactly what was happening, a response was got underway.

The RAF had already made a plan should such a situation arise, code-named Operation Fuller, and despite some panic, this was put into action, but not until 11.30 am. By this time the ships were nearing the Straits of Dover, their crews no doubt unable to comprehend their luck.

The story of the various attacks against the convoy of ships need not be retold here, nor of the sacrifices many flyers made in trying to damage or sink the vessels. For our story, all that needs to be recorded is that Stanislav Fejfar and 313 Squadron became part of the operation, which ended in success for the German navy, their heavy ships making safe haven in Norwegian waters, and although two were damaged by mines, they were not sunk. Eventually they were anchored in safer waters than Brest and although the damage was repaired, the ships ironically took no further active part in the war, Hitler being too fearful that they would be lost.

12th February 1942

At 12.30 pm we are brought to readiness. Our task is to escort Hurribombers in an attack on the *Gneisenau*, *Scharnhorst* and *Prinz Eugen* battleships. We are told their direction is northwards. Our course is ordered at 130 degrees. The flight under my control, with Hochmal, Fogler, Dohnal, Horák, Kresta and Stočes, is the first to take off, at 1.30 pm and we make rendezvous with the Hurribombers above the aerodrome at 500 feet.

We fly out just above the water and leave the English coast at 1.45. We can immediately see a large cloud of smoke which after clearing, reveals the three battleships which are enormous. We see a red signal but we know that for today, the colour signal should be green, so this is the enemy trying to fool us. We accompany three Hurribombers who make the first attack. We then observe another three following and soon the ships' anti-aircraft pom-pom guns make a thick forest of white tracer shells. We aim for the three large grey ships and dive towards them. All of us fire off our cannon shells towards their superstructures. Once over them we turn back towards England, after the Hurribombers have executed their role.

We land at 2.35 pm and await further news or orders. We are very tired, all of us, because it is a great strain to avoid the shell streams coming at you with such density. The attack is not successful. All three battleships escape and we are now counting the cost of this battle.

All Swordfish torpedo planes are lost along with 20 Hurribombers and 16 Spitfires. The RAF managed to shoot down 19 escorting Luftwaffe Me109s. One of our pilots – Špaček – landed with his undercarriage still up and so another disciplinary action will have to be taken.

Hurribombers were normal Hawker Hurricane fighters, which had been relegated to fighter-bombers now that Spitfires had taken over all day fighter operations. Two 250 or 500 pound bombs were carried, one under each wing, and as they made their diving approaches, they could open up with their four 20 mm cannon to encourage German ground gunners to keep their heads down. Four of this type from 607 Squadron were shot down on this operation with all pilots lost.

The Swordfish mentioned in the diary were those Fleet Air Arm boys led by Eugene Esmonde, in what was virtually a suicide mission. They nevertheless carried it out in full navy tradition, even though they were all shot down by flak and fighters. Esmonde, for his leadership and extreme heroism in the face of such defensive fire and German fighters, was awarded a posthumous Victoria Cross.

Fighter Command suffered greatly too with some 15 pilots lost, three more taken prisoner. Most were Spitfires or Hurricanes, but four were Whirlwinds of 137 Squadron, all of whose pilots were killed, all downed by Me109s. Several fighters returned damaged. Bomber Command sent a number of Hampdens, Blenheims and Wellingtons into the fray, losing 10 Hampdens, two Blenheims and four Wellingtons, with the majority of their crews killed. Coastal Command's torpedo-carrying Beauforts, and Hudson bombers, were also in the battle, at a cost of three Beauforts and two Hudsons.

RAF fighter pilots claimed an incredible 21 German fighters destroyed, three probably destroyed, plus 14 more damaged. According to the Germans they only lost three Fw190s, one Me109 and three Dornier 217s (although none of the latter were claimed), with 11 other aircraft of all types damaged.

The day had already started early for Fejfar although he does not bother to mention this in his diary. At 09.10 am he and Sergeant Jaroslav Dohnal were scrambled to patrol over base because there was a suspected enemy aircraft about but they saw nothing and landed.

13th February 1942

Today is Friday the 13th and some say an unlucky day. For us everything ended well. We were at readiness at 10.45 am with an order coming through to make an offensive sweep against enemy shipping. We made rendezvous with 18 Hurribombers at 12.45 at 1,000 feet. They will attack shipping in and around Calais, Dunkirk and Ostende. Heavy ack-ack greeted us off the hostile coast but the Hurribombers quickly completed their task and we were all soon returning to Southend unscathed.

20th February 1942

During the week we practise various wing formations as the weather improves. We ask our commanding officer to permit us, with our cannons, to attack Berck-sur-Mer aerodrome on the French coast, where not long ago I was flying Morane 406s. The AOC agrees and we set off flying just above sea-level, on a course of 150 degrees towards France. Unfortunately a thick wall of cloud faced us when we reached the target so we had to return home. Our revenge against the pilots killed here will have to await another opportunity.

22nd February 1942

I am very sad because my dear friend Bönisch was killed today.[5] While on a convoy escort his engine began losing power and although he made the coast he crash-landed 30 feet from the beach. We observed his Spitfire do this and also saw that a small ship was close by. The ship's captain manoeuvred his vessel as close to the beach as he could and in an endeavour to help, we even saw the captain jump into the sea and begin to swim towards shore in order to reach the crashed aeroplane. The captain, we discovered later, was 58 years old, but of course his efforts were to no avail. He needed hospital treatment, where our CO, Mrázek, visited him to thank him for his efforts.

We are on night flying practice once more, and it began well with a full moon. When the clouds started to arrive the landings became more difficult. I was in charge of my flight on the ground, armed with a Very pistol to signal aircraft when it was safe to land. One aircraft, which I later discovered was mine, crashed and is a complete write off. The pilot, I am glad to say, escaped with just a few minor scratches.

Another operation Fejfar does not mention in his diary is the day the squadron escorted eight Hurribombers to about a mile off the French coast, where they found a large flak-ship together with another of medium size. The Hurricanes

---

[5] František Bönisch hailed from Prchalov and was 28 years old. His body was recovered and he is buried at Hornchurch.

flew in and bombed from 400 feet, scoring a direct hit on the larger vessel, and then the Spitfires went in.

Squadron Leader Mrázek (Red 1 in AA869) targeted the bridge of the second ship, two of his men also attacking, then escorted some of the Hurricanes back home. Fejfar (Yellow 1 in AA757) and Sergeant Dohnal (AA765) flew escort to two of the Hurricanes and found a medium-sized flak ship with an armed trawler in attendance. Both pilots attacked after the Hurricanes strafed them, and they and the Spitfires scored hits on the flak ship.

Assessing the results later, Mrázek had scored hits on the ship's bridge, Sergeant Řezníček (AA918) hit the boat's aft area, while Sergeant Fogler (AD380) had hit the vessel amidships. Both Fejfar and Dohnal reported scoring hits on their target amidships.

7th March 1942
Two days ago all of us returned to Hornchurch, but had to leave our comrade Bönisch in Southend cemetery. We celebrate our return with a party in the mess.

Today we practise more flying manoeuvres within the wing formation but ops decided that we should train to be part of the 'air sea rescue' service. So we are sitting in our cockpits for 40 minutes but nobody, it seems, needs to be rescued! Naturally someone begins to joke by saying: 'For heaven's sake, why do they not shoot somebody down so that we can take off?' This type of black humour shows that we are still living on the edge.

Spring is approaching and I am suffering from headaches. I see the doctor and I am not allowed to eat anything and I must also stay in my room. My friend Kučera visits me there with the sad news that Captain Kulhánek was shot down while on an escort mission with his squadron, and has been reported as missing. That happened on the 13th of February but quite a few of us believe that perhaps he crash-landed and will be coming back via the French underground resistance movement and Gibraltar.[6]

18th March 1942
A year ago on the 15th, I left hospital and it looks like I shall be returning for further examination. I am furious and envy all those who can fly, especially now that the weather is improving every day.

Whilst I am forced to stay in my room, I faithfully follow the exploits of my squadron and comrades. As a result of strafing a German airfield, two of our pilots have been reported as missing, believed killed, since

[6] Unfortunately Flight Lieutenant Jaroslav Kulhánek did not return. This 34-year-old experienced pilot, came from Prague, and was with 124 Squadron, RAF. He was shot down by JG26 over St Omer during Circus 114, a raid on the Hazebrouck marshalling yards. He is buried in Leubrighen Cemetery, Calais.

the attacks were at very low level and the enemy ack-ack fire is, we regret to note, improving daily.

Warrant Officer Špaček and Flight Sergeant Zauf will have to be replaced as soon as possible.[7]

23rd March 1942

Three days ago I was taken off flying duties. Today our squadron has been detailed to fly above London during the celebration of 'The Warships Week'. Sergeant Kresta's engine began misfiring just above Trafalgar Square and he began searching for a long, wide street where he thought he could land. He took the Thames-side [Embankment?] and just when he thought that he could possibly make a landing his engine began to fire properly and he quickly returned to the first airfield he could find. He was later congratulated by the station commander, and the ops room people had been in a terrible state, afraid that his aircraft would end up killing a lot of innocent Londoners.

24th March 1942

Another Circus operation, this time to Comines in France [Circus 116A]. The wing consisted of aircraft of 313, 411 and 64, and these were escorting the bombers. Although it seemed that the bombers were to be attacked at all costs by the Luftwaffe fighters, our aircraft despatched two Me109s as soon as they appeared on the scene. Squadron Leader Mrázek shot down the first one while Sergeant Horák got the other one.[8]

27th March 1942

On the 25th the boys flew escort on Circus 117 but over France the operation was aborted. Today we go back to Ostende as bomber escort. Our 313 Squadron found themselves suddenly alone with the bombers, since 64 and 411 Squadrons had flown too far to one side. When the Me109s went for the bombers, 313 could not sit tight while alone, which is normal practise, but had to fight off the attackers. The result was that Flying Officer Vancl and Sergeant Horák each managed to

---

[7] Otto Špaček, just nine days past his 24th birthday, was not lost this date, and in fact survived the war. However, Milislav Zauf was killed. Zauf came from Brodek u Přerova, and he was 27. He was brought down near Condette that afternoon and is buried in Boulogne eastern cemetery.

[8] It looks as if Fejfar was incorrect in his dates, and even the names. 313 Squadron did not make any claims on the 24th, although Mrázek did destroy a 109 on the 28th, while Pilot Officer Jicha got a Focke Wulf. The target was indeed a power station at Comines plus the marshalling yards at Abbeville for another Circus, No.116B.

damage a 109, but in accordance with strict RAF protocol were not allowed to watch them to the ground or claim them as destroyed.

Horák's Spitfire was so heavily damaged in the fight that it was a miracle he ever managed to reach England in one piece. Only the day before yesterday Horák and his flight commander shot down another Me109, and no doubt this sergeant will be commissioned very soon. Not everything ended up well for we lost Pilot Officer Michálek, whose Spitfire was seen to dive into the ground. Fortunately the bombers, despite being left unprotected for a short while, all returned safely.

Pilot Officer Vladimír Michálek came from Závišice. He has no known grave but his name is on the Runnymede RAF Memorial. He was six days past his 24th birthday. He was shot down at 4.40 pm by Hauptmann Josef 'Pips' Priller, commander of JG26's III Gruppe, and was the German ace's 60th victory. He had engaged the Spitfires some 10 kilometres west of Ostende. Two of JG26's FW190s made forced landings, with one pilot, Feldwebel Karl Willius wounded. Willius would become a top ace later, and 313 came close to stopping his career permanently.

28th March 1942
As a special order, four Czech Spitfires were assigned to escort two Hurribombers in an attack upon Berck aerodrome. The operation was to begin from RAF Manston and they took off at 11.39 am. The two Hurribombers did not find the prescribed target and so they returned. However, Sergeant Vykoukal, one of our escorting pilots, spotted a machine-gun nest on the aerodrome of Le Touquet, which he attacked with cannon fire. His colleague, Sergeant Kresta, fired at a military bus he saw travelling around on the aerodrome perimeter. As he opened fire he saw German soldiers jumping out and running for cover.

Meantime, Flight Lieutenant Hájek fired at a railway signal box and with ammunition left, opened up on some small barges he saw on a beach. Upon their return to base, they found that the Spitfire flown by Flight Lieutenant Vykoukal had been extensively peppered by machine-gun fire. One strike was only six inches from his head. That is what I call 'The Fortune of War'!

During the afternoon the squadron flew out again, this time with 64 Squadron, being ordered to sweep an area between Dunkirk-St Omer-Calais. Whilst looking for something suitable to harass, they were attacked by patrolling Luftwaffe fighters – both Me109s and FW190s. A furious dog-fight ensued and it carried on out over the sea. Squadron Leader Mrázek destroyed one Focke Wulf, while Jicha severely damaged another. All our aircraft returned although Řezníček's Spitfire was shot about somewhat.

So, whilst I sit at dispersal and hear all that has been going on, I am hoping that the promised medical in London will prove that I am fit to fly. 313 Squadron, for the month of March, has 9 officers and 17 NCO pilots on strength.

According to the Germans, JG26's First Gruppe had engaged the Hornchurch fighters over Guines and then out to sea. They claimed one Spitfire shot down, and 64 Squadron did lose a pilot, who became a prisoner. Oberfeldwebel Erwin Leibold was shot down over Marquise and injured, while another 190 had to make a belly-landing near Guines with a damaged engine.

This action almost merged with Spitfires of the Kenley Wing who arrived and were themselves engaged by other elements of JG26. They shot down a number of Spitfires, including the famous station commander of Kenley, Group Captain F V Beamish DSO DFC AFC, who was killed.

10th April 1942

Whilst sitting in the officer's mess, an order arrived to come at once to the flight dispersal area. I arrived soon afterwards and those on readiness take off for France. In another hour the intelligence officer answers the telephone and looks quite worried. Apparently two packs of fighters, one of which in fact were Focke Wulf 190s, formidable, fast machines, had arrived on the scene and in a fight, Flight Sergeant Fogler damaged one whilst Flight Lieutenant Fajtl claimed another destroyed. Flying Officer Hájek also damaged a 190. However, two of our pilots

Fejfar, right, in the crew room awaiting the time for take-off with P/O Václav Jicha.

are missing. One, Flight Sergeant Truhlář, was attacked by four FW190s and Flight Sergeant Pokorný is reported as killed in action since he was attacked by a 190 whilst trying to force land with his engine knocked out, and was seen to dive into the ground.[9] I am confident that Flight Sergeant Truhlář will return for he is one of our best.

12th April 1942
The skies are blue and at once we have a job of escorting twelve bombers to hit Hazebrouck. The Hornchurch Wing is split: two squadrons covering the high ceiling whilst our squadron is at the bottom. The fighter escort is soon busy after the bombers leave the English coast. Furious fighting occurred over Gravelines where Squadron Leader Mrázek shot down a FW190 but will not be able to be credited with it since he did not follow it down to see it crash. Flight Lieutenant Fajtl was luckier because his opponent, another 190, disintegrated after just one burst of cannon fire. The same happened with Sergeant Brázda, whose 190 went down vertically. Pilot Officer Jicha damaged a 190 and so did Flying Officer Kasal. Lastly, Flight Sergeant Hloužek did the same. However, everything is not perfect because Flight Sergeant Kresta is missing.[10]

This was Circus 122, Bostons attacking Hazebrouck railway yards and the various RAF fighter squadrons lost 12 or more Spitfires to JG26. 41 Squadron lost four with a fifth crash-landing in England! Kresta also ended up a prisoner, in Mühlberg PoW camp, on the Elbe, east of Leipzig. Oberleutnant Rolf Hermichen of JG26's 7th Staffel claimed the Spitfire flown by Kresta, his 13th victory of an eventual tally of 64.

13th April 1942
I am returning to duty as a flight commander, and today I am flying over France at 22,000 feet. Four enemy aircraft are reported over the radio but the task of engaging them is assigned to 64 Squadron. The Luftwaffe, as usual, are surprised that whenever they fly above or below us there is always the RAF waiting for them.

---

[9] František Pokorný was indeed killed this day. He came from Pavlovsko, and was aged 25. Václav Truhlář survived to become a prisoner of war. He ended up in Wistritz bei Teplitz PoW camp, which was situated just inside the north Czech border, due south of Dresden. He died in October 1947, aged 30. The fight had been with JG26 again and they had two pilots killed.
[10] Otakar Kresta survived as a prisoner of war. He was 23 and from Klokočov. He survived the experience and died in 1992.

We are flying in new machines with stronger engines and a faster climb, and this with a two-stage supercharger is noticeable whilst flying above 16,000 feet. After our return I am advised that Flight Lieutenant Vykoukal is being transferred to a British squadron as a flight commander.[11] I am wondering who we will get as a replacement.

14th April 1942

I think we shall soon know northern France like the back of our hand and that includes Belgium too, as we are escorting the bombers again. We are informed that with continuous high-altitude flying the supply of oxygen is paramount and if one begins to feel even slightly confused, we must reduce height at once.

After landing we are off once more patrolling over Le Touquet-Desvres-Cap Gris Nez. During our return flight we notice high above us that there are at least 20 enemy fighters but we are not advised to do anything about them. After I return I am informed that a replacement, Pilot Officer Příhoda, will fly in my flight and the squadron is pleased to have George [Jiří] Kučera, who at long last wears an officer's uniform. I flew with him in North Africa.[12]

15th April 1942

We are aware that England at last is bombing Germany every night and during the daytime, the Yanks have their own targets. We are jealous that we do not carry enough fuel to range deeper into Germany ourselves. I personally would shoot-up anything German just to repay the brutalities inflicted upon our nation. But today was busy for us. The first sortie before lunch we escorted Hurribombers with their cannons shooting at Cap Gris Nez and Dunkirk [Circus 124]. As escort, we kept watch for Luftwaffe fighters but they do not want to play today.

Our second sortie was at 6.10 pm and this time the bombers had a special task of destroying a particular factory at Calais [Circus 125]. We

---

[11] Karel Vykoukal was posted to 41 Squadron at Merston, but was killed in action on 21 May 1942, shot down by flak during an anti-shipping sortie to the Seine estuary. He came from Chotěboř, and was 25 years old. He has no known grave.

At this time František Vancl and František Fajtl both held the rank of flight lieutenant.

[12] Josef Příhoda came from Vlašim, Benešov, and was 26. He would be awarded the British DFC later in 1942. He had already seen considerable action with 1 Squadron in 1941, claiming several victories, and then with 111 Squadron in early 1942. He was lost over Brest on 6 March 1943 in a fight with JG2, while escorting American Liberators.

Jiří Kučera was 27 and came from Roudnice n. Labem. He later became a flight commander and then a staff officer. He survived the war.

flew above 20,000 feet and realised that breathing in all this oxygen every day is cracking our lips and is also affecting our sense of taste. The flak over Calais is formidable and the coloured shells is something one never gets used to because one day this colourful stream may hit you!!

16th April 1942

Today is the ninth consecutive day we have flown over our usual targets in northern France, but this time it is a Rodeo, which means fighter operations only [Rodeo 10]. We climb right up to 28,000 feet. By flying so high, plus the atmospheric conditions, we produce vapour trails which would be a give away to the Luftwaffe, but where are they? The German ack-ack fire, being so high, is useless. We land without any encounter and take off again at 18.30 pm. This time we fly at 21,000 feet and go quite deep into France – to St Omer. We are seeking the German bastards but no luck again. Later on we saw some FW190s approaching but they were too far away and only one bullet hit Jicha's machine, which considering the distance was a miracle. We landed at 19.30 pm.

The RAF had worked out during the latter stages of the Battle of Britain, that German fighters sweeping over southern England posed no threat, and these were ordered to be ignored by the AOC of 11 Group, Sir Keith Park. This is why some of the Me109s began to carry small bombs to attack targets of opportunity, forcing RAF fighters to engage. The Germans, in 1941 and now in 1942, were equally happy not to engage the RAF in pure fighter versus fighter actions, where both sides were likely to inflict similar damage upon each other just for the sake of it. There was no percentage in shooting down two enemy fighters and perhaps losing two of your own. The German fighter pilots generally only attacked if they were in a good tactical position whereby they could make a swift pass, shoot something down, and then dive away home.

Chapter Nine

The Final Weeks

Mid-April 1942 found 313 Squadron and Stanislav Fejfar still part of the Hornchurch Wing under Wing Commander Peter Powell, along with 64 and 122 Squadrons. 122 had replaced 411 Canadian Squadron on 2 April, and in fact 64 were actually based at the satellite airfield of Southend. They would return to Hornchurch at the end of the month.

In his book *Raiders Approach*, an account of RAF Hornchurch in both world wars, Squadron Leader H T Sutton OBE DFC, made the following comment about 313 Squadron:

> The Czech squadron stayed at Hornchurch... and during this time they earned the respect of the station as fearless and skilful fighter pilots. These quiet and strangely polite men will always be remembered with admiration by the Royal Air Force who fought alongside them. They were a small force amongst our now numerous allies, but their great individual experience and ability placed them on more than equal terms with their contemporaries. Such gallant Czechs as Flight Lieutenant Karel Kuttelwascher, with his bag of eighteen enemy aircraft destroyed and five damaged, and the almost legendary figure of Sergeant Josef František, who destroyed sixteen enemy aircraft in three weeks of the Battle of Britain – these men placed this small band of exiles in a class of their own.

Karel Miroslav Kuttelwascher, from Svatý Kříž, had been born in September 1916, and had joined the Czech air force in 1934. Three years later he was a fighter pilot but the following year he was one of the many who decided to escape via Poland. He also got into France and like Fejfar found himself a member of the French Foreign Legion, and in North Africa. Flying Dewoitine 520s in the Battle of France with GC III/6, he claimed a couple of shared victories and when he too reached England eventually served with 1 Squadron in 1941. He gained a few successes during sweeps etc, over France but then began to fly night intruder missions in a Hurricane, attacking German bombers at night as they took off or returned from bombing raids over England. He gained considerable success at this dangerous game and received the DFC and

154

Bar. From his own countrymen he received the Czech Military Cross with four
Linden Leaves on Riband, the Medal of Merit with 3 Linden Leaves on Riband,
the Czech Bravery in Silver and the War Commemorative Medal (Bars for
France and Great Britain). He survived the war and flew as a BEA captain but
suffered a heart attack in August 1959 from which he did not survive. He was
42.

Josef František came from Otaslavice, born in October 1913 and was also a
member of the Czech air force, escaping into Poland, then Roumania and on to
the Middle East. Eventually reaching England in June 1940 he became a
member of the famous 303 Polish Squadron and during September claimed 17
victories and won the DFM and Bar. Sadly he was killed in a flying accident on
8 October. The Poles awarded him their Virtuti Militari, 5th Class, and the
Cross of Valour with three Bars, while he also received the Czech War Cross.
At the end of the war he was posthumously commissioned as a first lieutenant.

17th April 1942

Took off at 11.35 am and there were six of us from my flight. Myself,
Kasal, Příhoda, Dohnal, Horák and Čáp. We have a special job of
escorting six American Bostons that are tasked to bomb a railway
station. Several groups of enemy fighters were reported but they were
not interested in us at all and we just do not know why this is so.
Perhaps the next few days will prove something. We return as
unemployed once more.

At 14.55 pm we receive a new order, this time as an escort of
specialist bombers whose task was to destroy the radar towers at
Lumbres. We are ordered to climb to 28,000 feet which we consider as
too high and naturally we are soon in the clouds and therefore are
unable to observe the bombers. We are then told to reduce height to
18,000 feet, but our task was carried out without any hindrance
whatsoever. The Luftwaffe were once again, nowhere!

Returning via Boulogne we encountered the ack-ack barrage stronger
than we have ever experienced before. The space above, below and
under was just a mass of streamers of death, but despite all the intensity
they didn't even hit the slower bombers.[1]

18th April 1942

Today is my day off, which means a lie in followed by a relaxing bath,
without being disturbed. After breakfast and reading the newspapers in
the officer's mess lounge, I determine to visit my flight at our dispersal
area later.

---

[1] Operations this day were mainly flown for diversions in order to aid a deep
daylight penetration by RAF Lancaster bombers that were attacking the
Messerschmitt factory at Augsburg, which resulted in its leader, Squadron Leader
John Nettleton, winning the Victoria Cross.

The squadron took off later and it was another escort job. Pilot Officer Jicha comes back early due to engine trouble and lands on the long concrete runway at Manston. This aerodrome has saved hundreds of lives especially bomber crews returning at night, or Yanks who had no hope of reaching Lincolnshire.

I was told confidentially, from our man in ops that Hermann Göring [commander of the German Luftwaffe] was supposed to visit a place in France. However, there were no details or briefing, so the result for us was nil. The squadron was so furious that they went out and strafed every fishing boat in Boulogne harbour, so there will not be many fish and chip suppers in France today.

20th-23rd April 1942
Not flying weather – fog. You would never see this on the continent but we welcome the rest and the ground staff are able to use the time to catch up with major repairs and servicing.

24th April 1942
A special and dramatic day. At 1.55 pm we took off to escort American Boston bombers in an attack on Ostende[2]. It was a success but on our return journey we were attacked by a group of Focke Wulfs but once we turned to face them on this, for us, welcome occasion, they quickly disappeared. However, we had an unhappy loss as Sergeant Brázda's Spitfire was hit by flak over Ostende and suddenly everyone was advising him to land on the grass and not try to get back across the sea to England. He was closely watched by Pilot Officer Jicha who tried to protect him from another bunch of Nazi FW190s and succeeded in shooting down one of them. It was quite an achievement since he was still worried about how to protect Brázda. It was to no avail as Brázda wanted desperately to reach the English coast but he must have been wounded because only some 300 yards from the beach he went into a spin, crashed and was killed instantly.

---

[2] While Fejfar records the bombers as American Bostons, this is because they were built by the American Douglas company in the USA. The RAF's 2 Group of Bomber Command had exchanged their Blenheim bombers for Bostons and used them on these Circus operations during 1942. This day the Bostons belonged to 107 Squadron RAF, on Circus 132, and the fighter opposition came from JG26's III Gruppe, led by Pips Priller. Obviously they made no claim for 313's loss as it was not seen to go down.

We are all depressed because we all liked Prokop Brázda.[3] We barely recover from this depressed state when ops asked us once again to take off in order to escort some bombers, this time flying as top cover, at 27,000 feet. Fortunately this was on the way out as my engine lost power completely and I was forced to glide down to the aerodrome. As soon as I landed the propeller stopped turning and I had to leave my Spitfire and walk back to the dispersal hut.

The squadron had taken off at 16.45 pm and made rendezvous with the North Weald Wing over Southend and then crossed out over Folkestone and headed towards Cap Gris Nez, where Fejfar had to break off. The wings headed along to Desvres, crossing the patrol area of the Kenley and Tangmere Wings. While Fejfar was getting down safely, the patrol was heading for Le Touquet, then St Omer, and out via Gravelines and Calais. No enemy aircraft or flak were encountered or seen.

25th April 1942

We were on readiness at dawn. Visibility is nil and yet we were to take off. Just a few yards during take-off a red flare warned us to return at once. We were then called for a briefing with the station commander himself [Broadhurst]. Our job is as close escort to Hurribombers in order to destroy some special factory in Calais. No Luftwaffe about and we land and refuel. The mission was a success, but we took off once more, this time for Abbeville as rear support for bombers.

As soon as we cross the Channel I find Germans on my tail. Their propeller hubs are painted yellow. Our orders are, of course to escort and not to engage in individual air fights. However, imagine my surprise when, on glancing in the rear view mirror, almost at once one of the FW190s is replaced by four Spitfires. The German veered towards the sea but suddenly I saw bullets dancing on my wing. I closed the throttle as fast as I could and a Focke Wulf overshot me – I swear by just inches – but I levelled up and there he was in my gun-sight. I pressed the firing button without stopping and soon bits and pieces were flying above and below me. Naturally I was out of squadron formation after this, when I saw four Spitfires not very far away. I thought I would be more comfortable if I joined them, being suddenly alone.

But this is not the end of the day it seems, because I saw two arrows

[3] Flight Sergeant Prokop Brázda came from Kosov and he was 26 years old. Prokop can be a first or surname in Czechoslovakia, the name of a Czech/Bohemian saint. He actually crashed near Colchester and is buried at Hornchurch. He was lost, as mentioned above, on Circus 132, the Bostons attacking oil installations at Vlissingen, on Walcheren Island. 122 Squadron were also attacked and had two Spitfires shot down, one by Oberleutnant Karl Borris, the other by Leutnant Paul Galland, a younger brother of Adolf Galland, both of the 8th Staffel.

coming for me from out of the sun. I kicked the rudder, pulled back on the throttle again, and one after another, Focke Wulfs were passing me. Once more one is in my gun-sight so I pressed the firing button again. I am only about 35 yards from it and again bits and pieces, including a bit of tail aileron, were passing me by. I stay no longer in the vicinity and with full boost I aim for England. One final glance at France [and] I notice one FW190 gliding down and one above him acting as escort. If I were not alone I would probably go after it, but today's action is enough for me!

The squadron's Form 541, recording flight times and pilots involved in these operations, reports the following for 25 April.

> First mission – Escort Bombers. 1105 – 1240 hours. [Ramrod 28]
> Hornchurch Wing (10 Spitfires VB 122 Squadron – including W/Cdr Powell and 12 Spitfires 313 Squadron) led by G/Capt Broadhurst together with 12 Spitfire VB 64 Squadron, rendezvoused over Eastchurch at 6,500/8,000 ft, with 8 Hurribombers and [the] Biggin Hill Wing. Out across Manston and Deal, in over Gravelines stepped up from 14,000 to 16,000 feet, No.122 below, No. 313 middle and No.64 top. Bombers escorted well south of target where latter dived down sun into haze. Wing dived to 11,000/13,000 ft, skirting Guines and out at Gris Nez. Turning east, wing climbed to 18,500/20,000 feet. Then North back towards Calais, along coast to Boulogne, up to Gravelines, round to Calais and returned to Base via Dover. E/a not engaged. Black flak observed over Calais at 15,000 feet. Weather, haze forming cloud at 6,000 feet over English Channel. Thick haze over France.

> Second mission – Escort Bombers. 1535-1725. [Circus 137]
> Hornchurch Wing (Nos.64, 122 and 313 Squadrons) led by G/C H Broadhurst DSO DFC AFC, flying with 122 Squadron and W/C P Powell, rendezvoused at Beachy Head with Kenley and Biggin Hill Wings. French landfall 2 miles N. of Le Touquet where many e/a sighted at various heights. After several attempts to engage by all three sqns and owing to large number of e/a having advantage of height and sun, the G/Capt ordered wing to return to Base, having ascertained that bombers and other wings were en-route for home. Two pilots of 313 Squadron fired without result, and another (F/L Fejfar) attacked one of the FW190s which was claimed as damaged.

The strange thing here is that from his diary, Fejfar seems to have scored hits on two FW190s and also been hit in one wing, but the action report only alludes to the second 190 and no mention of damage to his own machine – BL973. This Spitfire had arrived on 313 Squadron from 28 MU on 30 March and was usually flown by Fejfar. He was flying it again on the 26th so if there was any damage it was minimal and repaired overnight. Fejfar was in combat with elements of the Second Gruppe of JG2 (although JG26 was also around) and they did have some 190s damaged in the action.

26th April 1942

St Omer rail station was our target today but we think only that somebody is joking, since after all our recent sorties there cannot be anything left of it. The bombers despatch their greetings downwards and we were then warned that Luftwaffe fighters are now flying above the waves and they endeavoured to attack us from below during our return flight but to no avail.[4]

We ate as our aircraft were refuelled, and in no time we were up on another escort job. This time we were at 16,000 feet which is far from comfortable as German ack-ack fire can reach us here. During our return a lone Me109 suddenly appeared but no sooner does it do so than it quickly disappears. They do not like to fight against the odds. In the officer's mess later, somebody told us that Hitler made another speech but I bet it is no longer as bombastic as his previous ones.

27th April 1942 am

We take off at 11.25 am and it is another Hurribomber escort to St Omer railway sidings [Circus 142]. This time the Luftwaffe attacks our squadron and our newly arrived pilot, Pilot Officer Příhoda shoots down a Me109. It was our 13th victory for the squadron. It costs Příhoda some beer in the mess during the evening.

Part of the escorting force was 71 (Eagle) Squadron, manned mostly by Americans who had volunteered to fly and fight with the RAF in 1940-41, before the USA came into the war in December 1941. JG26 engaged them and 65 Squadron, part of the Debden Wing, and four Spitfires went down, three from 65 and one from 71, with another badly damaged and written off. Pips Priller was again in evidence as leader of the Geschwader's Third Gruppe, and he claimed two of these victories, bringing his personal score to 67.

27th April 1942 pm

We had another mission during the afternoon but I do not see the necessity to write things down if nothing occurs. One of my sergeant pilots complains about battle fatigue and is given a special 7-day leave.

---

[4] The morning sortie, Circus 138, was flown between 09.40 and 11.10 am. 313, led by Squadron Leader Mrázek (BM242) made rendezvous with 64 Squadron over base and linked up with the bombers over Gravesend at 5,000 feet. Crossing out over Deal they set course for Dunkirk, climbing steadily to 15,000 feet. Course was set to Cassel then St Omer (the target was the railway station as Fejfar says). After the bombing the formation flew out via Mardyke and Gravelines.

My best friend and the commander of A Flight, František Fajtl, is leaving the squadron and is going to command the British 122 Squadron.

The time is coming fast now, that we are coping in English, and can cease duplicating the squadron leader posts. We roomed with each other and I remember him so well from our days in the foreign legion, and our happy days in Paris before our uniformed duties put an end to all that.

28th April 1942

As our Czech president, Beneš, is due to visit us during the afternoon, ops sent us out at dawn as an escort on a mission to St Omer. Apparently it is a very important rail junction. It is a show for only one flight so sergeant pilots are allowed to sleep on, and we are all officers on this job. The return flight was once more impossible, with coloured tracer all around us. In Czech we call it a 'Venice Carnival Night'.

A second sweep takes place at 10.30 am but I was off duty. I am told that I volunteer far too much and that other people want to fly operations as well. Quite a few FW190s arrived on the scene but were far too high and they never dived down, the cowards.

The president arrives at 5 pm and after an inspection, Czech medals are awarded to many of the Czech pilots flying with these British squadrons: 1, 32, 41, 65, 111, 121, and 501. The medals are the highest degree and are called the Czech Military Cross 1939. I am awarded a medal for bravery, first class, and perhaps having flown 142 operational hours and destroyed three German aircraft in France, it is a fitting occasion.

The president talks to us a long time as usual, and we just surround him like friends and comrades. He thinks that with America now with us, everything in the Third Reich will soon go downhill. His remarks and his presence provoke our thinking about our dearest ones left behind.

29th April 1942

Our first operational flight is at 15.15 hours and we are escorting six Bostons while they are dropping their eggs. [This is Circus 145 to Dunkirk and the Bostons are from 266 Squadron.] Some Me109s turn up but fly right through us and vanish. This is quite boring especially for our new pilots who desperately want to prove themselves in combat.

We return for a late lunch and in the late afternoon we have the sad duty of accompanying Sergeant Brázda's body to Hornchurch cemetery, and listen to the 'Last Post' trumpet call. Prokop, we shall avenge you, our brother.

Later still we fly to our new RAF base at Fairlop, but instead of landing we are directed to escort bombers to Holland. When the usual pack of FW190s arrive, they lose one of their machines almost at once, to one of our newly arrived sergeant pilots who has only 20 hours of operational flying time. He is Sergeant Hloužek.[5] We suffer no losses and the total hours in my B Flight this month are 281 plus 127 of practice flights.

30th April 1942

We are ordered to patrol in the Calais-Boulogne area. Again quite boring since the Luftwaffe is simply not paying any attention to the RAF, but naturally the ack-ack, the swine, are always firing, reaching up for us pilots.

Our new aerodrome has just been built and not quite finished, but after the experience of our Czech aerodromes we are used to it. In order not to allow us too much rest the squadron takes off at 14.05 hours and once more we are over Holland. Nothing much occurs [except for Hloužek's Spitfire being damaged]. In fact I was off duty today.

Fairlop was not exactly new, but perhaps appeared to Fejfar to be so. The airfield had been used in World War One for home defence squadrons operating against day and night raiding airships and bombers. It had been reactivated in September 1940 and became operational just under a year later, having had three good runways built in that time. As a satellite to RAF Hornchurch, squadrons from this main base each took turns in living and operating from here. 313 Squadron would operate from here until June 1942, so it was from Fairlop that Fejfar flew his last missions.

1st May 1942

The month of love is here, but you cannot be sentimental which a take-off at 09.10 am proves. We are escorting Hurribombers. Unfortunately the other side of the Channel is completely closed with nil visibility so we had to return to Fairlop at once. At 18.40 another escort – yes, you guessed it, without briefing – to St Omer. The Bostons decimated part of the marshalling yards and then two Me109s appear to shake us out of our regular timetable. They dive towards us, but they are only

---

[5] Jaroslav Hloužek was not yet 22 years of age and came from Jackov. In fact he was not only credited with a 109 destroyed, but also with a FW190 damaged. He would be lost on 18 November 1942 flying a low-level Rhubarb operation (in AR606). He had led a bit of a charmed life, having his Spitfire shot-up the day after his victory (BM127), and being hit by flak while over Le Havre on Circus 227 (EP560) on 15 October.

pretending to attack, and quickly vanish without opening fire.[6]

3rd May 1942
Yesterday the clouds were down to the ground and we did not fly. Today, though, we were on a Rodeo operation to the area of Dunkirk-Le Touquet and Paris-Plage. We were flying top cover and whilst we observed some Luftwaffe mob approaching the area we were ordered homewards because the job of meeting them went to the North Weald Wing, the lucky devils. If they had arrived three minutes earlier it would have been our fight.

5th May 1942
We make rendezvous over Hornchurch aerodrome with Boston bombers, at 28,000 feet. The sky is so blue that you cannot believe there is a war on, but the black tracers from underneath us confirm the constant danger. Ops are reporting 20 to 25 enemy fighters but after twisting our necks round and round nothing arrives in our area.

After landing, Jiří Kučera, with whom I flew in North Africa, is posted to A Flight and I am delighted since being no longer in a sergeant's uniform, we can talk about our experiences more easily.

At 14.00 hours we come to full readiness and take off at 14.40. I am delegated as a squadron leader for this operation. Our wing crosses the Dunkirk-Mardyk area at 15.15, with everything deadly quiet, just like it is before a storm. Suddenly the wing leader is shouting that there are 20 enemy fighters at 15,000 feet. With ack-ack exploding around us at this height, we are trying to dodge the flak shells as the bombers drop their loads. Then we are turning for home, but suddenly our flight path is full of Me109s – six of them. I am warning my colleagues but then more enemy aircraft appear from the right, at first eight, then a further nine.

I am sweating a bit and immediately order the 'Tally Ho!' At this altitude this fight is for life and quite possibly, death. I attack the nearest 190 in that micro-second and after pressing the firing button I see the enemy pilot climbing out of his cockpit, but I do not see the subsequent parachute canopy. I cannot and must not muddle my thoughts because I now notice white tracers approaching my Spitfire. I flick my machine into a spin at once – what else can I do? – to avoid two FW190s that suddenly appear. However, they pass me and head towards some Spitfires below me.

---

[6] This was Circus 150, flown by six Bostons from 107 Squadron. While 313 saw no real action, the other Hornchurch squadrons did, and so did other escorting fighters. Hauptmann Pips Priller in fact claimed his 69th victory, a Spitfire of the Kenley Wing. Eight Spitfires failed to return, with others damaged. Hornchurch's 122 Squadron suffered one of the losses.

Whatever happens and whether the Spitfires are flown by Polish, Czech or English pilots, I have to dive at once to help, lining up one in my gun-sight. I fire without hesitation but in my mirror I spot another Fritz, this time the horrible yellow propeller hub of a FW190. My knees tremble. My usual trick is to close the throttle, but I almost black out from the g-force effect, and I go into another flat spin. When I recover and start to climb, a 190 without one wing just passes me by.

The battle is far from over and I see another three FW190s are now after me. I am alone and can only do one thing – full throttle, engage emergency boost for more power – and aim for England. The German pilots do not like the Channel much and this has saved my bacon I believe! Yet the danger is still present because I estimate my remaining fuel is no more than ten gallons, Merlin engines consume 40 gallons an hour, and I am now over the sea with nothing below but a milky fog.

I immediately request Hornchurch for a course home and am given 280 degrees. I make it to Manston and land. After refuelling I head back to Fairlop and to find out how my squadron has fared in the battle.

The outcome of the fight is as follows: Pilot Officer Kučera made an emergency landing and is reported as wounded. Pilot Officer Jicha has his machine so badly shot-up as to be unfit for repair. I myself claim one enemy shot down and two probably so. Příhoda damaged one and so did Dohnal. However, we have lost Sergeant Pavlik, who was killed during an encounter with three Luftwaffe fighters.

During our supper in the mess, news comes that the new commanding officer of 122 Squadron, my friend Fajtl, only posted in a few days ago, is missing. I refuse to believe this at all and feel terribly depressed. I keep talking about Frank and in my heart I hope fervently that he is still safe and in good health. How could anyone shoot him down or out-manoeuvre him in the air? Now that you are not here with us you will not be able to celebrate the birthday of this squadron. 'Au Revoir, Frank', and I can assure you that I will avenge you!![7]

As it happened, Fajtl was alive. Circus 157 – six Bostons of 226 Squadron going for the power station at Lille – were met yet again by Priller and his III Gruppe of JG26. He had led his men in a broad sweep to the west of their base and gained height looking for a position to attack. As the RAF formation turned away from the target area, he dived onto 313 Squadron, and shot down

---

[7] Here, when Henry Prokop translated Fejfar's diary, he made the comment that he thought it a pity that Squadron Leader Mrázek did not seek Stanislav out and talk him out of this depressive feeling before Fejfar tried to take his revenge upon the Luftwaffe, with tragic results. But then again, one cannot blame the Slavonic soul for the depth of feeling and his lack of the British self-control that he so admired. After all, he had only been among the English for two years.

Sergeant Pavlik, who crashed to the ground south-west of Ypres. It was his 70th victory.

Other 190s of his Gruppe headed down to attack 122 Squadron. These were the 190s that Fejfar had seen heading down for Spitfires below and had tried to engage. The other JG26 pilots, led by Hauptmann Johannes Seifert, picked off four of 122's machines, one flown by Fajtl (BM210), another by a Belgian pilot, Flight Lieutenant B M G de Hemptine (BM321). Boudouin de Hemptine was 32 years old and had been in the pre-war Belgian air force. Escaping to England he had flown in the Battle of Britain with 145 Squadron, and in 1941 with 609 Squadron. At Hornchurch he had been with 64 Squadron before being made a flight commander in 122.

Leutnant Artur Beese of JG26 had shot down Fajtl, who crash-landed at Hardelot and was fortunate to make a successful evasion back to England via Spain and Gibraltar. He was back in the UK by August 1942. A year later he returned to 313 Squadron as its squadron commander. Leutnant Beese scored his 4th victory this day, out of a total of 22, but he did not survive the war, being shot down by American P47s in February 1944.

Sergeant Karel Pavlik, from Plzeň, was 23 years old. He is buried in the cemetery extension, at the famous Menin Gate at Ypres, Belgium. The Menin Gate Memorial has the names of over 50,000 British soldiers on it, denoting those who gave their lives in World War One around the Ypres area, and who have no known graves.

313 Squadron's Form 541 reports the action as follows:

> Hornchurch Wing (Nos. 64, 122 and 313 Squadrons) led by W/Cmdr R P R Powell DFC, flying with 64 Squadron, acted as high cover wing for 6 Bostons bombing Lille. Rendezvous Clacton at 10,000 feet with bombers, North Weald and Debden Wings. Wing crossed out South of Clacton and made landfall over French coast 5 miles East of Dunkirk stepped up:
>
> > 64 Squadron at 20,000 feet.
> > 122 Squadron at 21,000 feet.
> > 313 Squadron at 22,000 feet.
>
> Wing proceeded to target and when 5 miles SSE of Furnes, 6 FW190s and Me109s were seen 3 to 5 miles away at same height as wing, coming from direction of Ostende and flying parallel to the wing. These e/a followed the wing to Lille and as bombers turned right after bombing, two formations of FW190s (8 and 7 a/c respectively) were seen coming from direction of St Omer about 2,000 feet above and behind. At the same time 6 more FW190s (probably those from Ostende) were seen diving to attack 313 and 122 Squadrons, which fell back while evading attack and became involved in various dog fights. F/L Fejfar (Red 1) leading 313 Squadron warned the wing leader of e/a and immediately ordered

his squadron to break formation. He himself attacked two FW190s out of a formation of 6 and he saw the pilot of one aircraft bale out. This FW190 was claimed as destroyed. Red 1 went into a spin and lost 4,000 feet in height. He pulled out, climbed again and saw 2 FW190s on his port side about to attack 3 Spitfires. He opened cannon and MG fire expending all his ammunition as he closed from 300 to 200 yards. Before he could observe results, he saw in his mirror another FW190 behind and, taking evasive action, went into a further spin. Pulling out, a FW190 passed him on its back, with half its wing missing. As he saw another Spitfire at the same time and as e/a passed him in its spin immediately after his attack, he claimed this second FW190 as probably destroyed. P/O J Kučera saw 4 FW190s about to attack his section. As he turned, he noticed a further 6 FWs about to attack. He immediately engaged one of the latter closing from 200 to 100 yards, making a port quarter attack. He saw a large part of the wing fall off and white smoke, then black smoke pour from the e/a. He was unable to follow as several e/a were behind him. The last he saw of it was at 15,000 feet when it was smoking and in a vertical dive. It was claimed as probably destroyed.

Sgt Dohnal (Red 2) fired at one of four FW190s and the e/a immediately rolled on its back. Apart from this, no result was observed as friendly aircraft got in his way. P/O J Příhoda (Blue 3) fired at two of the same FW190s. After his second burst, they turned on their backs, rolled and dived away.

F/S Řezníček (Red 3) was attacked by 3 FW190s. He took violent evasive action and climbed into cloud, was again attacked by two FW190s at which he fired without observing results. In taking evasive action he found himself 10 miles W of Flushing, where heavy flak was observed. P/O Jicha (Yellow 2) was attacked by 4 FW190s and his aircraft received several hits (Cat.B). He was protected in a magnificent manner by 2 Spitfires of 122 Squadron.

P/O O Kučera (Yellow 2) was attacked by 6 FW190s after leaving Lille and fired a short deflection burst from 100 yards at one. E/a immediately made one and a half quick rolls and grey smoke was seen to come from it. As pilot was again attacked, he lost sight of the e/a and made no claim. On reaching the French coast at about 6,000 feet, he was again attacked by 3 FW190s. He did a series of light turns down to sea level, but e/a continued to attack him, sometimes singly and at other times one from astern and the others from above and head-on. He got in four separate bursts at the a/c making head-on attacks but saw no definite results. Attacks continued until he reached a belt of fog somewhere in the North Sea. He eventually crossed English coast near Dymchurch and while searching for aerodrome, his engine cut out from lack of petrol and he force landed at Newchurch on Romney Marshes at 16.40 hours. His aircraft was severely damaged by hitting an obstruction post

(Cat.E) and the pilot slightly injured with abrasions to head and leg and with slight concussion.

Pilots involved and the Spitfires they were flying: F/L Fejfar BL973, Sgt Dohnal BM137, F/L Vancl BM248, P/O J Kučera BM209, P/O Jicha BM306, P/O O Kučera BM323, P/O Příhoda BM301, F/S Řezníček BM242, Sgt Kotiba AR397, Sgt Pavlik BM361, Sgt Kocfelda BM374, Sgt Borkovec BM328.

Deciding on a tally for any fighter pilot is never clear cut. Often there are several interpretations of a score by a number of different people. Chris Shores in his massive book on WW2 fighter aces and their scores, *Aces High* credits Fejfar with five destroyed, two probably destroyed and three damaged, although he actually lists six destroyed and two shared. Another, Czech, source indicates five destroyed, two shared, one probable, and one damaged.

Chris Shores also records two enemy aircraft damaged, one on 27 February (a FW190) and another on 12 March 1942 (a Me109). Although Chris points out that neither of these appear in RAF records he was told they apparently are shown in Fejfar's flying log-book. This is odd because he does not appear to have been in combat during this early part of 1942, nor are there entries in his diary about these combats. A photograph of his Spitfire which he flew in 1942, BL973, with his personal insignia by the cockpit of, presumably, the Disney dog character Pluto, with the words 'Tally-Ho' coming from its mouth, has six and a half victory marks (German crosses) which indicates that Fejfar himself counted this $6^1/_2$ as being his 'score'. Ordinarily this sort of personal tally on an aircraft would not include probable victories or those damaged.

Chapter Ten

The Final Days

The Hornchurch Wing were out again on the 6th, a Rodeo operation that began shortly after mid-day. 313 Squadron was led by Mrázek but Fejfar was not part of the 12-man sortie. Wing Commander Powell led the wing at the head of 64 Squadron, and they linked up with the boys from North Weald. Peter Powell was hoping that, after control reported enemy aircraft were to the east of them, by sweeping round behind them, therefore coming from the east, they might surprise them, but nothing was seen. No doubt by this time someone had called up the German controller to report there were no bombers in the RAF formation, so leave well alone.

7th May 1942

Today is my name day, but not celebrated here in England. Nobody would know except my mother, and possibly a tear or two are shed, but it is impossible to write to her to say that I am still alive, and that my time has not yet come. Perhaps tomorrow or a day after that it may come, or I may even survive all this unscathed.

At 10 am comes what I now refer to as an 'excursion' over France. As explained before I don't feel able to write about things, if nothing happens. Yet, yes, the Germans have their factories and railways bombarded every day.

I was given 24-hours rest and in the meantime my flight was on the other side twice this afternoon facing those horrible ack-ack streamers, carrying death for someone. Two Me109s appeared, but as usual, quickly vanished. And they call themselves the master race!![1]

9th May 1942

Today is the day before our anniversary of the founding of this 313 Czech Fighter Squadron in England. We were supposed to have a day

---

[1] The two shows on this day were Circus 164, six Bostons of 266 Squadron going for the power station at Ostende, and Circus 165, six Bostons of 88 Squadron, bombing the docks at Dieppe.

off and our planned Czech meal was to have been taken in the NCO's mess and the airmen's dining hall. It was booked for 3 pm but then ops had a job for us twice this afternoon. The first one I missed but the second one was over Belgium. This time FW190s arrived but flying as close escort we could not break off to attack, and instead, remained close to the bombers. Nevertheless, one of our pilots, Pilot Officer Příhoda, managed to shoot down one FW190 and when he landed, we discovered that the whole station was waiting to begin our 313 anniversary celebrations.

The officer commanding 11 Group of Fighter Command (Leigh-Mallory) was here, and also our Czech C-in-C, Air Commodore Janoušek, with several other visitors, so we totalled some 48 people. Our Czech cooks obviously prepared continental savoury specialities, much appreciated during a time of war utility meals. Air Commodore Janoušek then awarded some English pilots with the official silver wings such as those worn by Czech pilots on active duty.

Much later, Charlie Mrázek, with suitable alcoholic encouragement, began dancing like a Russian cossack on the floor, interspersed with those high kicking jumps. I eventually fall into my bed when *the* day has arrived – 10th May.

Today's operations were Circus 168, which entailed six bombers of 266 attacking the marshalling yards at Hazebrouck, and Circus 170, again six of 88 Squadron, this time bombing oil tanks near Bruges. Pips Priller and his III Gruppe of JG26 were in evidence but for once were unable to engage, as his pilots were cut off by German aircraft from II Gruppe. However, Priller re-grouped and managed to engage aircraft of the RAF's 10 Group, Fighter Command, flying in support, and shot down four Spitfires, Priller himself gaining his 71st victory north of Gravelines. JG26 lost two pilots in this action, both shot down by Spitfires, although three were claimed, with another probable and six damaged. Příhoda's claim was for a 'damaged' only.

The other Circus was also engaged by JG26 and they claimed just one Spitfire, and only one was lost by the RAF.

10th May 1942

You are not entitled to a rest after all those energetic dances, and I am back at the pilot's dispersal hut this morning. We are off to France and I calculate today that this will be my 40th 'excursion' to Belgium, Holland and France with the RAF. What else can I write about our squadron? Many are missing from our original group of escapees from our homeland back in 1939. All I wish to add, is that my present CO and dearest friend will be even more successful in downing more and more Nazi swine during the coming period of fighting!

This proved to be Stanislav Fejfar's final entry in his diary.

* * *

WHAT HAPPENED TO STANISLAV FEJFAR?
The weather was bad between the 10th and 16th, and nothing much occurred, although on 16 May some flying took place. Some pilots were assigned a convoy patrol late morning and again in the early afternoon, and at 15.30 pm, Mrázek led a practise formation flight for an hour and a half, which included Fejfar. Mrázek then departed and landed at Hornchurch, leaving Fejfar to take the others back to Fairlop. On this flight Fejfar was flying another Spitfire, not his usual BL973, but BM301, at least that is what is recorded in the squadron's Form 541.

* * *

The weather on 17 May 1942 was reasonable. Visibility was good, ten to twenty miles and clear over the English Channel. Above northern France there was 8/10ths cloud at 23,000 feet.

The Hornchurch Wing were once again scheduled for an operation, this time a Ramrod – Ramrod 33 – with 12 Bostons from 266 Squadron that were slated to bomb the docks at Boulogne. Squadron Leader Mrázek led 12 Spitfires off at 10.40 to join up with the other wing squadrons from Hornchurch and to make rendezvous with the North Weald Wing at 500 feet, then with the Bostons over Beachy Head, where they would cross out and head over the Channel.

313 Squadron comprised:

S/L K Mrázek	BM242	F/L S Fejfar	BL973[2]

[2] It is always dangerous to think that RAF Forms 541 are accurate and can be trusted implicitly. Generally they are only as good as the men who typed or wrote them up at the end of each day. It has been proven that from time to time, the compilers would just look up the previous day's flying times and note down the same aircraft serial number that such and such a pilot flew the previous day, irrespective of the fact they may have flown another machine. It has also been found that hard-pressed intelligence officers were not averse even to making up numbers rather than spend extra time checking out exactly who had flown what. A lot of the time it depended on how astute the squadron commander was when it came to signing the diary entries. Today this is a case in point for we know that Fejfar flew his usual BL973 on this operation. Whether he, for some reason, flew BM301 the previous day, and someone just copied this number down for the 17th will never be known.

BM301 was on the squadron, having arrived on 14 April, and is recorded as being written-off on 28 June with 611 Squadron, whence it had been sent on 17 June, after crash-landing near Eastbourne following a combat with JG26 over England. Two FW190s had been sent on an evening reconnaissance to southern England and two Spitfires had been scrambled after them. High over Beachy Head they clashed, the two German pilots each claiming one shot down. In the event only one Spitfire was hit sufficiently for its pilot to be forced to make a crash-landing, in which he broke an arm.

F/S F Vavřínek	BM248	Sgt M Borkovec	BM360
F/O V Jícha	BM207	P/O J Kučera	BM117
Sgt V Přerost	BM127	Sgt V Horák	BM203
F/O A Hochmal	BM317	W/O V Fogler	BM131
Sgt J Dohnal	BM322	Sgt P Kocfelda	BM314

* * *

The RAF formation set course for Hardelot from mid-Channel but turned slightly to port and had gained height to 22,000 feet by the time they crossed the French coast. Six large AA puffs were seen over the target area and eventually the whole harbour became enveloped in black smoke.

Course was then set for St Omer and then on towards Mardyck. However, before reaching Mardyck, and still slightly south of it, a right-hand orbit was made as enemy fighters were reported in the immediate vicinity. Six FW190s were then seen passing 313 Squadron to the right, 2,000 feet below but they were not engaged. Course was then set towards Ambleteuse but before reaching there, and when over Marquise, 313 turned slightly to starboard.

Jagdgeschwader 26 had been scrambled at 11.13 (German time) while the Bostons and their escort were still over Hastings, and they were ordered to assemble over St Pol. Once the bombers were over their target, the 190s found large formations of Spitfires between them and the Bostons, not only the direct escort fighters, but other wings flying in support. They were therefore in a good position to attack some of the Spitfires.

Leading his III Gruppe was Pips Priller and he was able to make what was described as a text-book stern attack on the rear Spitfire, which turned out to be from 313 Squadron. He closed in to 20 yards before opening fire and he watched as large pieces flew off the RAF fighter, which then burst into flames and went into a vertical dive to crash between Guines and Audembert.

Leutnant Johann Aistleitner, a wingman in Priller's staff-section (Stabsschwarm) also claimed a Spitfire and so did Oberleutnant Karl Borris, leader of the 8th Staffel. Meantime, Oberleutnant Johannes Seifert's I Gruppe's Focke Wulfs waded into the other two Hornchurch squadrons, 64 and 122, and shot down three.

II Gruppe of JG26, flying a little more inland, attacked Spitfires of the Kenley Wing and shot down one from 602 Squadron, then chased the others out over the sea, downing another from this squadron. A 10 Group Wing, flying rear support to the operation, was engaged by JG2, and this unit shot down a Spitfire of 402 Canadian Squadron.

When the action began, Flight Lieutenant Fejfar, Blue 1, and his Number 2, Sergeant Borkovec, had turned to port and lost height. Blue 3 and 4 followed, Blue 3 calling Fejfar telling him that the rest of the squadron had turned to starboard, but he received no reply, and then he lost sight of the two Spitfires. Blue 3 and 4 regained position with the squadron and they all crossed out over Ambleteuse, where they reformed with the rest of the wing and headed back across the Channel to Dungeness.

Upon landing back at Fairlop around 12.10, it was soon clear that Fejfar and his wingman were missing. For a while it was hoped that both or either of them would turn up, or at least call in from another airfield where they might have had to land to refuel. But as the time went by, it became obvious that neither would be coming home.

The wing lost two aircraft from 64, two from 122 and two from 313. Exactly who shot down the 313 pair is unclear. It seems fairly obvious that Pips Priller and Aistleitner had been the two responsible for downing them, but who got who is uncertain. Priller claimed that he attacked a rear Spitfire which suggests he attacked Borkovec, the wingman, and that therefore, Aistleitner had attacked Fejfar, but it might easily be the other way around. Priller's victory – his 72nd – was claimed at 11.33, south of Guines-Audembert. Leutnant Aistleitner claimed his at 11.43, 15 kilometres north-west of Calais. It was his 7th victory.

However, the fact that Priller saw his victim crash (see combat report below) seems to confirm it was Fejfar, whose remains were recovered and buried by the Germans, whereas Borkovec's remains were not, and as Aistleitner reports his victim going down 15 km north-west of Calais, this would be over the sea.

Miroslav Borkovec came from Brno, and was just a month short of his 26th birthday. He has no known grave and his name appears on the Runnymede RAF memorial to the missing.

The Hornchurch Form 540 records the operation as follows:

> The operation of the day was RAMROD 33. Led by Wing Commander Powell, the wing took off by 10.47, rendezvousing with 12 Bostons over Beachy Head. Our role was to act as target support (with Northolt) to the Bostons which were attacking Boulogne. Having gone in at Le Touquet the wing flew towards St Omer flying at 21-23,000 ft. Many FW190s were sighted and leaving 313 Squadron up above to act as umbrella, 64 and 122 Squadrons attacked. Many combats ensued and as a result, W/Cdr Powell destroyed a FW190, as did S/Ldr Smith, 64 Squadron, and S/Ldr Prevot and P/O Rolls, 122 Squadron. Besides this, F/Lt Thomas and Sgt Stewart, 64 Squadron, together with F/Lt Hallowes and F/Lt Griffiths, 122 Squadron, got probables (all FW190s) and Sgt Harrison, 64 Squadron, F/Lt Hallowes (2), P/O Dunkin, P/O Prest and P/O Rolls, all got FW190s damaged. Our casualties were P/O Baraw and Sgt Bennett, 64 Squadron, F/Lt Barthropp and P/O Muller, 122 Squadron, and F/Lt Fejfar and Sgt Borkovec, 13 Squadron. Flak from Boulogne and Calais was intense. Our aircraft landed by 12.20.

One pilot mentioned in this report, Flight Lieutenant Paddy Barthropp DFC, was a well known character in the RAF, and wrote an interesting little book in 1987, entitled *Paddy, the life and times of Wing Commander Patrick Barthropp DFC AFC*. Co-author of this book, Norman Franks, had the pleasure of meeting Paddy on one occasion and found him a lively character indeed. In his book Paddy records his last flight and his joining 122 Squadron having been posted away by the station commander at Heston, who had had enough of Paddy and his antics.

> ....Parker had now had enough of me, and sent me packing to 122 Squadron at Hornchurch. I drove down in my newly-acquired drop-head Rover, which my trustee had bought me for a twenty-first birthday present. I arrived on May 12th, and began a series of sector reconnaissance flights, interspersed with the odd convoy patrol with A Flight. At this time I had completed three hundred and seventeen operations for the loss of one Lysander and two badly holed Spitfires. Not a bad record. I didn't know it, but I was nearing the end of my war.
>
> I had been at Hornchurch five days when I took off with countless other Spitfires and six (*sic*) Bostons .... I hated sweeps over the Channel and realised just how the Germans felt in 1940. Around twenty thousand feet we were attacked by FW190s, a type I hadn't seen before.
>
> Jim Hallowes, a most experienced pilot, had always told me never to break away from the formation but, as the Huns whipped past us, I thought the opportunity was too good to be missed and off I went on my own. The exercise proved fairly costly.
>
> Two FW190s, flown by Hauptmanns Karl Willius and Rolf Hermichen respectively, appeared from nowhere. In the process of my dispatching Herr Hermichen to his ancestors, Willius had got behind me, letting me have it very forcibly with 20 mm cannon that removed the bottom part of the rudder bar and the control column. There was no alternative but to bale out, praying silently that Mr Irvin's magic silk device would function effectively.
>
> In a way, I suppose, it can be said that it did.... Although my parachute opened correctly my worries were far from over. Willius followed me down, doing dummy attacks, trying to collapse my canopy and, as I had previously witnessed pilots being shot at while making a parachute descent I really thought I was a goner. It was a beautiful day and below I could see little figures in uniform converging towards my anticipated point of arrival.
>
> The landing wasn't one of my best. I hit the roof of a barn, crashing to the concrete floor below. Having seen my free fall display into his barn, a French farmer appeared and I just had time to hand over to him the francs that had been provided for use in the eventuality of escape, together with my parachute, and then the dreaded Wehrmacht were entering the scene in force.

That evening Karl Willius visited Paddy Barthropp while being kept under guard in a house, and the two fighter pilots chatted for some time, and when Barthropp told him that his captors had stolen his gold Hunter watch and silver cigarette case, Willius was able to reunite them with their owner.

Karl Willius would achieve 50 combat victories before his own death to American P47s over Holland in April 1944. Most were achieved in the west, although he did score 17 kills on the Russian front. Like Priller, 11 of his victories were over four-engined bombers. It is not clear why Barthropp thought he had killed Rolf Hermichen, for he didn't die this day. Indeed, he went on to command JG26's 3rd Staffel till June 1943, gain 64 victories and survive the war. There are no reported losses in JG26 this date but perhaps in talking, Willius had mentioned that Hermichen's 190 had been hit and damaged, if not actually shot down.

Since the war it has been firmly believed that it had been Pips Priller who had in fact shot down Fejfar. Josef Priller came from Ingolstadt, Bavaria, born in June 1915. A pre-war pilot he had been Staffelkapitän of the 6th Staffel of JG51 and fought during the Battle of France and during the Battle of Britain. In November 1940 he had taken command of JG26's 1st Staffel and just over a year later, took charge of JG26's III Gruppe. His combat report for this action with 313 Squadron, translated, reads:

Josef Priller   Headquarters, 17.5.42.
Hauptmann and Gruppenkommandeur
III/Jagdgeschwader 'Schlagater' Nr.26

Combat Report

Take off: 11.17 hours   Landed: 11.55 hours
Engagement: 11.33-35 hours

On 17.5.42, at 11.17 hours, I started with the Group to repel the attack of the English enemy. At 11.33 I attacked from behind from a height of 5,000 metres, 2 Spitfires and fired from a distance of between 50 to 20 metres. I saw the last of the two Spitfires had large pieces disintegrate from it and it burst into flames, flipped over and went straight down and crashed. I dived through the clouds after him and saw the Spitfire crashing into the ground. I cannot exactly pinpoint the position; it might have been between Guines and Audembert. I cannot give the exact position because I was flying at a speed of 759 km/h. Immediately after that I chased several other Spitfires at low altitude.

Priller had been awarded the Knight's Cross of the Iron Cross (the Ritterkreuz) in October 1940 after 20 victories and then the Oak Leaves to this decoration in July 1941, following his 41st victory. He would go on to win the Swords to his Knight's Cross in July 1944 by which time his score was 100 – all scored in the West, rather than on the Eastern (Russian) Front, where victories were easier to attain.

In all he shot down 101 Allied aircraft, including 11 four-engined American bombers. On D-Day – 6 June 1944 – he gained fame as being, with his wingman, the only German fighter pilot to strafe the invading forces along the Normandy beaches. A larger-than-life character, he was one of the Luftwaffe's foremost personalities, as depicted, perhaps a trifle extravagantly, in the film *The Longest Day*. He survived Fejfar by three days over 19 years, dying of a heart attack in Augsburg on 20 May 1961, just short of his 46th birthday.

Johann Aistleitner, having risen to Hauptmann and leader of JG26's 5th Staffel, was killed in action with Allied fighters near Montdidier, France, on 14 January 1944, having brought his score to 11, although he had not been in combat for almost a year when he was killed.

*   *   *

Fejfar's comrades on 313 Squadron were extremely saddened by his loss. For a while there was always the hope that he and Borkovec had survived, even if downed over France. They may be prisoners, or even on the run, hoping to evade capture. Being Czech and with some knowledge of French, Fejfar was in a better position than many RAF pilots who tried to evade. If questioned by Germans there was every chance he could talk his way out of trouble. Sadly that was not to be. Stanislav Fejfar had not survived his last encounter with JG26.

In England most families were soon informed of the loss of a loved one on operations, whether their death was known, or if they were merely missing. For Fejfar's family back in Czechoslovakia, there would be no news, no devastating telegram, no consoling letter from a comrade or commanding officer. It would not be until the end of the war that his mother was given the news that her son had died three years earlier. In 1945 she finally received a letter from Stanislav's former CO with 313 Squadron, giving her the details of her son's last mission.

Dear Mr and Mrs Fejfar,

I knew your son since our pilot school and military academy in 1932. I am now saying goodbye to my colleague, after ten years on continuous service, including a period in the French Foreign Legion.

It is I Karel Mrázek whom you will find in his remarks throughout his diary. I was also his last commanding officer and we both were very sad indeed when our best friend from our 'Three Musketeers', Squadron Leader Frank Fajtl, did not return from an operational flight on 5th May. And today, the 17th May 1942, without the wound of Fajtl's disappearance being healed, it is the turn of your son Stanislav. I am left alone now from the three of us, but fervently hope that they will both return since other pilots did not see them fall to earth.

It is of course my duty to describe the events of the last flight on 17th May 1942. The task was to escort twelve bombers to destroy the harbour of Boulogne. We were flying at 24,000 feet and after the bombers were returning to England, we were following. Suddenly, Stanislav, with his Number Two – Borkovec – was returning towards Calais [and enemy aircraft are seen]. I called on the radio [to describe] what was occurring and perhaps he saw an opportunity of avenging Frank but by this time we could not observe anything untoward, except that no fight was seen to take place. Then again, by this time we were too far from the French coast.

After our return we quickly noticed that Stanislav and his Number Two had not returned. I am convinced that he and Borkovec sold their skins to the German fighters very dearly!

To you, dear parents, I can only thank you both on how well you brought your son up and that our dear fatherland had, in him, one of the best fighter pilots. This has been acknowledged already during our sojourn in France where he received one of the highest decorations, which is the Croix de Guerre, with two palms and a star. In England he was, after two years of flying, awarded the Czech War Medal 1939, three times, and also the Medal of Bravery twice.

You should be proud of your heroic son.

Signed, Wing Commander K Mrázek DSO DFC.

Another letter sent to his family was from General K Janoušek himself, a month after the war ended:

Inspectorate
Czechoslovak Air Force

15 Grosvenor Place
London, SW1

6 June 1945

Dear Mr Junek,
I am sorry to confirm the news I am sure you already know by telegram.

Captain Stanislav Fejfar, born 25.11.1912 in Stikov was one of the greatest members of the Czechoslovakian foreign air force. With his bravery and energy he promoted the good name of the Czechoslovakian air force in foreign countries. After his arrival in the UK he was posted to a Czechoslovak fighter squadron, and very quickly became one of its best pilots, which made the squadron proud. But on 17th May 1942 he did not return from an operational flight over occupied territory. Later that year, in December 1942, we received a message from the International Red Cross that Captain Fejfar was buried in an army cemetery in Pihen, near Calais.

He lost his fight with the enemy as a faithful son of his country and brave defender of our ideals and freedom. His personal belongings will be sent to you as soon as possible.

I do feel with you your pain and thank you in my name and that of the Czechoslovak Air Force for his sacrifice and our victory, which was achieved by the help of Captain Fejfar.

Janoušek

Pan Alois Junek,
Nová Paka,
Žižkova 11.

*   *   *

Also by the document shown here, dated 1946, the Czech air force in Prague gave Fejfar a posthumous promotion to headquarters group captain, with these words to his mother (see pages 208-209):

By giving you this information I assure you that the Czechoslovakian Air Force will never forget his sacrifice and will forever remember his brilliant example of self-sacrifice and the love for his country and to the Air Force.

*   *   *

Of course, by late 1945 many Czechoslovak airmen were starting to return to their homeland, but it soon became clear that the victory they had helped achieve was somewhat tainted by the people who were now running the country, mainly those of the communist regime. If the first couple of years proved difficult, in 1948 it became impossible. The new People's Democratic Constitution were suspicious of the returning 'heroes' who had fought in the west and very soon many of them began to be rounded up and arrested. Many were imprisoned without trial, while others were made to work in the mines, with their families being thrown out of their homes.

František Fajtl was one, and although he was told he was only being taken away for questioning for an hour or so, he was thrown into Mirov prison where he remained for 17 months. The worst of it was he had no idea why.

Karel Mrázek too was imprisoned, so both remaining 'Musketeers' were in jail. Even the great Karel Janoušek was arrested, having first been given trivial work in the Czech air force, and then spent 11 years in prison. He had been declared to be 'an enemy of the people'. Václav Šikl, a pilot who had served in 310 Squadron, was also under suspicion and his friends advised him to escape. He could not believe his liberty, the liberty he had fought for so long, was under threat, so decided to stay. As he was later to admit, it was the worst decision he ever made and it cost him 7 years in a communist prison.

Others acted more quickly and decisively and began to escape from their country yet again. It was a repeat of the exodus in 1938, except now there was no 'enemy' to fight against. As one man put it, in 1938 they knew who the enemy was. In 1948 you did not, nor did one know whom to trust. Many escaping former RAF personnel managed to return to England, where they remained, a number actually rejoining the Royal Air Force.

Perhaps it was as well that Stanislav Fejfar did not live to see his country ravaged by the regime of communism. It would have broken his stout heart.

Stanislav Fejfar's mortal remains were recovered by the Germans and were buried in Pihen-Les-Guines cemetery (grave C-8), located 10 kilometres south-west of Calais. When he was killed he held the rank of captain.

In 1947 he was posthumously promoted to major and on 1 August 1991 to the rank of lieutenant-colonel. On 3 May of the previous year he was made an honorary citizen of Nova Paká, his home town.

There is also a street named in his honour, by the Black Bridge in Prague, 14 District.

Fejfar's original grave near Calais. Note the German spelling of 'Czeck'.

Fejfar's CWGC gravestone at Pihen-les-Guines cemetery, Calais, France.

Appreciations

*Gordon Sinclair DFC and Franti*š*ek Fajtl DFC*

On 25 April 1996, Wing Commander G L Sinclair OBE DFC wrote the following letter in relation to Stanislav Fejfar, quoted at length in the Foreword to this book:

> 'Stanislav Fejfar was one of a group of Czechoslovakian pilots, who formed the nucleus of 310 (Czech) Squadron of which I had the honour of helping to form and build up immediately before the Battle of Britain in June-July 1940.

> 'Like the other pilots and the ground crew, Fejfar spoke no English when he arrived at Duxford, but his intentions were clear from the outset, to get at the Germans.

> 'That he and his fellow pilots fulfilled their intentions became abundantly clear from the moment that 310 Squadron was declared operationally fit to join the battle.

> 'I flew with Fejfar on many sorties, over the Thames estuary in particular, meeting up with the Luftwaffe bombers and their escorting fighters. I can only say that it was a wonderful comfort to me knowing that I was fighting with such gallant and determined men as Fejfar and his fellow Czechs.

> 'His diaries are a vivid reminder of what he represented in gallantry and courage.'

Gordon Sinclair died on 26 June 2005.

* * *

Major-general František Fajtl died a little over a year later, on 4 October 2006. However, he too left an appreciation of his friend Stanislav, in a letter to Simon Muggleton, which says:

> 'Flight Lieutenant Fejfar was a dear friend of mine and was an excellent fighter pilot and flight commander. He fought in France and was very successful in bringing down some Germans. Many years we lived together and both wrote diaries. I often think of him and his devotion to his country and to Great Britain. We brothers should never forget the terrific war effort of Great Britain during the Second World War and it should never disappear from our minds or hearts.'

Appendix A

Czech Air Force Students 1932-33

This is a list of student comrades of Stan Fejfar, with remarks concerning those who later made their way to England to fight with the Royal Air Force.

Holeka, Commander

Student	Birth date	RAF	Died
Jasmín Fikrle	25 May 1912	F/Lt navigator 311 Sqn	4 Jan 1989
M Jadrníček			
J Strejc			
Tomáš Vybíral	29 Sep 1911	W/Cdr pilot, France, BofB 312 Sqn, HQ CAF DSO DFC Ld'H CdG	21 Feb 1981
Vlastimil Veselý	20 Sep 1913	S/Ldr pilot, France, 312 Sqn BofB, 68 Sqn; DFC AFC	
L Fibikar			
Josef E Hýbler	18 Sep 1913	F/Lt pilot, France, 310 Sqn BofB, 234 & 286 Sqns.	9 Jan 1984
J Soustružník			
P Šulek			
V Janíček			
J Bohuslavický			
S Ferdus			
R Navara			
L Hajda			
V Jiříčka			
O Sidlák			
František Sýkora	24 Nov 1911	S/Ldr pilot, 68 Sqn	24 Dec 1988

B Petráš

Stanislav Fejfar	25 Nov 1912	F/Lt pilot, France, 310 Sqn BofB, 313 Sqn	17 May 1942

M Štěpánek
F Reichelt
J Maloušek

Josef J Hanuš	13 Sep 1911	W/Cdr pilot, France, 310 Sqn BofB, 32 & 245 Sqns, 600 & 125 Sqns 1942-43 DFC CdG, Czech War Cross	15 Apr 1992

K Štarman
J Smetana
J Falta
F Danda

Karel Mrázek	29 Nov 1910	G/Capt pilot, France, 43 & 46 Sqns BofB, OC 313 Sqn 1941-1942, Czech W/Ldr, DSO DFC	5 Dec 1998

F Štefančič
J Polák
B Kepert
B Klement

Appendix B

310 Squadron Pilots

Pilots who flew alongside Fejfar during the Battle of Britain

P/O Václav Bergman	France. W/Cdr RAF, OC 313 Sqn DFC (Bar to DFC during Korean War 209 Sqn.) Rt'd from RAF 1969.
F/Lt G D M Blackwood	213, then 310 Sqn. Czech War Cross. HQ 12 Group, Stn Cdr 10 Group, OC 134 Wing 2nd TAF. Died March 1997
F/O John E Boulton	Killed in action 9 September 1940.
P/O František Burda	France. PoW April 1943. Died in Feb 1988.
Sgt Alois Dvorak	Killed in flying accident 24 Sep 1941.
P/O František Fajtl	France. 310 and 1 Sqns. 313 Sqn, then OC 122 Sqn. Shot down and evaded back to UK and awarded DFC. OC 313 Sqn 1943. OC Czech Sqn in Russia 1944. Died October 2006.
P/O Emil Fechtner	France. Awarded DFC. Killed in action 29 Oct 1940.
Sgt Bohumir Fürst (Fiřt)	France. Czech MC, F/Lt RAF 1946. Died 2 Jan 1978.
P/O Vilem Göth	Also 501 Sqn – killed in action 25 October 1940.
P/O Josef J Hanus	France. 68 Sqn DFC. Rt'd from RAF in 1968 as a Sqn Ldr. Died April 1992.
S/L Alexander Hess	France. Awarded DFC. USA 1942. Group Captain. Lived in USA post war – died August 1981.
P/O František Hradil	France. 19 Sqn – killed in action 29 August 1940.

Sgt Josef Hubaček	France. Rt'd from RAF as F/Lt after the war.
P/O Josef E Hýbler	France. 234 & 286 Sqns 1942. Died January 1984.
P/O Svatopluk Janouch	France. Rt'd from RAF as S/Ldr.
F/Lt Jerrard Jefferies	France with 85 Sqn. DFC, Czech MC. Changed his name to Latimer. Killed with 106 Sqn (Lancasters) April 1943.
F/Sgt Miroslav Jiroudek	France. 68 Sqn 1942-43. 24 Sqn 1944-45, F/Lt. Airline captain post-war. Died March 1995.
Sgt Jan Kaucký	France. Rt'd from RAF as F/Lt 1946. Airline pilot post-war. Died August 1970.
F/Sgt Josef Kominek	France. Killed in flying accident 8 June 1941. Awarded Czech MC.
Sgt Josef Kopřiva	France. Rt'd from RAF post-war as a F/Lt. Died June 1976.
Sgt Josef Koukal	France. Badly burned 7 Sept 1940. F/Lt. Test pilot in Czechoslovakia post-war. Died February 1980.
P/O Miroslav Kredba	France. Killed in flying accident with 310 as a F/Lt 14 February 1942.
P/O Jiri J Machaček	France. 145 Sqn. Killed in action as F/O 8 July 1941.
P/O Jaroslav Malý	France. Took his own life in June 1941.
Sgt František Marek	France. Killed on active service 14 September 1940.
Sgt Stanislav Plzak	France. 19 Sqn. Killed in action 7 August 1940.
Sgt Edward M Prchal	France. 68 Sqn 1941. 511 Sqn. Airline pilot post-war, having become a F/Lt. Died December 1984.
Sgt Raimund Půda	France. F/Lt RAF, Rt'd 1954. Awarded the Queen's Commendation for Service in the Air (1953). Died in March 2002.
Sgt Josef Řechka	France. RAF F/Lt, awarded AFC. Died January 1984.

P/O František Rypl	France. Ended the war as a F/Lt. Died August 1973.
Sgt Karel Šeda	France. Later with 68 Sqn and became F/Lt. Died June 1992.
F/Lt Gordon L Sinclair	DFC and Czech MC. OC 313 Sqn 1941, then OC 79 Sqn. Rt'd as a W/Cdr in 1957. Died June 2005.
P/O Jaroslav Štěrbáček	France. Killed in action 31 August 1940.
F/Sgt Jaromír P Střihavka	France. Rt'd from RAF as F/Lt, having changed his name to P J Scott. Died July 1994.
Sgt František Vindis	France. DFC. 313 Sqn in 1944. Rt'd from RAF in 1961 as a F/Lt. Died February 1991.
W/O Josef Volpálecký	France. 68 Sqn 1941, became a F/Lt. Died in May 1995.
P/O Vladimir Zaoral	France. 501 Sqn. Killed in flying accident with 310 Sqn, 19 November 1941, as F/O.
Sgt Rudolf Zima	France. Left the RAF as a F/Lt. Died June 1972.
P/O Stanislav Zimprich	France. Killed in flying accident with 310 on 12 April 1942, as F/O.

* * *

Stanislav Fejfar's promotions with the Royal Air Force:
Pilot Officer   2 August 1940
            Flying Officer   27 December 1940
            Flight Lieutenant   27 December 1941

And the dates of his postings:
Attached to RAF   2 August 1940
            310 Squadron   6 August 1940
            No. 6 OTU   17 August 1940
            310 Squadron   8 September 1940
            Sick   1 November 1940
            Czech Inspectorate   21 March 1941
            313 Squadron   21 July 1941
            Non-effective   15 March 1942
            313 Squadron   13 April 1942

Appendix C

Czech Losses & Achievements in France

Czech personnel performed well whilst attached to the Armée de l'Air, claiming an estimated 158 enemy aircraft confirmed or probably so. Many were shared with other pilots.

The high scoring Czech pilots in France were:

Captain Alois Vašátko	GC I/5	12 victories[1]
Lieutenant František Peřina	GC I/5	11 victories[2]
Sergeant Václav Eric Cukr	GC II/3	9 victories
Lieutenant Tomáš Vybíral	GC I/5	7 victories[3]
Sergeant Josef Stehlík	GC III/3	6 victories[4]

The list of those Czech fighter pilots who died in France 1939-40 is as follows:

Name	Location	Date	Unit
Sergeant František Bartoň	Chartres	6 October	Fighter OTU
Sergeant Jaroslav Křížek	Toulouse	16 November	Bomber OTU
Corporal Jaroslav Novák	Villefort	15 December	Bomber OTU
Sergeant Vladimir Vašek	Malancourt	2 January	GC I/5
Sergeant Miroslav Rajtr	Chartres	11 January	Fighter OTU
Corporal Jaroslav Stoklasa	Pau	4 March	Bomber OTU
Sergeant Jaroslav Krákora	Chantilly	23 April	GC I/1
Captain František Novák	Paris	27 April	(Illness)
Corporal Zdeněk Eichelman	Toulouse	29 April	KIFA/bomber
Corporal Jan Cerny	Châteauroux	11 May	(Air Raid)
Captain Jindřich Beran (a)	Wettern	11 May	GC III/3
Captain Timoteus Hamšík (a)	Sedan	14 May	GC I/5
Lieutenant Vladimir Kučera	Etampes	14 May	Fighter OTU
Lieutenant František Dýma	Senlis	21 May	GC III/7
Lieutenant František Bieberle	Arras	25 May	GC I/6

[1] Vašátko was credited with two more confirmed victories with the RAF.
[2] Peřina was credited with one victory with the RAF in 1942.
[3] Vybíral was credited with one shared victory with the RAF in 1942.
[4] Stehlík was credited with four victories with the RAF and on the Russian front.

Lieutenant Antonin Mikolášek (b)	Paris	25 May	GC II/3
Sergeant Antonin Králík (a)	Amiens	27 May	GC 1/8
Warrant Officer Josef Novák	Toulouse	2 June	GC III/3
Lieutenant Josef Dekastello (a)	Thieux	3 June	GC I/8
Sergeant Stanislav Popelka (a)	Ozoir-la-Ferrière	3 June	GC I/6
Sergeant Josef Kosnar	Amiens	5 June	GC III/7
Sergeant Josef Hranička (a)	Compiègne	5 June	GC I/6
Lieutenant Otakar Korec	Amiens	5 June	GC I/3
Sergeant Josef Bendl	Amiens	7 June	GC I/6
Lieutenant Jiří Král (a)	Montdidier	8 June	GC I/1
Lieutenant Jaroslav Gleich (b)	Avord	13 June	GC II/3
Adjutant Emil Morávek	Langres	17 Jun	GC I/5

(a) credited with one victory; (b) credited with two victories.

The list of Czech pilots who served with GC I/6 is:

Captain Jaroslav Kulhánek *
Captain Svatopluk Janouch *
Sergeant Stanslav Popelka +
Adjutant Josef Hranička +
Sous-lieutenant Vaclav Jicha *++
Adjutant Miloslav Štandera *
Captain Stanislav Fejfar *++

Sous-lieutenant Jiri Kučera *
Sergeant Josef Bendl +
Adjutant Vladimír Horský *++
Lieutenant František Bieberle +
Lieutenant Bohuslav V Kimlička *
Adjutant František Mlejnecký

+ Killed in France
++ Killed with the RAF
* Served with the RAF in England

A number of Czech pilots received the Croix de Guerre from the French for their actions during the Battle of France, Stanislav Fejfar being one of them, including one Gold Star and three Palmes to this decoration.

*   *   *

Groupe de Chasse I/6 had had the following combat claims and losses during the Battle of France:

	Destroyed	Probable	Losses
7 Apr	1 Ju52	–	–
18 May	2 Do17s	3 Do17s	2
20 May	3 Me109s	1 Do17	2
21 May	2 Do17s	1 Fi156	2
24 May	1 Do215	–	–
25 May	1 He111	3 He111s	2

26 May	–	–	1
29 May	1 He111	–	–
3 Jun	2 Me109s	1 Me109	2
5 Jun	3 Hs123s	–	1
7 Jun	–	–	2
8 Jun	–	–	1
11 Jun	–	–	3
16 Jun	–	1 Do17	
24 Jun	–	–	1

Top scorers were 34-year-old Henri Raphenne with five plus one probable, Georges Tricaud with three plus a probable. He had been in the French air force since 1925. Fejfar scored two and one probable and Vaclav Jicha two and one probable (one of which was shared). Fejfar flew 76$^{1}/_{2}$ hours in France.

The escadrille had lost 19 Moranes and one Dewoitine in combat and two Moranes in accidents.

Appendix D

Fejfar's Decorations and Medals

Fejfar's medals from left:
  Czech War Cross with 2 Linden Leaves;
  Czech Bravery Medal with 1 Linden Leaf;
  Czech Medal of Merit in Silver (1st Class) with Silver Star;
  Czech War Commemorative Medal, with bars 'Velke Britannie' and 'Francie';
    British 1939-45 Star with Battle of Britain Bar;
    British Air Crew Europe Star;
    British 1939-45 War Medal;
    French Croix de Guerre with 3 Bronze Palms & 1 Gold Star;
    French Croix de Combattant.

Czechoslovakia
1939 War Cross with two Linden Leaves on Riband
Bravery Medal with one Linden Leaf on Riband
Medal of Merit in Silver (First Class) with Silver Star on Riband
War Commemorative Medal Bars 'Velke Britannie' 'Francie'
Pilot's Silver and Gilt Flying Badge

Great Britain
1935/45 Star with 'Battle of Britain' Bar
Air Crew Europe Star
1939/45 War Medal
Cloth Pilot Wings

France
1939 Croix de Guerre with 3 Bronze Palms and 1 Gold Star
Croix de Combattant
Pilot's Silver and Gilt Flying Badge

Appendix E

Squadron Form 'F' Reports

Examples of 310 Squadron's Form 'F' Reports during the Battle of Britain and 313 Squadron in 1942.

At the end of each action, the squadron intelligence officer had to complete a separate report for Fighter Command HQ, known as a Form 'F'. The Form 'F' for 9 September reads:

Number of Enemy Aircraft:	150-200
Type of Enemy Aircraft:	Do215, Me109-110, He112
Time attack was delivered:	1735-1740
Place attack was delivered:	South of London
Height of Enemy:	22,000 feet.
Enemy Casualties:	2 Me110. 1 Do215 destroyed.
	1 Me109, 2 Me110 Probable,
	1 Me110 damaged.
Personnel:	1 missing.

GENERAL REPORT

12 a/c of 310 Squadron took off from Duxford at 1705 hours to patrol North Weald at 20,000 ft. The squadron joined up with 19 and 242 to form a wing, 242 Squadron taking the lead. A formation of 75 Do215 escorted by about 150 Me109, 110 and He112 were sighted south of the estuary heading north west. The main formation consisted of bombers and fighters flying in close herring bone formation with alternate lines of Do215 and Me110, this formation being protected by further Me110 and He112. S/Ldr Blackwood ordered his squadron into line astern in preparation for an attack on main formation from the rear. An Me110 was sighted breaking away from formation possibly due to previous attack by other fighters as one engine was smoking. He dived after it but lost sight of the Me110 in the haze. At this time a collision occurred between 2 Hurricanes and was seen by other pilots of 310 Squadron, who, on a signal, broke formation to avoid further collisions and then engaged in a series of dog-fights. The only pilot unaccounted for is F/O Boulton who was possibly one of the pilots concerned, but

190

pilots of 19 Squadron – part of the wing – state they saw 1 Hurricane and 1 Me110 collide but cannot give squadron letter.

F/Lt Sinclair was hit by a cannon shell, baled out and is now at Henley slightly hurt.

F/Lt Rypl as a result of being chased by about 10 Me109s ran short of petrol and landed in a large field near Oxted which had been obstructed, crashed and aircraft probably a write off, cine gun not carried. R/T satisfactory. Weather haze up to 8,000 ft, cloud 4/10 at 7,000 ft.

Pilots taking part and rounds fired were:

Red 1 F/Lt Sinclair = 280 rounds
Red 2 P/O Göth = 280 rounds
Red 3 P/O Fejfar = 280 rounds
Yel. 1 F/Lt Malý = NIL
Yel. 2 Sgt Zima = NIL
Yel. 3 P/O Bergman, 1920 rounds
Blue 1 S/Ldr Blackwood 240 rounds
Blue 2 F/Lt Rypl crashed
Blue 3 P/O Zimprich 2520 rounds
Green 1 F/O Boulton missing
Green 2 Sgt Hubáček 1440 rounds
Green 3 Sgt Řechka 1960 rounds

ADDENDUM
Lt G D Cooper, Irish Guards, Caterham, saw a Hurricane (most probably piloted by F/O Boulton) collide in the air with F/Lt Sinclair's Hurricane. He saw F/Lt Sinclair bale out and met him when he landed. He also saw the other Hurricane collide with a Do215 and both these aircraft crash in flames. This confirms reports of pilots of 310 Squadron, that they saw a Hurricane collide with a twin-engined e/a. This makes an extra Do215 destroyed.

*   *   *

The Form 'F' for 15 September 1940:

Number of Enemy Aircraft:	150-200
Type of Enemy aircraft:	Do17, 215, He111, Me109 and 110.
Time attack was delivered:	1440 hours.
Place attack was delivered:	East of London.
Height of Enemy:	20,000 ft.
Enemy Casualties:	Destroyed 1 Me109, 1 Do17, 2 He111. Destroyed shared 1 Do215.
Our Casualties – Aircraft:	2
Our Casualties – Personnel:	1 slightly injured.

GENERAL REPORT
12 aircraft of 310 Squadron took off from Duxford at 1415 hours forming a wing with 611, 19, 242 and 302 Squadrons to intercept enemy raid on London.

Several formations of 20 to 30 enemy aircraft were sighted consisting of Do215, 17 He111 and escorted by Me109 and 110, flying above the bombers. 310 Squadron, led by F/Lt Jefferies with other Hurricane squadrons, had been detailed to attack bombers, but were attacked by a formation of Me109s which had been sighted above and overhead and which broke up the wing. F/Lt Jefferies ordered the squadron to climb to 24,000 feet into sun when another large formation of e/a were sighted approaching from south. 310 Squadron delayed attack until they turned and when they faced west, a head-on attack was launched with the sun behind him, he carried this out aiming at the leading section in the first formation. The starboard engine of No.3 of the leading section attacked by F/Lt Jefferies caught fire and [it] broke formation. As F/Lt Jefferies used all his ammunition, broke off engagement and returned to base. Sgt Hubaček, leader of Green Section, was hit by a cannon shell, baled out and landed, and is slightly injured in left leg. His combat report is not available being away in R.N. Hospital, Chatham.

S/Ldr Hess, Leader of A Flight followed the B Flight in line astern in sections. The enemy fighters which escorted the main bomber formation attacked from the port the aircraft of A Flight and a general dog-fight ensued.

S/Ldr Hess's aircraft was hit by a cannon shell and he baled out uninjured. Our pilots encountered single enemy machines and obtained results. Sgt Řechka, Blue 3 chased an He111 and attacked it with 2 other Hurricanes and he saw it crash on Foulness Island and this statement is confirmed by Sgt Prchal. P/O Fejfar, Red 2, attacked and shot down a Do17 which landed near Grain. 2 of the crew were taken prisoners and P/O Fejfar's statement can be confirmed by one Spitfire pilot, who chased the He111 also.

Sgt Vopálecký, Blue 2, saw a twin-engine a/c marked with black facets in a white circle on upper surface of wings, he delivered attack on it with 2 other Hurricanes but it disappeared in cloud. The leader of Yellow Section, P/O Janouch, sighted a seaplane when attacking another enemy aircraft from above and from the rear, he believes it was an He115.

Red 3, Sgt Fürst, followed a formation of Do215s and He111s. He attacked an He111 which was some distance from the formation, driving it down out of control to the ground.

Green 3, Sgt Kaucký, whose leader had been hit and baled out, attacked with 2 Spitfires, a Do215 which went down in smoke uncontrolled to the ground.

10 aircraft landed here between 1505 and 1715 hours.

A Flight
Red
S/L Hess A   Unknown
P/O Fejfar S   1104 rounds
Sgt Fürst B   1408 (re-armed at North Weald)
Yellow
P/O Janouch S   240 rounds
Sgt Zima R   168 rounds
Sgt Prchal E   2400 (re-armed at North Weald)

B Flight
Blue
F/L Jefferies J   1695 rounds (P3, S3, broken ejector)
Sgt Vopálecký J   200 rounds
Sgt Řechka J   2400 rounds
Green
Sgt Hubáček J   Unknown
Sgt Půda R   400 rounds
Sgt Kaucký J   160 rounds

Hurricanes flown by individual pilots in this action were:
Red Section: S/Ldr Hess R4085 (the machine S/Ldr Blackwood had flown earlier that day), P/O Fejfar V6608, Sgt Fürst P3143.
Yellow Section: P/O Janouch P3056, Sgt Prchal V6556, Sgt Zima V6579.
Blue Section: F/L Jefferies R4089, Sgt Vopálecký P3887, Sgt Řechka L2713.
Green Section: Sgt Hubáček R4087, Sgt Půda V6619, Sgt Kaucký P3612.

                         *   *   *

The squadron's Form 'F' for 18 September 1940 reveals:

Number of Enemy aircraft: 2 formations, about 15 a/c each.
Type of Enemy aircraft: Do215.
Time attack was delivered: 1700 hours.
Place attack was delivered   East of London.
Height of Enemy: 8-19,000 feet.
Enemy Casualties: 5 Do215 destroyed, 1 Do25 destroyed
                             (shared) 1 Do215 probable.
Our Casualties – Aircraft: Nil.
Our Casualties – Personnel: Nil.

GENERAL REPORT
12 aircraft of 310 Squadron took off from Duxford at 1615 hours forming a wing with 19, 242 and 302 Squadrons, to patrol Hornchurch at 20,000 feet. Two formations of about 15 Do215 were seen over London and the wing, led by 242 Squadron, attacked the first formation of Do215s. The Leader of 310 Squadron, F/Lt

Jefferies, drew level with the leading squadron and also attacked. The enemy formation turned towards the squadron and in order to avoid passing too close, the leader had to break away. In the ensuing dog-fight, all our pilots were attacking singly. F/Lt Jefferies (Blue 1) delivered 2 attacks on e/a with Blue 2 (Sgt Kominek) and Sgt Kominek reported that both engines caught fire and e/a spun down out of control.

Leader of A Flight, P/O Janouch, attacked together with Red 2, P/O Fejfar, one Do215 and reported that enemy a/c crashed in flames. The single friendly fighters were chasing the enemy bombers who were not escorted by fighters, along the north or south bank of the Thames, attacking all the time. The attacks were delivered in pairs or threes with Hurricanes of other squadrons as the enemy bombers were outnumbered.

Sgt Jiroudek, Red 3, delivered 2 attacks on e/a and saw both engines smoking and Sgt Pŭda (Green 3) who attacked the same a/c saw the crew bale out and a/c crashing about 3 miles from Stanford le Hope. P/O Bergman, Leader of Yellow Section, which was the last section of our squadron, attacked one Do215 which was far on the left flank of this formation and both engines caught fire. P/O Zimprich (Blue 3) in the leading section also attacked one Do215 from the last section. E/a broke away and was attacked by another Hurricane. Then he saw some distance away another Do215. He attacked from starboard from about 300 yards, closing to 100 yards, and then again from port. He saw one of the crew bale out. He made another attack from below and heavy black smoke was emitted from the engine. The e/a glided towards the sea level. He wanted to deliver another attack but had no ammunition left.

F/O Fechtner, Green 1, delivered an attack on a formation behind the leader of enemy formation from rear and above. E/a was hit and broke away from its formation. Green 1 followed it through clouds. Over the shore he fired at it again and petrol tank started burning and then the port engine caught fire. He delivered another attack and starboard engine caught fire and the e/a fell into the sea.

Sgt Prchal (Yellow 3) delivered an attack on a formation from about 400 yards and fired 5 bursts. The port engine and the petrol tank on one Do215 caught fire and the e/a went down. He attacked it again and gave a short burst and the e/a went into a spin and crashed near a railway station, South Benfleet. Two of the crew baled out. The Dornier was marked by letter 'F' on fuselage.

The enemy bombers were flying in 2 vic formations about 15 a/c each. Usual camouflage and markings. Along the south bank of the Thames the squadron had to break off engagement owing to the very close proximity of A.A. fire. Weather thin cloud 22,000 feet. Low cloud 7,000 feet. Visibility good above cloud. Aircraft landed Duxford between 1740 and 1800 hours.

Pilots taking part in engagement and rounds fired as follows:

A Flight	Rounds fired
Red 1 P/O S Janouch	2400
Red 2 P/O S Fejfar	2160
Red 3 Sgt Jiroudek	1504
Yellow 1 P/O V Bergman	2400
Yellow 2 Sgt Zima	2000 stoppages port 2 gun charge.
Yellow 3 Sgt Prchal	1328

B Flight

Blue 1 F/Lt Jefferies	2400
Blue 2 Sgt Komínek	800
Blue 3 P/O Zimprich	2110 port 2 gun weak charge.
Green 1 P/O Fechtner	2400
Green 2 Sgt Kaucký	1400
Green 3 Sgt Půda	150

Hurricane serial numbers for this action were:

Red Section: P/O Janouch V6556, P/O Fejfar V6579, Sgt Jiroudek V6542.
Yellow Section: P/O Bergman V6608, Sgt Zima P3056, Sgt Prchal P3143.
Blue Section: F/L Jefferies R4089, Sgt Komínek V7304, P/O Zimprich P3612.
Green Section: P/O Fechtner P8809, Sgt Kaucký V6619, Sgt Půda P3889.

*   *   *

313 Squadron's Form 'F', which only refers to Fejfar's combat on 25 April 1942, reads:

Type and mark of our aircraft:	Spitfire VB.
Time attack was delivered:	16.35-16.45 hours.
Place attack and/or target:	5 miles off Berck.
Weather:	sunny-clear.
Our casualties – aircraft:	Nil.
Our casualties – personnel:	Nil.
Enemy casualties in air combat:	FW190, damaged.

General Report: I was Blue 1, flying over Berck at 27,000 feet and on receiving a warning, turned to port and, climbing up sun, saw below 4 Spitfires which shortly went into a dive. I then observed two smoke trails coming down in my direction from out of the sun and soon after, tracer passed on my port side. I throttled down and two FW190s went by to starboard. I immediately attacked getting in a 3' burst on the second e/a but the range opened from 50 yards to 300 yards as the e/a had the advantage of the dive. I saw strikes and small pieces falling off. The e/a turned slightly to starboard towards

France, being shepherded by the first FW190. I then called up my
leader and set course for home. I claim this FW190 as damaged.

* * *

Stanislav Fejfar made out the following combat report, written out as a Form
'F' in regard to his combat on 5 May 1942:

Type and mark of our a/c:	Spitfire VB
Time attack was delivered:	1535 hours
Place of attack:	Over Lille
Weather:	4/10 cloud at 25,000 ft., hazy below.
Our casualties – aircraft:	2 Spitfires Cat.E.
Our casualties – personnel:	Sgt K Pavlík missing.
	P/O J Kučera slight head injuries.
Enemy casualties:	1 FW190 destroyed.
	1 FW190 probably destroyed.

GENERAL REPORT

I was Red 1, and after crossing Lille I saw 9 FW190s pass the
squadron on my right at 24,000 feet. The e/a then turned and came
from behind. I immediately warned the wing commander, and gave
the order to break formation. In this manner I turned to the sun and
saw 6 FW190s on my left followed by two lots of 4 FW190s. I went
in to attack two of the 6 FW190s and opened fire 4/5 secs burst from
port quarter at an opening range of 200 yards and a closing range
of 100 yards. Immediately after this burst, the pilot from one of the
FW190s baled out. I saw him jump, but did not actually see his
parachute open. I then went into a spin losing 4,000 feet in height,
and after coming out of the spin climbed again and saw 2 FW190s
on my left about to attack 3 Spitfires. I went into attack, and opened
fire at one of the e/a from port quarter at an opening range of 300
yards and a closing range of 200 yards, expending all my
ammunition. Before I could observe the result of this attack, I saw
in my mirror a FW190 very close behind me, and in taking evasive
action went into a further spin. As I pulled out of this spin an
FW190 passed me on its back and with half of its wing missing. As
I did not see a Spitfire at this time and as the e/a passed me in a spin
immediately after my attack I claim this as probably destroyed apart
from the e/a probably destroyed in similar circumstances by P/O
Kučera. I crossed the French coast west of Dunkirk, and asked for a
homing being short of petrol. I landed at forward base at 1625
hours. I claim 1 FW190 destroyed, and 1 FW190 probably
destroyed.

F/Lt Fejfar.

Appendix F

Fejfar's Combat Credits

1940

20 May	Me109E	Amiens	Morane 406	GC I/6
25 May	He111 (shared)	Denain	„	„
29 May	He111	Denain	„	„
5 Jun	Hs123	Chaulnes	„	„
9 Sep	Me110	Croydon	Hurricane P3143 D	310 Sq
15 Sep	Do 17	Grain	Hurricane V6608 B	„
18 Sep	Do17 (shared)	E of London	Hurricane V6579 J	„

1942

25 Apr	FW190 damaged	off Berck	Spitfire Vb BL973 S	313 Sq
5 May	FW190	Lille	Spitfire Vb „	„
„	FW190 Probable	„	Spitfire Vb	„

Appendix G

Pre-War Certificates of Appreciation

Čís. kat. *5.*

Vysvědčení dospělosti

ze státní průmyslové školy v Pardubicích.

Kolek 8.- Kč.

Stanislav Fejfar, narozený dne *25. listopadu 1912*

ve *Štíkově* v *Čechách*,

absolvoval strojnickou vyšší průmyslovou školu při státní průmyslové škole

v *Pardubicích ve školních roích 1928/29*

až 1931/32,

a podrobil se před podepsanou zkušební komisí

zkoušce dospělosti

podle předpisu o zkouškách dospělosti na vyšších školách průmyslových a jim

na roveň postavených školách odborných.

Podle výsledků této zkoušky byl uznán za

dospělého s vyznamenáním

CERTIFICATE OF ADULTHOOD

Government Technical School in Pardubicich.

Stanislav Fejfar born 25th November 1912 in Stikov in Czechoslovakia.

Graduated from the engineering technical school in the courses (attached) at the Government Technical School in Pardubicich during the second year 1928/29 till 1931/32, which was submitted to the undersigned Board of Governors.

EXAM OF ADULTHOOD

By the rules covering these exams in Technical Schools and Colleges.

The outcome of this exam was confirmed as an Adult (with full marks).

Číslo 14/33.

Vysvědčení zachovalosti.

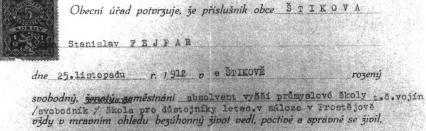

Obecní úřad potvrzuje, že příslušník obce ŠTIKOVA

Stanislav FEJFAR

dne 25.listopadu   r. 1912   v e ŠTIKOVĚ   rozený

svobodný, ženatý, zaměstnání absolvent vyšší průmyslové školy t.č.vojín
/svobodník / škola pro důstojníky letec.v záloze v Prostějově
vždy v mravním ohledu bezúhonný život vedl, poctivě a správně se živil,

takže se proti němu nevyskytlo dosud nic závadného.

V e Štikově   dne 14.dubna   1933.

Starosta:

VOCATIONAL CERTIFICATE

The Burgher and Local Authority of Stikova acknowledges that

Stanislav Fejfar
Born 25.11.1912 in Stikov Unmarried.

Graduated from College for Air Force Officers in Prostejov as a Leading Aircraftsman.

He was always respectable with high morals, lived honestly and correctly and supported himself. In so far that nothing was found to be wrong with his way of living.

Signed Chief Magistrate Stikov 14th April 1933.

JMENUJI VÁS

PORUČÍKEM

S ÚČINNOSTÍ OD 1. července 1935

A USTANOVUJI VÁS ZÁROVEŇ

ČEKATELEM

NA SLUŽEBNÍ MÍSTO VE SLUŽEBNÍ KATEGORII DŮSTOJNÍKŮ

ABSOLVENTŮ VOJENSKÉ AKADEMIE. ZÁKONITÝ SLUŽEBNÍ

PLAT ČEKATELSKÝ NÁLEŽÍ VÁM OD 1. července 1935.

POŘADÍ SE VÁM STANOVÍ OD 1. července 1935.

PRAHA,
24. červen 1935.

MINISTR
NÁRODNÍ OBRANY

This is to appoint you in the Rank of a Pilot Officer with effect from the 1st July 1935.

I also ordain that you are given a place in the services as a commissioned officer having graduated from the Military Academy.

Your regular official salary in your rank will be paid to you from the 1st July 1935.

Prague 24th June 1935

Signed Minister of Air

Ministerstvo národní obrany.
Čj. 1451 - osob. odděl. 1936.

DEKRET.

Dne 30. června 1936 dovršil jste jednoroční čekatelskou dobu ve služební kategorii důstojníků absolventů vojenské akademie.

Propůjčuji Vám tudíž s účinností od 1. července 1936 služební místo v 8. platové stupnici beze změny dosavadní hodnosti v téže služební kategorii, avšak s podmínkou, že stupeň Vaší kvalifikace za kvalifikační období 1935/36 bude aspoň vyhovující.

Služební plat důstojnický Vám náleží od 1. července 1936.

Praha,
1. července 1936.

Ministr
národní obrany.

Pan poručík let.
        Stanislav Fejfar,
            let.pl.3.

ORDER

On the 30th June 1936 you finished your one year
as an aspirant in the nominal category of officers
who graduated from the academy.

I am offering you a nominal place of 8 earnings
group from 1.7.1936 without a change in your rank.
This is on condition that your capability between the
qualifying period 1935/36 is suitable.

Functional salary for officers is yours from 1.7.1936.

Mr Pilot Officer Stanislav Fejfar
Air Regiment 3

Prague Czechoslovakia 1936

**Minister of National Defence
Machinik**

Appendix H

Post-War Certificates of Appreciation

MINISTERSTVO NÁRODNÍ OBRANY
hlavní štáb, velitelství letectva

Čj. 24.298 .... 4. odděl. osob. 1946

Praha, 31/12 194t

V uznání největší oběti, kterou položil na oltář vlasti, a v ocenění zásluh, které si získal o osvobození Československé republiky ve válečných letech 1939—1945, byl povýšen Osobním věstníkem ministerstva národní obrany čís. 101 z 26/10. 1946 na věčnou paměť

kpt. let. Stanislav Fejfar,

narozený dne 25. listopadu 1912

příslušník československého zahraničního letectva,

na štábního kapitána letectva

Čest jeho jménu, práci a památce!

Velitel letectva:

div. gen. ALOIS VICHEREK

206

Ministry of National Defence   Prague 31.12.1946.
Air Force Headquarters

In appreciation of the highest sacrifice which he
made for his country and in appreciation of credit
which he gained by the exoneration of
Czechoslovakia in war years 1939-1945, is
commissioned by the Ministry of National Defence
Number 101 from 26.10.1946 forever.

Captain Stanislav Frejfar
Date of Birth 25.11.1912.

A member of the Czechoslovak Foreign Air Forces
and Headquarters Air Force Captain.

With Honour, his name, work and memory.

Signed Air Officer Commanding
Div General Alois Vicherek

MINISTERSTVO NÁRODNÍ OBRANY
hlavní štáb, velitelství letectva

Čj. 24.298 _____ 4. odděl. osob. 1946

Praha, 31/12 _____ 1946

Věc: **Stanislav Fejfar,škpt,let.**
oznámení o povýšení

Pan — Paní — Slečna

Marie J u n k o v é ,

Nová Paka,Žižkova 11.

pošta

Osobním věstníkem ministerstva národní obrany čís. 101
z 26/10 1946 _____ byl povýšen na věčnou paměť

kpt.let.Stanislav F e j f a r ,

narozený **25.listopadu 1912**

na **štábního kapitána letectva**

Podávaje Vám tuto zprávu ujišťuji Vás, že československé
letectvo nezapomene jeho oběti a zachová navždy jeho světlou
památku jako zářivý příklad obětavosti a lásky k vlasti a letectvu.

Velitel letectva:

div. gen. ALOIS VICHEREK

Tiskárna MNO v Praze IV — 46-1722

Ministry of National Defence   Prague 31.12.1946.
HQ Air Command
No 24/298

Stanislav Fejfar Air Force Captain

By Order no 101 from 26th October 1946.

Captain Stanislav Fejfar born 25 November 1912
was commissioned as

Headquarters Group Captain

By giving you this information (news) I assure you
that the Czechosolvakian Air Force will never forget
his sacrifice and will forever remember his brilliant
example of self-sacrifice and the love for his country
and to the Air Force.

Signed Air Officer Commanding
Div General Alois Vicherek

PRESIDENT

REPUBLIKY ČESKOSLOVENSKÉ

UDĚLIL

V UZNÁNÍ BOJOVÝCH ZÁSLUH, KTERÉ ZÍSKAL V BOJI

ZA OSVOBOZENÍ REPUBLIKY ČESKOSLOVENSKÉ

ŠKPT.LET. STANISLAV F E J F A R

přísl.čs.zahr.letectva

DRUHÝ

ČESKOSLOVENSKÝ VÁLEČNÝ KŘÍŽ 1939

V Praze dne____9. dubna____1947

Číslo matriky:___37.548

PRESIDENT CZECHOSLOVAKIAN REPUBLIC

In appreciation of Merit in Battle, which he received in the battle for the freedom of Czechoslovakia.

Headquarters Captain Stanislav Fejfar
Member of Czechoslovakian Foreign Air Forces

CZECHOSLOVAKIAN WAR CROSS 1939

In Prague 9.4.1947.

**Fejfar received a similar document for a bar (Linden Leaves) to the War Cross.

VELITEL LETECTVA A PVO ČSFR

vyslovuje

Stanislavu FEJFAROVI

ČESTNÉ UZNÁNÍ

při příležitosti morální a politické rehabilitace
čs. zahraničních letců, bývalých příslušníků RAF,
účastníků bojů za svobodu ČSR
na světových válčištích v letech 1939 ‹ 1945

PRAHA 13. ZÁŘÍ 1991   genmjr. ing. JAN PLOC

Air Force Headquarters a PVO

DECREE

The Air Officer Commanding Provisional Variation
Orders Czechoslovak Federal Republic

Gives

Stanislav Fejfar

CERTIFICATE OF MERIT

On the occasion of moral and political restitutions
to Czechoslovakian airmen, former members of the
RAF, who fought in the air war between 1939 and
1945.

Prague 13th September 1991

Signed General Major Jan PLOC

Bibliography

Aces High, by Christopher Shores and Clive Williams, Grub Street, 1994.

Armee de L'Air, by C F Shores and Paul Camelio, Squadron/Signal Pub., 1976.

Airmen in Exile by Alan Brown, Sutton Publishing Ltd, 2000.

Denik Stihace [Fighter Diary] by Stanislav Fejfar, Circle-Hradec, Kralove, Cz, 1970.

Men of the Battle of Britain, by Ken Wynn, CCB Associates, 1999.

Na Zemi A Oblose Západní Evropy [On the Ground and Over Western Europe], by Ladislav Kudrna, Our Army Publishing, Prague, 2007.

No.310 (Czechoslovak) Squadron 1940-45, by Tomas Polak, with Jiri Rajlich and Pavel Vancata, Graphic Sud, France, 2006.

Paddy by W/Cdr P P C Barthropp DFC AFC, Howard Baker Press Ltd, 1986.

Raiders Approach, by S/Ldr H T Sutton OBE DFC, Gale & Polden Ltd, 1956.

The Battle of Britain – Then and Now, Winston G Ramsey, Ed., After the Battle Publications, 1980.

The Rise and Fall of the 3rd Reich, by William L Shirer, Secker & Warburg Ltd, 1960.

Index